The Personal Letters Of John Alexander Dowie

John Alex. Dowie

The Personal Letters

OF

JOHN ALEXANDER DOWIE

COMPILED BY

EDNA SHELDRAKE

WILBUR GLENN VOLIVA

Zion City, Illinois, U. S. A.

PUBLISHER.

$1.25

Foreword.

A few men—of all the millions born in their day and generation—leave an impress upon their age. When one does this, it is the part of wisdom to mark such, study him, and note wherein he differed from the commonalty—for along this path lieth truth and progress.

That John Alexander Dowie was such an one is conceded by foe as well as friend.

To discover the inner springs whence a man's actions flow, is to know the Man—and is rarely vouchsafed to his comrades along the way.

The world first began to hear of John Alexander Dowie in Australia, where after receiving ordination to the ministry in the Congregational body, he repudiated the organized church and became an Independent. He quickly assumed place as a leader in the fight against the liquor traffic, and in pursuance of his methods was arrested, fined, and served a prison sentence of thirty-four days rather than surrender his principle; stood for Parliament, was defeated by the liquor interests, founded a Free Christian Church, taught the doctrine of "Divine Healing," preached constantly and prayed for physical healing for many hundreds who testified to receiving the same, founded a Divine Healing Association, started a magazine as a vehicle of propagation, and when he left Australia for a world tour in 1888, he had gained many adherents to his religious faith and possessed a strong personal following throughout that continent and the Islands. Contra, he had made many enemies.

After a few years on the Pacific coast in America he located near Chicago; then, in 1893, building a "tabernacle" just outside the World's Fair grounds —of so poor and flimsy a character it was dubbed by the press "an old wooden hut."

After a period of comparative inaction, he awoke over night to find his name known. The press ridiculed and fought him. Incidentally, it told of cures being wrought. The big wooden structure became all too small to hold the crowds of sick and maimed and halt and blind—body-sick and sin-sick souls who gathered from every point of the compass and every stratum of society. Ever one indisputable fact existed: cures were wrought. And the opposition of press, pulpit, medical fraternity, state and civic authorities were but avenues which spread abroad the new propaganda and recruited the ranks of John Alexander Dowie's following.

His strong, pungent, denunciatory words and aggressive methods concerning the practice of medicine and surgery aroused the State Board of Health to action, in which they were defeated. The city authorities then instituted action under the Hospital ordinance, causing the arrest of himself and wife on more than one hundred separate charges

He fought this fight, which lasted nearly a year, to a finish, winning success in the upper courts, which declared the ordinance under which the arrests had been made, invalid.

From this time his rise to great power, influence and wealth was phenomenal His following grew into the thousands, he engaged and filled to overflowing each Sunday the largest auditorium in Chicago, founded a church in 1896, sent out his paper and other almost innumerable literature from a printing plant which he owned and operated, bought a large downtown hotel as a "Home" and headquarters, rented another, established a college with full equipment and faculty, started a bank, established in America a new industry—lace making,—the machinery and lace makers being imported from England, and in 1901 founded Zion City, forty-two miles north of Chicago, which within a few

years reached a population of 8,000 people, all
adherents of the faith and living under the rules and
regulations prescribed, leases taking the place of the
ordinary deeds to property—the land, 6,500 acres, being "dedicated to God" and practically held in per-
petuity, the talents of one of the best corporation
lawyers in the country being expended upon these
leases.

About this time he made public declaration to his
church and the world that his mission was to "restore all things spoken by the holy prophets" and
that he came in "the power and spirit of Elijah," according to Biblical prophecy to do this.

Millions flowed into his hands, and his power and
activities multiplied. He spent himself prodigally.
Besides his ecclesiastical, educational and political
work, he kept his hand upon and gave personal attention to no less than thirty-seven industries, all a
part of the Zion undertaking. Wide reaching plans,
world-wide in their character, occupied his tireless
mind. These embraced the Christianizing of China, of
colonization in various countries, and questions of
state which presidents conferred with him over, some
openly, others secretly. He believed, with all his being,
that a new order was to be ushered in. He preached
a wide and all-embracing brotherhood of man, knowing no distinction of race or color. He heralded a
pure Theocracy, and gave that name to his political
party. Though men may not have agreed with him,
they reckoned with him.

His life was often endangered, by reason of mobs
and through secret agencies.

John Alexander Dowie made application for citi-
zenship in the United States, April 17, 1903. The
oath of allegiance was administered by Judge Joseph
Gary, the Nestor of the Illinois bar, who on this occasion added: "I think I may say, that since the days of
the revolution this country has never had a better ac-

quisition, nor has a more wholesome citizen been added to the United States."

At the zenith of his power and success, after a trip around the world, he suffered, in 1905, a stroke of paralysis, from which he never recovered.

Financial clouds, which had been darkly hovering, assumed portentous shape, and on April 1, 1906, the management of affairs passed into other hands.

The large property known as "Zion Estate," with value variously estimated into the millions, was immediately thrown into litigation. The contention, pro and con, has no place here. It is not, at this writing, an interim of six years, yet ended.

In the midst of complicated conditions in both church and finance, John Alexander Dowie passed away March 9, 1907.

His mortal remains lie buried in a corner of a little country grave yard in Lake county, Illinois, within the boundary of the city he founded.

These cold, bare facts constitute the skeleton of a life's history, made rich, glowing, palpitating with life, as revealed through the personal, intimate letters left by him. They tell their own story, and are given without interpolation or interpretation, this being the first volume.

In those long, last days, when disease had clouded his mind and battled for supremacy, the writer was associated with him almost daily.

As the life forces visibly ebbed, the immortal spirit looked forth from the dim, sunken eyes,—clear, undaunted, triumphant, compelling.

On one of these days he sent for me, and after some instruction concerning certain matters, his features relaxed and his closed eyes betokened sleep.

Suddenly opening them, he fixed his gaze upon me, and earnestly said: "Write—write, tell it."

I shook my head negatively, but again he insisted—commanded: "Write, you will find some letters—I give them to you—they will tell the story."

A few weeks after, he died.

My work took me to another state, and in other scenes the incident passed out of mind.

By a strange chain of circumstances, some months later I again found myself in Zion City, which I had never expected to see again. Without knowing why, and against my judgment, I remained, month after month.

Yielding one day to an impulse, without purpose or plan, my steps led me to an attic, filled with rubbish and old papers. I sat down beside a heap and idly yielding to this strange whim, began turning over the piles of debris, fit only for the ash heap. It was there I turned to the light a number of old, yellowed letter press books. The peculiar hand writing at once arrested my attention. I recognized it as that of John Alexander Dowie, and turning to the inscriptions, found they were indeed the "letters" he had referred to, which, I now remembered, he had said, I would find, and which it was his desire should "tell the story."

I gathered them together and preserved them, as a sacred trust. A few days later the attic was cleared and the rubbish burned. If there is any incompleteness in the story which these books give, it is no doubt due to my over-sight in rescuing them.

Thus do I keep the trust imposed upon me, in the publication of two volumes, the first of which is here presented, and covers that period of his life preceding his career in America.

EDNA SHELDRAKE.

THE PERSONAL LETTERS

OF

JOHN ALEXANDER DOWIE

(Explanatory)

But little is known of the ancestry of John Alexander Dowie. His father, John Murray Dowie, with a younger brother, escaped a cholera epidemic in Alloa, Scotland, which swept away their father, one John Dowie, and other members of the family.

John Alexander Dowie was born in Edinburgh, May 25, 1847, his mother being Ann Macfarlane-McHardie, a widow, who, previous to her marriage to him, gave lodgings to John Murray Dowie, then a youth of twenty, a tailor by trade. She was considerably older than he and is reputed to have been a woman of strong character, though illiterate.

Certain facts concerning his birth led John Alexander Dowie in his later years (these coming to his knowledge only at this late date) to deny this paternity, and was the cause of a bitter estrangement between himself and John Murray Dowie which lasted to the day of his death.

A second son was born Nov. 29, 1849, and the births of both are registered in the same office as sons of John Murray Dowie and his spouse, Ann Macfarlane.

Of his childhood, he wrote: "We were poor, I was often sick, my life being more than once despaired of. For some time before we left Edinburgh (which we did when I was thirteen) I was quite unable to go to school, partly because of the condition of my clothes, and partly because we were preparing to go to Australia, and partly because I was still sick. I had a joyless childhood, for the most part, so far as circumstances were concerned, and it was only my intense love for God and His work that gave me any joy. I accompanied my good father as often as I could in his preaching journeys, taking long walks with him to Gorgic and Hawthorne and attending the street preaching of Henry Wight, whose words first brought peace to my longing heart. Often did I long to be of service to the poor and miserable, and bitterly did I suffer from the consequences of the intemperance of some I dearly loved. This led me to sign the pledge when I was only six years old. I gave myself to God when a child, and although so poor and having so little opportunity for getting a really good education, I was diligent

13

and obedient and people kindly helped me, lending and giving me good books, which I read eagerly."

Upon the arrival of the family in Adelaide, South Australia, the young boy at once went to work for his uncle, Alexander Dowie, who was then laying the foundation of what became later a prosperous boot and shoe business, and whose daughter he later married. For his services young John Alexander received his food and eighteen shillings per week.

After a few months, he left to better himself, advancing from time to time and in various positions until while still in his minority he commanded a considerable salary and was accounted a more than ordinary promising business man.

At the age of twenty he left commercial pursuits, and took up study, under the guidance of a tutor, to prepare himself for the Christian ministry.

After fifteen months tutelage he entered Edinburgh University as an Arts student, where he remained for three years, taking voluntary courses in the Free Church School.

While in the midst of study and work he was called home by a cablegram from his father, the reason being unknown to him. He soon found, upon examination of the books of the partnership firm of which his father was the senior member, that an assignment was inevitable.

After the winding up of affairs, the young man, handicapped by the debt incurred in bringing him out from Scotland, set himself to his chosen life work—the ministry.

It was at this time he began to keep the record of his correspondence which extends over the whole of his life, and at which point this volume begins

The first three letters are dated at Alma, South Australia, his first field of labor, May, 1872.

My Dear R—:

Yours of March 2nd reached me duly; but I delayed an answer until I could say something definite as to my position

The Committee of the Congregational Union passed a resolution in February last pledging themselves to support me in opening up a new sphere of labour in any part of the colony. This I declined. Then other representations were made to me in reference to various places, to none of which I felt any special inclination and so spoke.

Still undecided as to returning to Scotland or not,

I came here towards the end of February on a visit to a friend.

This place was without a minister. I was asked to receive a call and at first declined; but eventually feeling that God's providence had been removing difficulties and clearly indicating my way, I accepted on April 1st a call to the pastorate of the Congregational Church here. At the annual meetings of Cong. Union I was admitted, on 16th, a ministerial member by a unanimous vote, and three days since, (21st), I was, in presence of a large assembly, publicly ordained "a minister of the gospel, in connection with the Congregational or Independent body of South Australia." Revs. F. W. Cox (Adelaide), J. C. McMichael (Gonder), J. R. Ferguson (Salisbury), J. Gibson (Angaston), P. Barr (Turo), M. Williams (Kapunda), and W. Oldham (late Alma), all took various parts in the ordination service.

Now you know the position to which God has led me, in ways of His own.

My district is quite an agricultural one, divided, for the most part, into very large holdings of from one to four and five square miles of splendid land. Consequently it is sparsely populated and that population widely scattered. There are about 1,000 souls in 90 square miles. My central church is about two miles from the little post town called Alma and my house is two miles farther north, being twelve miles from the nearest railway station and about 60 miles north of Adelaide. It is a level country, bounded on the east by a range (I live in a gully at the foot of this range) and on the west by a dense scrub about 25 miles broad, between us and the sea. North and south the country is flat. I have preaching stations at Lower Alma (Wednesdays), about seven miles south, Salter's Springs, about six miles north (Sabbath afternoons and Tuesdays) and Dalkey Plains (Mondays) about 12 miles west. The last named is

15

being established. The others, with my central work at Alma (Morning School and twice on Sabbaths and meeting on Thursdays) are fully established. God gives me the most cheering tokens of success. The people are above the average in morals and intelligence. There is only one wine shop within ten miles on every side, and I have entered opposition against its license at the forthcoming Bench of Magistrates on June 10th, and hope to be successful. My health is better than for the last five years. I have much time for study. Preparation for four original sermons every week (six sermons are preached by me weekly in full work) and keeping up in certain studies fully occupies me.

I have furnished my house nicely and God has provided me with a model housekeeper—a person about 50 years of age, a widow, no children, of quiet, lady-like ways, a good cook and a prudent manager.

Whenever you visit South Australia I give you a hearty invitation to come and spend some time with me. You can have a horse and scamper over all the country. I shall be right glad to see you.

May you increase daily in Christ-likeness, experiencing greater peace and joy in the Spirit.

Your affectionate friend in Christ,

John Alexander Dowie.

Dear Father and Mother:

This is the first letter written from my house—I shall soon doubtless get to feel it is my home.

On Wednesday evening after writing to you I rode to Joseph Smith's farm and opened my Lower Alma Plains preaching station. It was a terribly stormy night —wind, rain and darkness—and yet there were about twelve persons present. I firmly believe it will be one of my best stations

As a young man at the beginning of his ministry.

As Pastor in Sidney.

I got home about 10, thoroughly drenched—could not see my horse's head greater part of the way, midst heavy rain and hard wind   None the worse for it all.

On Monday morning I brought up Mrs. S—and took her first to Mr. F—'s where she had dinner, and in the afternoon drove her here and left her for my meetings.   I only came back this evening and have now taken up my abode and getting all my books, etc , into order.

Mrs. S— will, I think, suit me well.   She takes to her work and the place generally.   I trust this is truly a good housekeeper from the Lord

Last evening there was no church meeting and only three at evening meeting.   Probably I will come down on Wednesday

I am very tired and can scarcely hold my pen   It is 2 30 a. m.   Good morning.   God will guide.

Love to all.

Your affectionate son,

John Alexander Dowie

––––––––

Dear Father and Mother:

I am a little uneasy not having had any letter from you for more than a week   I sincerely trust that you are all well.   Please tell me how matters are going with you every way.   Do not, if anything is adverse, keep me in suspense; because it prevents any action on my part of a helpful nature, until the matter is over, and that is not right

As I already told you, I think, Angaston and Truro were not very satisfactory nor profitable to God's work as far as I could see.   Many little things occurred which were painful to me.   It is anything but pleasant, when one's mind is realizing deeply the value of perishing souls, to walk into a brother minister's room and find, item: one bottle brandy, one decanter wine, (getting low down), one tumbler (with sugar standing by

17

and spoon in tumbler) and three or four wine glasses, evidently used; and more, a brother minister lying back in an easy chair, legs crossed, hands folded, head reclining, face flushed, talk quick and thick at intervals, courtesy forgotten: "Ha ha! Dowie, how are you?" And this man has only come ten miles or so of a pleasant drive across country to do the Master's work and seek the lost drunkards and pleasure seekers—the sinners perishing in Truro. And the work there seems, as also at Angaston and Kapunda, in a very bad condition. The Rev. R. L. Coward (fine, good old Christian and an abstainer) with whom I stayed, told me that there were not more than four regular hearers at Mr. Barr's, out of the township of Truro, and there seems to be a population of at least two or three hundred there

But I could write for a day about it. The result with me is to cling more firmly than ever to my own way of working, looking only to God for clearer light and help May He enable me to do so incessantly, humbly and prayerfully, and actively.

Last evening, Sabbath, a man of about thirty-five from Salter's Springs was in my room here for several hours under deep conviction of sin. I trust the Spirit is leading him into rest in Christ; in fact, I believe it is so Drink was one of his besetting sins, and I told him he must, before God, forever renounce it. His name is in my pledge book.

There are many painful discouragements, but the work is going on, and will, if I am only faithful. Love to all.

Your affectionate son,

John Alexander Dowie.

(Two months later—July 5th—finds discouragements in new field.)

Dear Father and Mother:

Many discouragements,—or are they encouragements? A month ago, when writing to you, I said they were, and that Paul thought so; and now, although I have felt bowed down under them, if I am preaching, by God's power, people into the church—and this blessing is given me—there can be no doubt that, in the process, I am preaching some out.

My church here has been cruelly neglectful from the beginning, though I would not even to you say it, and now I fear there is something like open opposition impending, on account of the too searching character of my preaching. Dissimulation, wicked hypocrisy and Pharisaic formalism have been unmasked; and only Divinely given wisdom can help me through.

Details it would be almost impossible to give in a letter. Never have I felt more keenly, in all my life, anything like the anxious, sharp sorrow that I have during these past few days. But, thanks to the Lord, I begin to feel now the consolation of His gracious Spirit aiding, enlightening and strengthening me. All must be well.

Conscious of my integrity (not that I claim perfection of action, very far from that) I will not fear, though an host should encamp against me; for God knows my speech and action have been from a loving, earnest heart, for the welfare of the souls around me; and my most searching examination fails to show anything in either contrary to the Word of God (I speak regarding my feelings and actions in my ministry) nor can anyone even allege the opposite My only fault is too great faithfulness and diligence—not sleepy half-heartedness in preaching or action. So they seem. But I know full well that I shall never attain to the honour of such a charge being wholly true, while I thank God it is partly so; for if ever I worked for Him it has been here.

Thursday evening was appointed for my church meeting, before which at my house here is held the deacons' meeting. Mr. F— is now sole deacon.

There were only two members of the church present. I quietly announced to them that, there being no quorum, no meeting could be held

Doubtless all this must appear very sudden and puzzling to you, especially as I cannot trust myself to details just now. It cannot appear more so to you than it does to me It seems a perfect mine of evils sprung in the midst of the nominal church here. Oh, how it has perplexed and grieved me.

But in the midst of all, I have the cheering tokens of God's blessing among the unsaved in all parts of the district under my ministry. Of members of my church there are some, I trust, thoroughly sound, while of those Christians attending and being evidently most deeply interested there are men who would doubtless stand by me in the event of any wicked attempt by an unfaithful majority in the church—not to speak of worldly men whose souls seem attracted by the truth But in all such supports is not my trust. "My grace is sufficient for thee; for my strength is made perfect in weakness" These words of God strengthen me For weak in myself indeed do I feel, but I feel I am right, and therefore strong in God His promise can never fail. Now do pray for me. I value much your sympathy and fervent prayer to God for me.

And now I scarcely like to tell you of what happened to myself on Wednesday night, lest it should needlessly alarm you. But it is one of the many tokens of God's care which I am now receiving that I really dare not keep it back. Returning late from Lower Alma (roads awful, night very cloudy and dark) it was only safe to amble along at a little more than a walk When nearly a mile or more from home, my feet seemed benumbed and cramped with the cold, and as riders often do when similarly affected, I took my feet out of the stirrups and let them hang loose for a minute. My horse was walking quietly and steadily, I had just replaced the right foot, when, sud-

20

denly, something which I could not see caused the mare "Clem" to shy and bound some yards to the right side of the road. Of course with one foot out of the stirrups I came off, "flying", but excepting a little shake, now nearly gone, there was not a single scratch to my body. Clem stood like a guilty thing, quietly, for the good part of a minute, but when I went towards her she set off at a trot which quickened into a half canter and in less time than it takes to write, she was off into the darkness. I followed down the road for some distance, soon saw my folly, and walked over dark paddocks and arrived home feeling my cup of trouble full—new mare and she lost! In the morning, at daybreak, I dispatched Johnnie to Mr. D—'s for a horse to begin the search for Clem, but before he returned Clem was here. She had turned into Mr. Kelley's paddock, they found her there and sent her home to me, neither horse nor saddle was in the slightest degree injured. Today I rode her and found her better than ever. I can see now quite a mark of God's goodness in not letting me come home upon her. Had I done so, I had intended making a visit which, if made, would tonight only be a bitterly regretted memory. No fault in the horse. But my gratitude for life perserved is great to God.

It is a long time since you had so long a letter, I think. Tomorrow I hope to hear from you. Love to all.

> Your affectionate son,
> John Alexander Dowie

(Sept. 25th—moved to action by havoc wrought through intemperance.)

Dear Father and Mother:

I enclose 14 pounds, which is almost every penny I have, to meet bill due tomorrow. If you can get Murray's people to retire it for me, I shall probably pay the balance, 11 pounds, within a week or two, for I have 12 pounds due for second quarter now ending of "Union" grant to church here.

This comes very hard upon me just now and causes me to be in debt for various small current accounts— store, butcher, blacksmith, etc , which brings a consciousness of "owing," very worrying. Economical and careful as I am, this is one of the things which "ought not so to be."

However, I will doubtless get through, though depression is more present than hopefulness, I must confess. I trust there will be no difficulty made about retiring the bill.

It is very uncertain whether I shall be down at half yearly meetings of the "Union" or not. If I do I have fully made up my mind to table the following notice of motion for the annual meeting in May, 1873: "That this Union deeply deplores the great evils resulting from the licensed traffic in intoxicating liquors; and earnestly calls upon all members of associated churches to endeavour, by every private and public effort within their power, to diminish and eventually suppress so man-destroying and God-dishonoring a trade." You know that I have for years past determined to work from the inside of the church, for the most part, in regard to that worse than slave trade.

The time has come for action. What could possibly be gained by delay? I am sick at heart with the cool indifference with which the church regards great moral evils, such as this traffic produces.

I foresee something of the obloquy which would be heaped upon me by the worldlings inside and outside of our communion; the sneering satire of "youthful enthusiasm"; the trimming and time-serving obstacles which for years might hinder the passing of such a resolution; and the insinuations as to seeking public prominence, etc.

Shrinking from such an ordeal is only natural. But

when I think of the mighty moral forces which the destruction of that fearful trade would liberate for the destruction of ignorance, crime, disease, insanity and destitution; when I think that the cutting of that one cord would undo a thousand more of Satan's weaving —surely that would be a triumph—the grace of God which bringeth salvation.

Drunkards "clothed and in their right minds;" homes made happy; children cared for, clothed, fed, and seated in the house of God—surely the Saviour would become more precious were these blessings brought about by the instrumentality of the saved— the true Church of Christ.

Effects beyond the most uncontrolled imagination's power to conceive are bound up in the salvation of even one soul. What mighty hindrances have we removed, now absolutely preventing the salvation of thousands, when we even partially crush this traffic.

It is worth bearing, were there a hundred fold more to bear than will have to be encountered. Quickening power from God and the conversion of thousands may be looked for by the church when it goes out against the mighty social evils which Satan has established, of which, none can dispute successfully, the Liquor Trade is one.

My work is moving slowly along All the energy of mind and body and soul which I can apply scarcely moves the lethargic souls around me, few as they are. I trust God will give more grace and manifestly bless. During the last week or two I have been frequently feeling unwell The season is very trying. I hope you are well in every way. Love to all.

Your affectionate son,

John Alexander Dowie.

23

(Nov. 1st—resigns from his first charge—resignation accepted.)

Dear Father and Mother:

Yours of Wednesday received. This will find you, I hope, quite well

Mrs McD— brought the helmet today, and the vegetables, etc., for which I thank you. The helmet was too small, but, with some sharp stretching, I have managed to wear it today It is a very nice one, and the cover is especially neat. On such a hot day as this has been, it was most welcome

Today I have made three visits and ridden probably more than thirty-five miles, four or five hours being spent in the sun, at "Nellie's" best speed.

Last night's experience of Alma has quite filled up the measure of my discontent, and my mind is now fully made up to leave

Only think, usual service and monthly church meeting announced: How many present?

Two men, who were camping out on the road near, whom I invited, Mr D—, Mr. F—, Mr. McD— and my boy Johnnie—six in all Fancy, a full service and discourse, and my riding five miles, and losing three or four hours, besides the preparation time. Only think of the church—two members! It would be a sinful waste of my life, when so many would gladly hear elsewhere, of my time, and of whatever talent God has given, longer to use (or abuse) them thus Spiritual results are utterly disproportionate God cannot bless, apparently.

And besides, material results are utterly disgraceful. Since April 1 to October 28, (leaving out my February and March labour) my church has raised 36 pounds and, including some received from Home Mission, 58 pounds, which magnificent sums have not even paid my expenses. Surely, after this, it would be monstrous to delay—it will be utter ruin, almost

24

every way, to my efficiency. Into the hands of God
I put it all.

> Your affectionate son,
> John Alexander Dowie.

Dear Father and Mother

Yours of 4th duly received.

I write this early this morning at a time when I
am very weary, after a day's hard riding in visiting and
a long night's conversation with the McD—'s.

Were it not that you are doubtless anxious for this
letter, I would really defer writing. As it is I shall only
give you the two most important events on Thursday
night, leaving a long account of details (D. V.) until
Tuesday.

The following is my letter of resignation:

> "Alma, December 5, 1872.

To the Church of Christ, meeting in the Congregational
Chapel, Alma Plains.

Dear Brethren and Sisters

After much anxious consideration and prayer for
Divine guidance, I have determined to relinquish my
office as your pastor, and now, therefore resign it into
your hands I propose that this take effect on Sabbath, December 29th.

It is with much regret that this decision has been
arrived at My hopes in accepting your call have not
been realized; but I can only view this result as of
God's appointment

I shall ever feel the deepest interest in your spiritual
condition, and that of the people amongst whom I
have here laboured for the Redeemer.

In all your future movements, I now earnestly im-
plore the direction of the Lord by His gracious Spirit.

When this time of probation has merged into the
eternity of bliss purchased by Christ's work for our

souls, I trust there to meet you where pain is unknown
Until then, may "the God of peace make you perfect
in every good work to do His will."

I am, faithfully yours in Christ,

John Alexander Dowie "

This letter I laid upon the table, after conducting
all ordinary business, and retired.

The following resolution was the only formal decision of the after meeting. It was moved by Mr. D
McD—, seconded by Mr G. F—, and carried unanimously: "That this church hereby, with profound sorrow, accepts the resignation of the Rev. John Alexander Dowie as pastor, such resignation to take effect
on Sabbath, December 29, 1872. The church desires
to express their very high sense of his ministry in the
Lord to them, most reluctantly accepts his resignation,
and earnestly prays that God would bless him in all
his future work, abundantly crowning it in the salvation and strengthening of many souls."

The above comprises all the **formal** results of
Thursday evening's meeting. Informally much was
said before and after my retirement from the meeting,
which I am too tired to venture upon writing now.
This at least seems clear, that financially, nothing from
them is to be expected

Tomorrow I hope to hear from you. I hope you
are well Love to all

Your affectionate son,

John Alexander Dowie

(*New field at Manly Beach, near Sidney, New South Wales—writes
friend under date Dec. 3, 1873.*)

My Dear Friend:

Since writing to you on November 22 I have received—indeed only yesterday—your letter dated Nov-

ember 18, and though time is by no means plentiful with me, yet I wish to let you know how things are on with me here.

I was glad to get a letter from you—the first since leaving—and to know from it that you were well, and that, so far as you could then see, you were likely to have a good harvest. The grasshoppers are becoming yearly a serious source of danger, and it is only by, I suppose, a good supply of grass provided for them that they condescend to hop past the wheat. But what when grass is scarce?

There seems, in prospect of a dry season, to be serious grounds for apprehension, owing to their increasing numbers.

I am sorry that from other causes the crops in many places will fall short. But I am quite sure that what is given will be far in excess of the deservings of the reapers; for God never deals out to us the full deserts of our sins, nor rewards us according to our transgressions, either individually or nationally. We are, however, so used to His overflowing bounty that we demur and bitterly complain, as if wronged, when He checks its superabundance.

How foolish and wicked that is! Yet it is a folly of which thousands are daily guilty, and that folly is also the basest ingratitude. Every moment comes laden with God's goodness to all men, and that whether they are just or unjust, yet not only does it pass onward laden with human indifference or repining, but only too often with sins of deepest wickedness through man's misuse of God's gifts, and through his turning those gifts into engines of destruction. It amazes me daily more and more as I extend my actual knowledge of man, when I reflect upon God's forebearance and continued goodness to so rebellious a creature. Wherever I turn the same facts continually meet me—in myself and in the world of men around me—there are mighty and rebellious passions continually leading to

27

disobedience of God   And the struggle is so hard,
needs such continuous watchfulness and strength—
while too often there are friends within us of the
enemy which from without assails us—traitorous desires that would have us surrender the fortress of our
hearts to sin and Satan.   Well may we sing in the
words of the "bairn's hymn"—

"My home is in heaven, my rest is not here,
Then why should I murmur when trials appear?
Be hushed, my sad spirit, the worst that can come,
But shortens my journey and hastens me home

It is not for me to be seeking my bliss,
And building my hopes in a region like this;
I look for a city which hands have not piled,
I pant for a country by sin undefiled."

Do you not find that the more you know of the
Christian life leads you to see more clearly, to feel
more keenly, the fact that "rest" is not here, that
life for Christ is a journey onward, ever onward, a conflict ever raging or impending, a scene where to live
purely and Godly means often to live far from, out-
wardly, peaceably; but with all that, is it not blessed
to find that this is the path which Jesus trod, and
every step the story of His life reveals to us as more
painful and terrible than it can ever be to us, while
His words come back to us as we journey on in these,
His footsteps: "These things have I spoken unto
you that in me ye might have peace. In the world ye
shall have tribulation; but be of good cheer; I have
overcome the world." And as these words of the
Saviour, the Captain of our Salvation, come down to
us they fall upon our listening ears like a soul-stirring,
fear-destroying melody—sweet and strong, causing our
hearts to chant back—"Yea, Lord, Thou hast overcome the world, and following Thee so may we—for

28

'who is he that overcometh the world, but he that be-
lieveth that Jesus is the Son of God?'"

Yes, we can so sing, as we press daily forward,
with calm, undaunted confidence, in the path which
God appoints, and as one by one the Christian pilgrims sink and fall, to the world's eye just as others
on its path, do we not hear the angel hosts of heaven
re-echo our song in theirs, saying, "Write, Blessed
are the dead that die in the Lord from henceforth:
Yea, saith the Spirit, that they may rest from their
labours, and their works do follow them"   .   .   .
These are glorious songs for such as we to sing and
hear, they are among the songs of the redeemed, and
among them are not we?

By the way, you must tell me how you like Spurgeon's "Morning by Morning" There is a companion
volume entitled "Evening by Evening," which you
could probably get from some Adelaide bookseller
easily, if you wished.

Thanks, many thanks, for the way in which you
write of the portrait which the sun drew of me in
South Australia, for a photograph means literally "a
thing drawn by the light." It is good for me to feel,
when my heart is craving for some human sympathy,
to remember you and such as you who do sympathise
with and pray for me, that I may be kept faithful and
blessed in the work of the Blessed Master Often and
often my memory recalls your face, your words, your
deeds, and all the unuttered and perhaps unutterable
desires you have had on my behalf—these things are
"things drawn by the light," true photographs, upon
my heart.

Is it not astonishing when we place a photograph
of a dear friend before us, look straight into the eyes,
mark all the well known, hidden to others, expression
which rests upon every part of the countenance, how
memory after memory rushes in upon us, like a high
spring tide filling all our hearts, and causing us to feel

even a keen sense of pain as well as pleasure, compelling us sometimes to put the picture back again, or to turn away from so close a scrutiny?

This often happens to me, and that with whom I most love. Yet, it is a pain which is only in many cases produced by too keen a remembrance of former recollections, which comprise a treasure of pleasure. Strange that pain and pleasure should be so intermingled. . .

From the enclosure in my hasty letter of November 22 you will know the circumstances connected with my coming here, and to that I have only to add the fact that the work of Christ continues to prosper under my ministry. The church is filled to overflowing with a most earnestly attentive audience every Sabbath, especially in the evening,—a Sabbath School, which I only organized three Sabbaths ago has considerably over 70 scholars on the roll, 11 of whom were youg men between 15 and 30 years old, who form a Bible-class. My people are very enthusiastic about their new minister, and I have been most honorably treated by my brother ministers, who have shown me every kindness, and welcomed me to their gatherings on a footing of perfect equality. Next Sabbath, I leave my pulpit here for the day, and preach in Sydney two sermons on behalf of Camden Congregational College funds; and it is one of the good signs, that even for the day, the people are very unwilling to have me replaced, even by one of our most successful city ministers These things and many others, more indeed than I can put on paper, are very cheering, and everything seems bright and prosperous; the necessity for increased reliance upon God the Giver is more deeply impressed upon me The frail tenure by which all human happiness is held can never be forgotten, I trust, by me; and often do I seem to hear the voices: "Watch and pray, lest ye enter into temptation."

There are indications of higher blessing, too, in

manifestations of spiritual awakening among rich and poor, educated and ignorant, in this small community; and while, of necessity, it is evident more in general, wide-spread desires after holiness of life, yet I am not without cheering cases of distinct decision. These have happened very recently. It is the Lord's doing, and marvelous in my eyes.

I know how truly you sympathise with me in my work, in joy or in sorrow; and I say again, it does me good to tell you how it is with me, assured that I have your prayers for increased wisdom and guidance. Therefore, I have written

When I next write you I wish to give you a short description of the beauties of the natural scenery here, which surpasses everything I ever saw in my life—a sort of terrestial paradise; and I cannot help saying how much joy it would give me to see you here . . Now South Wales appears to me a very much finer country than any of the other colonies; and the accounts which I receive of the interior lead me to believe that you can find in many parts of it almost an English climate for coolness, and an Australian one for clearness.

I am invited to visit Bathurst, about 150 miles from Sydney, westward beyond the mountains, about the beginning of the year. A new Congregational church is to be commenced there and a large number are going from Sydney to assist at the meetings in connection with the laying of the foundation stone. If I go, I shall be able to speak of the country as an eye witness and will tell you my impressions.

You see what a long letter I have written to you with mine own hand. It is a pleasure and not a toil; and I could only wish that it was more carefully written. When I look over it, I shall be sure to wish I had written many other things; but it is quite impossible to please oneself in these matters.

I hope soon to hear from you and meanwhile say good-by again, praying that the Almighty Father

31

would guide you in all your ways, making you, by His Spirit, more fully to know and to follow Jesus Christ as your only Saviour and Eternal Friend; and

I am, in Him,

Affectionately your friend,

John Alexander Dowie.

(Three months later.)

Dear Friend:

You will remember that I promised more fully to reply to your last letter.

Your account of affairs at Alma is a very saddening one; but just what my experience of those nominal Christians warranted me in expecting.

It was quite clear to me, long before I left, that the institutions of a Christian church could not be carried out by those whose lives and actions exhibited nothing of, but on the contrary, were sometimes diametrically opposed to—Christ's life, actions and precepts.

This is still my opinion, and, therefore, I deeply sympathise with you as a member of the church whose sole desire, I know, is to walk by our Saviour's own right line of life: for those most prominent in church matters, troubled by no such scruples, are only desirous to carry out their own will—crooked, ignorant, selfish and worldly as these wills are. Consequently, your power to do right in the church, seems to me to be only limited to a protest against wrong; and such protest it is your duty to make so long as you remain in fellowship there.

God's way with sinners is known only to Himself.

I would not anticipate His dealings; but this I know, that though hand join in hand, yet shall the wicked not go unpunished. Only a true penitence, deep humiliation of self and faith can avert that stroke of Divine wrath.

Christ's work in this city is in a sad state. Church

going there is; but a perfect malaria of spiritual disease with it, slow fevers of indifference and cowardice, leprosies of pride, hatred and vanity, burning fevers of money and pleasure seeking, and an epidemic of vice. 'Tis a doubtful picture, I know, to draw; but falls far below the reality.

There are doubtless many who have not bowed the knee to Baal, but, like Elijah, I don't see many of them.

And oh, how powerless, paralyzed almost, I feel in the midst of it all! Sometimes I feel I ought to cry out, but then again—almost literally—my mouth is shut. God has His time, I know, but I am tempted much to weary for its manifestation.

It seems clearer that the British climate would be too severe for my constitution; but I have so deep a heart's longing to work there for Christ that it is trying, indeed, to acknowledge it. Then, if not there, Where? comes the question. My heart says "not here"; and God has not yet made it clear. But I will not perplex either you or myself with that which I desire to cast in simple faith upon our Father's care.

I shall expect some time during next week to hear from you. May the power and soothing sweetness of the Saviour's love be all your portions, making you to feel calmness and confidence in the midst of joy or sorrow, looking to Jesus, making you to gaze steadfastly through all the mist of time into the clear light of Eternity where He stands waiting to crown you— the Finisher of Faith.

Affectionately yours in Christ,
John Alexander Dowie.

(*Written to a young man whom he has rescued from drink habit and assisted, and at time of writing has position on newspaper.*)

. . . The paper does you credit in its way, though there is always a good deal of pettiness which will force itself into country papers. I am glad that you

2

have dropped the rubbish "poetry" from "Lucknow." I could imagine Carlyle pointing to it with a fierce chuckle. Do try and get your "cynic"—Diogenes or Antisthenes would not own him—to follow "Lucknow" into the realm of shades. Get some strong, pithy sense, in short, pungent, clear sentences, into your writing. Men have no time or patience with stupid rodomontade You are engaged in very important work. Go in hard for it Give them glimpses into British social life in every way you can: for generally speaking, colonials are dreadfully ignorant of these matters. Aim high in thought; but express yourself more and more in volleys of words which sweep low enough to hit the meanest capacity. Let a glorious sense of doing Divine work sweep all paltry ideas away and ever stimulate your endeavors. While writing, I am reminded of quaint old George Herbert's words in that wise old poem of his "The Church-Porch":—

"Pitch thy behaviour low, thy projects high;
"So shalt thou humble and magnanimous be:
"**Sink not in spirit**: who aimeth at the sky
"Shoots higher much than he that means a tree.
"A grain of glory mixt with humblenesse,
"Cures both a fever and lethargicknesse."

And now that I have the volume before me, I shall. for your edification and my own, quote another verse—greatly needed to be observed by all pen and voice preachers —

"Be calm in arguing: for fiercenesse makes
"Errour a fault and truth discourtesie
"Why should I feel another man's mistakes
"More than his sicknesses or povertie?
"In love I should, but anger is not love,
"Nor wisdom neither; therefore, gently move"

These words will bear five minutes earnest reflection, and we will be the better for getting them into daily realization But ho! a truce to sermonizing!

How easy it is to glide away into essay-writing in letter-writing. But it is not the most interesting, nor perhaps instructive way of writing. Let me ask you to look up friend Herbert, though. There is true piety, rich spiritual experience, sweet thoughts of Jesus and His love, and a deep, fresh, manly well of true and cool and clear Christian philosophy in his poetry. Take for instance his poem "Man." It is a grand conception, though oddly expressed. Read it, and tell me what you think of it.

"Oh, mightie love! Man is one world, and hath
    "Another to attend him."

"Effectual calling," by God's gracious Spirit—it is a glorious doctrine—is a blessed experience. To Him be all the praise for His marvelous work in leading you to accept the gifts of pardon, reconciliation and eternal life in Jesus. It rejoices me to know that you are growing in grace. Oh, keep very near to Jesus always. Get down very often in prayer, and you will rise in power to do and bear His will in all things. O that we loved Him more, and looked to Him more steadfastly! Blessed Lord, Eternal Saviour, Friend of sinners, Intercessor for us and in us, shed abroad the fire of sin-consuming love in our poor hearts! Jesus, Lord, come quickly; visit us with reviving grace and power!

May God bless all your scholars. Do you pray for your class daily, by name, and **expect** a blessing? What a joy, if God saves them, and by your means! A Christian effectually called can always exercise, if he will, effectual fervent prayer. May God bless you in that work. Prepare well. Pray earnestly before going to teach. Let prayer be your spiritual atmosphere. You will reap, not now misery, but the fruits of the Spirit, if you are willing.

My work is steadily maintained. About 14 persons have become abstainers, within the last two or three weeks, and have signed my book. In other ways there are signs of God's presence; but how I long to hear of decisions for Christ! No doubt we are being blessed, but God's promise is to bless us "until there shall not be room enough to receive." What a blessed time will come when we have faith to **try** Him with that promise!

I sadly feel that I want more room, more population, to work upon, and cannot stay much longer here Let us, meanwhile, do what lies to our hands to do with all our might Keep up your weekly letter and do not be surprised if I am a little irregular. I have such **heaps** of work before me.

May the Lord very graciously strengthen, comfort, guide and establish you in all your thoughts and ways

Ever yours in Jesus,

John Alexander Dowie

(Oct. 29, 1874—deeply impressed with state of society about him— feels his own weakness.)

Dear C—·

Though I have neither married nor died—and sometimes it had been better to die than to marry for not a few sons of Adam—yet my delay is capable of explanation. I have been overworking, and have really not found time to write to you All yours have duly reached me, and gladdened me I look now quite regularly for your weekly letter.

I am glad you had a good communion time and that Mr. W— seems to be growing in your esteem. Truly it is a glorious thing to know the oneness of all followers of Jesus, and I am increasingly desirous to manifest this practically. My present position, too, as Secretary of the "Monday Mid-day United Prayer Meetings" enables me to do this in some measure; and I have also, in a fortnight's series of united evangelistic meetings, been able to bring together, in a work among the masses of Sydney, ministers and people of all denominations of Christians. The work has been blessed but has involved prodigious labour, and my presence and help for the greater part of both weeks. The awful sights and sounds which I saw and heard in the neighborhood of the Australian Hall, and elsewhere, have deeply impressed me with the conviction that there is a terrible amount of misery and evil in this city. The half could not be told of what is known, and it is my firm belief that not one tithe of the wickedness is apparent to the onlooker. In all classes there is a terrible flood of moral evil, and while men are discussing mere metaphysics on the one hand and mere externals on the other in religious matters, vast numbers of souls are hardening in vice and wholly slaves to bodily and corrupt passions. Nine tenths of infidelity in all classes has, in my opinion, its roots in immorality; for instinctively the human soul cries out for the living God until it is silenced by sins consciously opposed to all ideas of His purity, and only then does the fearful and guilty heart question God's existence, deny His laws, reject His Son, and flee from His presence.

Therefore, to destroy all sin and infidelity, the Gospel of mercy and pardoning love, with its consequent life of Christian truth and purity must be pressed upon men in all conditions, as a complete panacea for all human woes and necessities.

Smart telegraphy, snorting rail trains, delicious cookery, witty and silly literature, explorations into fossils of the earliest period, floods of lip talk, oceans of newspaper talk, with "news"—these things will not lead to more peace or joy in the soul. But a living, Christ-like love for an inward reality, and an outward unceasing self-sacrificing life of true charity will speed the day along the track of a Divine life such as would speedily solve all earthly problems, by carrying men away onward into such conceptions of the life beyond as would lead them to a more and more perfect life here.

Neither Caesarism nor Ultramontanism nor Materialism nor any revised Ecclesiasticism in any church will ever raise the human family to a Divine life and true, loving unity But true Christianity will; and before true religion can reach its power it must be freed from the sins in which social and political and even church organizations have bound it A pure, clear, firm trust in the words of Jesus; and a fearless and thorough endeavour to realize them fully, in every step and moment of the daily life—these principles must operate. But ere they can there must be, for the whole Church of God, a more thorough belief in the presence and power of the Holy Spirit—and no doctrine and fact is at present less prominent than a simple reliance upon the Holy Spirit. The baptism of Repentance, rather than the baptism of the Holy Ghost, is too much insisted upon. And the recognition that all true progress must be the work of the Spirit is most sinfully ignored or forgotten often times When floods of spiritual light and life are poured down, in copious showers of quickening inward grace, upon the churches of Jesus, **then** shall we see sinners flocking to the Cross and finding pardon there—then shall we see saved ones bearing the Cross in all its glorious, attractive power, as the Banner of Liberty from all oppressions among all nations Now, there are flocks of miserable creatures squabbling as to **who** shall carry, and **how** they shall carry, and **when** they shall carry, and **where** they shall carry, and **for what** they shall carry to a ruined and lost race the restoring grace of Christ's eternal power in His glorious Gospel Is it not destestable? **Who?** All! **How?** In every possible form! **When?** Now and at all times! **Where?** Everywhere! **For what?** Nothing!—for Christ's people will, or ought to, see all Christ's followers, their brethren, fully supplied by a true and faithful, Christ-like communism in material things.

Think of all these things, and pray over them.

God will grant true liberty and comprehensiveness of soul, and fire your heart with the grandest and holiest aspirations, while you make His will your **only** guide.
. . . Of course you will be saying, what is really true—off again into a pulpit discourse. However, you know my frailty. Like Carlyle, a firm believer in the grandeur of silence, and yet at all possible times the most inveterate of talkers and scribblers.
. . . Oh, how miserably weak and empty of goodness and power do I feel! My heart fairly aches with its weariness and langour! God give me more strength and fill me with grace! My physical health is good, despite my having taxed it most severely, and I am deeply grateful to God for this and His other innumerable mercies

Now remember that you are ever in my prayers, that the Lord may protect and direct you in all your ways, ever enabling you to adorn the doctrine of God, your Saviour, in all things. Ever pray for me. Let us continue to fight the good fight of faith; let us, amid fierce storms of fearful temptation, hold fast to Jesus.

"And we, on divers shores now cast,
Shall meet, our perilous voyage past,
All in our Father's house at last."

Never again shall we then mourn over sin-marred days   With sincerest love,

Yours in Jesus,

John Alexander Dowie

(*Expresses views on Spiritism*)

My dear Mr. L—:

Enclosed I return the pamphlet on "Spiritism" which you kindly lent me.

Permit me to say, in reference to it, that it is more ingenious than ingenuous, and deals with criticism most unfairly by withholding the main arguments.

The trumpery stuff which is appended as illustrations of spirit manifestations, and especially the eminently silly "angelic ministrations," stamp the whole affair at once as foolish and unchristian—nay more, anti-Christian, from whatever source it proceeds

Now, I have striven for the greater part of my life to regulate my thoughts and words and actions by the teachings of the Lord Jesus Christ, as I find them in the Bible. Therefore, I can experimentally testify that there can be no comparison between the two systems, Christianity and Spiritism: for separate and opposed systems they certainly are, and every day multiplies evidence of this assertion. Experience has proved to me, that there is one, mighty, omniscient Holy Spirit, and that there is **neither need nor room** for any other teacher and guide into the way of all Truth, than that Spirit who, to every faithful follower of Jesus, gives strength, purity, love and eternal peace all through life here, to immortality hereafter.

When I find God's revealed will insufficient for my spiritual guidance; when I find nobler precepts and greater principles of truth than Jesus has declared; when there directly comes to me a more blessed Consoler and Guide than the Spirit which daily "helpeth my infirmity" and teaches me how to pray, as well as pleads "with unutterable groanings within me" when I am weak and err,—then, and not till then—when I shall have lost all faith in the eternal and loving Father whom the Bible reveals—then I shall listen to these childish fables and devilish lies. Oh, what unutterable misery is coming down upon this wretched, blasphemous, vicious, drunken, sin-cursed world of ours, by wandering away from a simple faith in Jesus! His grand and yet tenderly compassionate words, His clear, unmistakable directions, and His atoning life and death here and intercessory reign above, are still,—not the Gospel of glad tidings,—but the words of "foolishness to them who are perishing." May God in His mercy grant us deliverance from the spirit of pride and disobedience and unbelief, which in manifold forms in still endeavoring to destroy all faith in Jesus as the Christ, and all belief in the direct accountability of man to God.

I beg that you will consider these remarks as conceived in a kind and unpresumptuous spirit and that you will not for a moment consider them as intentionally disrespectful. I only mean them as a candid declaration of my views as a neighbor and as a minister of Christ's Gospel, and my earnest prayer to our common God and Father is that He would bless you and yours, and lead you into an entire trust in Jesus and the Truth as it is in Him.

> I am,
> Very sincerely yours,
> John Alexander Dowie.

(Feb. 25, '74—discouraged, but refuses to retire.)

Dear Father and Mother:

A reproachful conscience, who can bear? He answers that he cannot, and therefore perforce has commenced to write, though strongly tempted to put it off again: for he is tired and desirous of a little rest. But, doubtless he will forget it all as the pen and the mind and the stiff, unpliable hand gets used to their occupation.

Your letters are always interesting; but they are always too short. You need patience. Writing is about as irksome to me as to you; but I overcome that a good deal by persistent pegging away. Do write more fully. It develops one's own thought, and leads to greater facility and precision in the use of God's great gift to man—language. This you know, doubtless; but by way of remembrance I find it necessary to stir up your thinking powers.

Your remarks as to the contrast between the South Australian and New South Wales churches are, in

41

the main, just, but attentive observation always reveals special dangers and defects in all human systems, which just leads up to the conclusion that in regard to all church organization, it is simply a choice of imperfections which is afforded us. I am more inclined than ever to maintain a very observant attitude in regard to church matters here, and yet, of course, wish to be helpful as well as watchful, which is a desire difficult to realize.

Absorption, if not identification, is almost a necessary consequence of anything like effective help, and in that case critical—I use the word in a good sense—observation is trying to the strongest mind. However, I must try do do both

To think of "retiring from it all' is not what a Christian should say Keble's verses often occur to me when tempted to think as you have expressed yourself

"I journey,—but no step is won,
Alas! the weary course I run,
Like sailors, shipwrecked in their dreams,
All powerless and benighted seems "

Then comes the revulsion

"What, wearied out with half a life?
Scared with this smooth, unbloody strife?
Think where thy coward hopes had flown,
Had heaven held out the martyr's crown "

We dare not think of retiring from it all, much less of doing so. What a terrible commentary upon that sort of thing is afforded by the history of Plymouth Brethrenism, American Shakerism, Roman Monasticism, etc. No, "let us not be weary in well doing: for in due season"—here and hereafter—"we shall reap, if we faint not." Old words, ever true.

If W— comes, I shall have as little as possible to do with him, for in temperament and thoughts and church action we are an exact contrast—in fact I feel, antagonistically opposite; because it seems to me that it is just such men as he who hinder Christ's work, in at least some important respects. In an earnest, restless, busy age, they are listless, lethargic and idle—sometimes obstructive. Let him at least not hinder. If he does, I for one will not have any difficulty in refusing to go into the traces with him, or any who are like him, for time will soon be all gone.

Nothing is becoming more deeply impressed upon my mind of late than the principle of absolute non-reliance upon one's fellow men, no matter how good.

It is well when I and others can thoroughly co-operate in any portion of Christ's work; but I feel that one must be ever ready to part company with even the most valued co-operator who strikes off to pursue some other path or plan in which we either cannot or dare not share. This feeling ought to draw us close to God, as workers together with Him, and thus cause us more fully to rely upon Him.

The work of God in my church is still steadily progressing; attendance, notwithstanding very inclement weather, is large on Sabbaths, and there must have been between sixty and eighty persons present at my meeting tonight, though it is a windy, rough night, and has rained heavily today.

My health has not been all that could be desired. Pains in head and sleeplessness have caused me much trouble, and rather reduced me in physical vigor—making all study and pulpit work to be a very heavy burden sometimes.

A most painfully interesting case is now occupying much of my attention here:

One evening, more than three weeks ago, I was walking alone through George Street, one of the principal streets in Sydney, from an anniversary meeting

at Waterloo, near Sydney. A young man, very shab-
bily dressed, came close up to me and in a voice which
gave me a thrill of pain to hear, he implored me to
give him money for food and a bed that night. His
clear, Scotch accent and appearance at once impressed
me, and I quickly discovered that he was an Edinburgh man and that drink had caused his plight. Re-
lieving his immediate wants, I gave him money to
pay his fare to Manly on the Thursday—it was a Tuesday eve I saw him—when I would more fully talk
with him and see what could be done He came down
here on the Tuesday and I asked him to tell me who he
was and what his former position. It fairly astounded
me, when he with tears replied that he was the young-
est son—he is 26 years old—of the late Rev. C—, Edinburgh, and that he had been a saloon passenger in
the "Loch Lomond" to Melbourne which reached
there September last, but that though he had got a
good situation, he had fallen again through drink, as
he had several times before at home.

Ashamed and disgraced, he shipped as a common
seaman in a vessel to New Castle, New South Wales,
an American ship which, owing to contrary winds
was about a month in reaching that port. There he
could get no employment and sold his clothing, excepting that in a bag, which along with his letters,
etc., were detained by a lodging house keeper for
money owing. Stowing himself away in a steamer
sailing late at night for Sydney, he managed to get
here and out of the steamer unperceived. But in Sydney week after week passed without his getting work,
until for the first time he begged, and in that deepest
depth of his degradation God had led him to me Here
he was fairly crying now, telling me that it was he
who had broken his father's heart and caused his
death, and that now even hope had almost completely
forsaken him and that it was "too late." My answer
was, "By God's help, no! We shall at least have a

44

fight with the Devil for you, son of many prayers; I shall ask God to answer them and help you all I can." There and then I fed and clothed him—angels' work is sometimes given to man—and got one of my people to take him and keep him comfortably in return for God's blessing and the work he could do about the place. That day he signed the pledge and ever since has wholly abstained.

Prayerfully penitent, he has now for more than three weeks given me every encouragement. Oh, how cunning and strong the demon is! but, "Greater is He that is with us than all that can be against us;" and in the Lord's name and strength we shall measure swords with this enemy of souls. In many ways my hands are full. Pray for me. May all needed grace be yours from a merciful and gracious Father.

Your affectionate son,

John Alexander Dowie.

(Writes to friend regarding the latter's work.)

. . . . The press has fast become—the newspaper press, I mean—so wholly secular that it is fast developing into a foe to all that is sacred. It is so unsectarian that it often becomes unchristian and often anti-Christian. It is so thoroughly devoted to material things, an intellectualism devoted merely to material and temporal things, that it ignores and sometimes denies the importance of spiritual and eternal things— it talks as if merely humanly framed economics and ethics were to be all mens guide, and as if Christianity were to be adapted to them, rather than that these sciences of mind should be adapted to the mind and will of Christ. Beware, O Press, or else the place which now knows you will know you no more! Learn the awful responsibility which God imposes along with your power: for if your power does not run in the true rail tracks of Divine Direction, then you are like a steam engine off the track, and rushing onwards to depths unfathomable!

O John, my friend, do what you can in preventing a collision between the truth speaking Word of Christ, from pulpit or otherwise, and the press,—the newspaper press. I see both, in many places and nations, tearing along in opposite ways, not directly opposite it may be always,—but across the line of truth, the press train is speeding. "Look out for the train!" is all I can say You see, I doubt not, that my anxiety is to see you and myself on the right and true track, which is the only track, and which it is woe to us and yet more awful woe, if we willfully get off it. Let us remember, too, that all who aspire to be thinkers and speakers and writers are intellectual locomotives who have trains behind them—alas, some of us have only coal wagons and turnips attached, with here and there a man; and there are some (may we be among these) who have noble freights of men—ay, men in all classes —and they have attached themselves to said engines

Most men do not keep on think, think, thinking— they link on to some thinker; and puff, puff, puffing, away they go after him, liking the motion! . .

There is no doubt a great tendency in local papers to magnify the importance of local magnates and to throw them all sorts of little sops, and every now and then to wave as incense in their nostrils expressions such as "Most worthy citizen," our "Respected" or "Highly honoured" or "Greatly esteemed" or "Well known—fellow townsman." Get rid of it. It is the quintessence of snobism, prevents the use of thorough-going, wide-embracing writing, and the "store-keeper" and the "country attorney" element have the appetite of the horse leech and her daughters for this sort of flattery—and when it is with-held are greatly offended. Discontinue at once and forever,—unless you can get an entirely new language for local flatteries alone . . .

46

Do not yield to the depressing influences around. The robust, vigorous, thorough-going piety of our Scotch religious life is far more preferable; and with a little more of the sunshine of love, is by far the most beautiful I know . . . . .

The Lord has been very gracious to us, and continues to give evidences of His presence and blessing. Yet there is not that evident result for which we naturally so long; but when I think of my sinful and unworthy heart, I wonder not. Oh, to be wholly true and faithful and loving! Mighty indeed is the Spirit. Oh, that we saw evidences of God's saving power among our perishing masses in all classes of society!

(July 28, '74—writes of his work—deprecates slothfulness in ministers.)

Dear Father and Mother:

Yours of 13th duly reached me, and terminated all my fears as to whether my letter had miscarried. I am greatly pleased to find you are all well, and that you are beginning to write longer letters. This is written in good average health; but after a very great deal of work, and, indeed, in the midst of work. However, work is pleasing when it is for Christ, and is still pleasanter when we know that it is not labour in vain, but manifestly owned by Him in its effect upon souls around. Humbling and self-destroying as all prosperity in the Savior's work is, it is calculated greatly to impress the worker with a solemn sense of God's presence; and these things I have recently experienced.

Everything is prosperous in outward things in my work, and increasing signs of deepening and awakening interest are seen on every hand. My work seems to be steadily consolidating and strengthening in all directions, and since it is for, and I trust with, Christ I labour, that is the greatest of blessings.

Since writing to you I have had much in hand, much anxiety, much exertion: for though I speak gratefully of much blessing, it is scarcely necessary for me to say that there has been much difficulty and toil that is inevitable: for labour is the Divine road to all success.

At the close of Monday I begin this letter after a very hard day and night's work, and trust to finish it tomorrow. When once the first procrastination is overcome, then I feel writing a relief; but it is hard to begin. However, after this rambling preface, I throw down the pen and give up the task for tonight, hoping tomorrow to write more pointedly and connectedly . . . .

About my housekeeping: I am doing quite comfortably, all things considered. My housekeeper's name is Mrs. Taylor; about fifty-five years old; a widow; tall, dark, strong and active, quiet and kindly in manners; a good cook and laundress, economical in her ways. All these treasures are, so far as money goes, procured for ten shillings a week; and if I were a cynical bachelor (into which state teasing drives one speedily) I would say that it would take more than that to keep most wives in gloves and ribbons every week—to say nothing of gowns, and frills, and feathers, and flounces, and parasols, and bonnets, and boots, and laces, and scents, and brooches, and bracelets, and carpets, and a new house, and a servant, and a washerwoman, and perhaps a boy, and often a cat, and perhaps a nurse maid; and the awful prospect of being relegated to the smallest room in the house for a study, and an end to all book buying, and envious eyes noting the minister's wife's new raiment, with calculations of cost, and confidential communications of the minister's most private affairs, with notes as to visitors, and—well, what would all these things cost in money (which I have not), in peace of mind (of which I need more), in loss

John Alexander Dowie and seven members of his church who suffered imprisonment in Melbourne jail, 1885, rather than pay a fine imposed for alleged violation of ordinance prohibiting street preaching; they were freed by an unconditional release from the Governor. Reading from left to right: H. Martin, J. S. Wallington, H. G. Mence, John Alexander Dowie, W. Foxcraft, J. L. Morrish, R. Hood, J. Ray.

of time and influence (of which I have too little)?

Thus might the cynical bachelor (do not confound me with him if you can charitably help it) argue when driven to bay by a chorus of mammas, his own included. Let those who read try to understand. It is a painful truth, that many a true word is spoken in a jest.

Were I to speak seriously about what, after all, is a most serious matter to all men, and especially to a minister, I would say that seeing "a good wife is from the Lord," I had better just keep on waiting until I can see some one clearly sent by Him in my way, and if no one comes, then so be it—and that is final. Therefore let mother just be content to leave it where I do, and not to let her loving desires for my welfare run counter to what may be the Divine plan. There are worse things far than "a tim hoose and auld servant and a cat": for a bad wife seems a gift from the Devil, and would make a hell of what might be a heavenly home—and a foolish, peevish, silly wife is only a shade less trying. In many ways, I am unfitted for ordinary home life, and not merely my present habits of Christian action, but those which an altered sphere of labour would impose are not likely to be congenial to any one who had not the same mind, or at least the fullest confidence in the general course of my thinking and doing; and, I say it seriously, it would require to be one who made up her mind to leave the reins entirely in my hands.

Am I at last clear; and will you kindly, therefore, rather aid me with your sympathy and prayers, than disturb me with kindly, most lovingly meant advice, which at present cannot possibly be taken?

After all, this is of very minor importance to the great importance of my work for the Redeemer; and I ask you to pray that it may ever remain so to me.

Poor Mr. White, I am sorry to hear of his illness and that the doctor says it is incurable. If any words of mine will cheer him, he shall have them; and I have just entered his name in my diary for Monday next at latest.

There is One "who healeth all our diseases" who, he knows, can most effectually cheer him, and on Him, doubtless, he trusts.

Lately I have bent over several dying beds, and have seen "how sweet the name of Jesus sounds, in a believer's ear," and more and more do I feel how precious it is to thrust Him, and how gloomy and cheerless it is to distrust Him. Weary and sad and labouring and sorrowing, where can the soul find rest but in Him who "wearily" sat down often in His toilsome journeys through a world which hated and scorned Him, Who bore our sins, carried our sorrows, bowed His head, poured out His soul unto death and wrought out by a life of labour and pain and by a death of ignominious shame, our redemption, our salvation?

He is the glorious Intercessor He is the eternal Saviour, the continual Advocate; and His **sympathy** is as complete as His **power**: "For in that He Himself hath suffered being tempted, He is able to succor them that are tempted " And the old paraphrase comes sweeter and more consoling as all human help disappears, and eternity alone is before us, but the Saviour beside us:

"In every pang that rends the heart,
"The Man of sorrows had a part;
"He sympathises with our grief,
"And to the sufferer sends relief."

And believing **that**, how comes it that prayer is restrained before God, and that the next words of the paraphrase are so little acted upon? If we cast away all garments of sin and weights which oppress our souls, **then** we can say

"With boldness, therefore, at the Throne,
"We come to make our sorrows known;
"And ask the aids of heavenly power
"To help us in this evil hour."

. . . As a specimen of W—'s way of looking at his work take the following as an almost verbatim report of a short conversation at the School of Arts in Sydney the other day, where we happened to meet. "D" represents myself and "W" our friend.

After the usual greetings and inquiries for each others' health, the conversation proceeded: D. "How are you getting on with the work at Petersham?" W. "Oh, pretty well, fairly, you know. They have had so many changes, you know, and the population is thin." (He has four or five times the population to work upon that I have.) "It will take time." D. "I suppose you begin to see things improving?" W. "Well, a little, you know; but it will take time, a great deal of time and patience. I told the deacons when I came that it would take about two years to do any thing."

At which wondrous exercise of faith and patience and Divine energy among dying men and perishing souls, I fairly collapsed.

I cannot understand such a man. Coming to a church which has been under a well sustained ministry for years, to a church fully constituted and ready for work, it amazes me.

Had I looked at Manly in the same spirit, I would have fled from it in absolute despair; for here there was a small population, a congregation of about twenty-five, and no church, while the chapel had been, often inefficiently, supplied for ten years by lay preachers, and even now there is only one thorough old Congregationalist among the whole audience and workers.

'Tis very sad to see this. And sadder still to hear the chorus of resounding praise over this mature,

51

richly stored, powerful pastor! Doubtless the man is a Christian, but in him there are little enough evidences, to my mind, of the right sort of power at a time when the energy, the intelligence, the power, the position, the influence and the numbers of the Evil One's emissaries amazes the thoughtful Christian Such men as W— have their place, and a most important place, too, in the ranks of a church; but certainly all the great qualities of a leader—strong faith, undaunted courage, catching, enthusiastic, passionate love for souls, keen watchfulness, quick decision, prompt action, hard-hitting, 19th century speech, and high, Christ-like, Pauline daring—these seem all wanting in our friend, with a wondrous lack of tact and adaptation of the highest source, and a gradually acquired consciousness of matured-wisdom-talk and self-appreciation, which he was never born to, never acquired, but which has, nevertheless, been thrust upon him, and which he has naturally enough appropriated. The Lord knoweth, and I know, how in writing these words, I have neither conscious ill-will to W— nor any consciousness of self-gratulation in thinking of myself as possessing the qualities of which I declare him to be, for the most part, entirely lacking. Doubtless there may be many points in which he is, as a Christian and scholar, immensely my superior; but he is one of those **ministerial sloths**, I was going to say, and it may as well stand, to whom I have an instinctive antipathy, which is yet without sin, I trust

I feel sadly my shortcomings in the great and responsible position in which I stand, but, if I thought I appeared to many as he appears to me, I would relinquish my ministry without a pang tomorrow: for I would be clearly unfit

Really, I ought to apologize for my long digression, but it seems inevitable that W— should always appear my ministerial **bete noir**—not the man, so much as his nature.

Hodge's "Outlines" are highly spoken of, and you will greatly benefit by their perusal. Is it not singular that the terms "System" and "Systematic Theology" are now so generally, and I think deservedly, disesteemed and therefore disused? It is a suggestive fact. "Outlines" seems a better term than "System." Please tell me what you think of Hodge as you proceed.

Archbishop Manning is very boldly taking up the gauntlet thrown down to him by Fitz James Stephens in the Review, and after answering him in the Romish way has, I see, assumed the offensive in an article on "Christianity and Antichristianics" in June issue. I most unhesitatingly say that Romanism has been greatly strengthened by German interference with the principles of religious liberty, to the full privileges of which all men may claim a right. Overt acts of force and conspiracy against civil liberty, from any source whatever, may be met by the firm execution of just civil laws; but no civil law is just or right which interferes with conscience, and demands that I, if a theological student, shall study in accordance with the state enactment. That is what the great physical force tyranny of Germany has imposed; and it is a cruel wrong, and a sad blow to the spread of true Gospel light and liberty, since it gives an enemy of Gospel liberty a vantage ground which ought never to have been given. I have little hope of good in Germany until kingly and aristocratic and military tyranny shall give way to a truly national government, in which the corrupt Lutheran State Church shall have no political sway.

Manning has seized his vantage, and fights with our weapons the cause of Romanism, and brings out the undeniable Divine truth which alone has kept

Rome alive, which is the most skillful way of weakening the attack upon his church, at a time when all men thought that the infallibility dogma and the loss of the temporal power had sealed its doom.

Between German political tyranny and Roman Catholic ecclesiastical tyranny there is no choice—it is simply, at it were, a choice between Satan and Beelzebub. God grant that Christ and His conquering, men and nation subduing, Gospel may prevail!   .

Surely this letter is long enough, yea too long, but it has been a pleasurable toil

May every needed grace be ever with you.

Your affectionate son,

John Alexander Dowie.

(Oct. 12, '74—considering change of field—decides to remain in Australia.)

Dear C—.

The quiet evening hour has come, and I sit now to answer your last two letters, while the rain and wind and heavy swell of the sea outside all mingle in one moaning sound, as if the elements were weeping over darkened, ruined nature   'Tis cold, dark, wet and windy without, and inside, though light and warm and quiet, yet my mind seems to sympathise more with the storm and darkness outside.   How strange a thing is mind and its various moods

I have been doing a long, hard day's reading and have not once gone outside my door   Truly, much study is a weariness to the flesh, and there is no end to reading.

What an awful age we live in!

When I look at the piles of unread literature even around me in this room, and the Himalayas of thought which lie within sight, I am saddened   Toiling wearily on, down in the valleys and then standing on some little hill, I get now and then glimpses of the Knowable, towering away in the distance like vast mountain ranges, even the base of which I feel as though I could not reach. Then what am I, and what can I do?

A sense of ignorance, of sin, and of infinite unworthiness so oppresses that I often feel so troubled I cannot speak aught but Hezekiah's prayer: "O Lord, I am oppressed, undertake for me."

And then it is,—even while I write it is so—that the sense of oppression is removed and the darkness and mists o'er the path roll away, while from the Mount of Faith and Prayer I look upon the Eternal Hills from whence cometh my help and whither I am journeying—and oh, how glorious, how glorious it is! Xenophon's weary army, after their long fighting in an enemy's land, suddenly came upon the sea, the broad, deep, still sea, and with a shout they rushed into its cool waters: so would I into that boundless Ocean of Eternal Love which is sometimes within my view. Meanwhile I must fight the good fight, and so must you; and then, by and by, will it not be glorious to rest by the "River of pure water of life, clear as crystal, proceeding out of the Throne of God and of the Lamb?" Let us be men in Christ.

. . . As to returning to Scotland, all is changed. I remain in Australia. Where, I know not yet. My present desire is to settle either in Sydney or Melbourne, and to leave Manly about the beginning of the year, by which time I hope our alterations and enlargement will be finished and paid for. I trust to be Divinely guided. It has been, in some ways, a great trial; but must be one of the "all things." I am in correspondence with Melbourne. Many wish me to remain here; but the way is not clear. I am waiting.

I know the books of which you write. They are delicately and touchingly written, and present the most terrible pictures of child misery through parental sin, with a vividness and moving Christian pathos, which draws out one's heart insensibly; and before you can analyse your impression the fountains of emotion are touched, the tears flow, and now you see 'tis Jesus' love and sympathy which have been guiding the writer's pen until you, too, are ready to weep with her as you look upon the sins and sorrows of the city.

Yes, it is a sweet and stimulating thought that we are partakers of Christ's holiness. But in the command, "Be ye holy," implied in Matthew, 5.48 and many other places, there are calls to perfection in that which we only now realize in **part**. It is of His own holy nature by His own Holy Spirit that we partake, in living by faith and love in Him always.

Go on with a Band of Hope by all means, and try to interest others in aiding you There is much trashy, but there is also much beautiful Temperance literature

As to the Communion: I am often perplexed about the way in which it is viewed by Christians. Extreme views are dangerous here The Via Madia seems safest The ordinance is not an eucharistic transubstantiation sacrifice, nor a useless optional ceremony. There is a deeply spiritual meaning; and the commemoration may be a very blessed time, when the union between the saved and Saviour may become more consciously blessed. The memory, and imagination, and reflection, and all the emotional powers, find fitting exercise at the Lord's table. Do not undervalue it. Strive to realize in it something of the depths of Christ's sympathetic love in view of His awful sufferings on that most awful of nights—the midnight of the world. The Romans and we begin the day after the midnight hour The dawn of Christ's eternal day was in that darkest hour of human misery. Often do we realize that our brightest hopes begin, when all our human hopes seem to expire. At the same time it is true we must be in active and daily communion with Jesus in private devotion and in public devotion —adorning His doctrine in all things.

About your question, "were not the sufferings of Christ complete in themselves?" That question shows a misapprehension of the meaning of the Apostle's words in Collossians, 1:24. Christ's own atoning sufferings were complete in themselves; but He did not from thenceforth make the path which His followers, His Church, should tread in this temporal world, a path painless and sinless. The path is yet one of temptation; the suffering still awaits all who will live godly; and the Christian has ever to contend against sins which would seduce or crush him. In all the sufferings of the Church (His body) even in its meanest members, Christ (the head) feels the most perfect sympathy—even as when, say, our little toe is trodden upon, our countenance at once expresses the pain our **head** feels, so in the highest spiritual sense with Christ. In every persecution of His members He is persecuted ("Saul, Saul, why persecutest thou **me**?"); hence the sufferings of Christians for Christ's cause becomes "the sufferings of Christ." The whole of the age-long trials of the Church are "the sufferings of Christ," wrought out in the persons of its members; and in fact constitute the training and preparation of the Lamb's Wife—the whole redeemed Church—for the consummation of her union with her lord in that day which ushers in her eternal happiness. This is to me briefly the meaning of the passage . . . .

The prospect seems fair and clear, and no dangers appear; but since we do not know what a day may bring forth, we can only watch and pray and labour on, leaving it all to God, whose wondrous forbearance and favoring love and constant guidance, call for my most perfect confidence and devoted consecration. When I have such an Advocate and Redeemer as Jesus, such an Enlightener and Comforter as the Holy Spirit, and such a Father and God, ought I not to "be

calm and free on any shore, since God is there?" It
is at such a time as this that Lady Guyon's beautiful
hymn recalls the wondrous fullness of God's thoughts
toward us, and I have been feeling the third verse,
lately, to be especially true:

"While place we seek or place we shun,
The soul finds happiness in none;
But with my God to guide my way,
'Tis equal joy to go or stay."

This is, indeed, just as I am wishful wholly to feel,
and so that I may be ready to say fully, "Father, Thy
will be done," I say, (slightly altering Madam Guyon's last verse).

"Therefore I will to God's Throne now repair,
And plead in Christ I am no stranger there;
From hence that love Divine shall come forth as my
    guard,
And peace and safety become my reward."

You will, I know, even while you read, pray that
I may be faithful and fitted to do and suffer God's
will in all things, and to find therein my highest pleasure In any event, I shall need strength and wisdom
for special trials soon.

To go to Newtown is a most important step, should
I be asked to take it; and should God place no hindrance I feel I would be likely to go. It is next to Pitt
Street in importance in the opinion of many. It stands
in the midst of a rapidly increasing population, afford-
ing room for the exercise of a many-sided ministry
and church work The demands for a high order of
preaching, and yet for that adapted to a large working population too, will call for special gifts and
graces—when you remember that the young gentlemen boarders at Camden College, the theological
students, with a highly cultivated professional and
merchant class, attend there, and also that it is the

only Congregational church among a population now numbering about 8,000 and rapidly increasing.

The increase in pastoral and perhaps public work, will require a large increase of strength and adaptation in every sense   But if with all I have a united and loving people, throughout loyal to Christ and His truth, and having confidence in me; and above all, the sense that it is the way wherein God would have me to go, then, in that event, what can I fear? Surely God who leads will give me grace to follow;   and surely God who calls me to feed, to lead, and guard one portion of his flock, will give me power to guide into the sweet pastures of Divine truth, courage to press on with the sheep through every danger and temptation, repelling every assault of the insidious foe; and with patient love and wisdom to call the wanderers home, who are pining with hunger and consumed with thirst in the enemy's country, striving to feed on filthy, sensual, or empty intellectual husks, and drinking deep of the naphthaline rivers to which the enemy leads their wrecked souls

Again I say, I am desirous to be quite prepared to go or stay; but I also feel I ought to say, if God make the way clear, I will not dishonour Him by any unworthy fear

-----

(Written to his father and mother—Dec. 10, '74, discusses political and religious movements—feels need of a wife.)

. . You ask about our United Religious Movements in Sydney, of which I am the clerical secretary Well, we are in the midst of an election, and the most inflamed   and   bitter   political   passions   are   raging throughout the land, and in Sydney specially; and I am sorry to say that ministers, and more particularly Congregational ministers, are fighting   away,   with "coats off," metaphorically speaking, in the thickest of the fray.

When I tell you that it is a contest precipitated, first by a contest between the one half of the Legislative Assembly, the Government of the astute and able Henry Parkes, and the gambling, horse-racing Governor in consequence of which the House was dissolved after the Governor escaping severe censure by the Speaker's casting vote only, then, second, that it is embittered by the action of two "Leagues"—one of which defends in toto the present Public School System, and the other of which wishes to abolish it, so far as would be necessary in introducing a system of education which would be "National, Secular, Compulsory and Free," then, third, when you know that Irish and English Orangemen and Irish Papists, and Roman Catholic and Episcopalian Clergymen and Non-conformist Ministers are, along with the usual herd of political harlequins, clowns, assassins and quacks, all making as much noise as their lungs, and as much mischief as venom-tipped tongues and pen can create—when I tell you that all this yelling pandemonium is in full force now in Sydney, you will not wonder that there are many who do not feel they can come on Monday to the calm, mid-day hour of sacred prayer and communion and conference in reference to Christ's Kingdom and perishing souls

There is much that is most painful in the controversy; and many ministers of our own body who have pleaded want of time to attend to prayer meetings, ministerial conferences, and evangelistic services, have found plenty of time for months past to stamp and talk on political platforms, far away into the night, in and around the city and suburbs.

I do not wish to press in an unduly hard way upon brethren; but while the Christian Church is so cold, and the world with its education and vice so aggressive—while Christians are pining for food, and the Christless masses, leprous in their social condition, are dancing and laughing in their chains of infidelity, immorality, frivolity, indifference and greed—while the wailing cries of perishing souls are ringing in our ears from the passion-tossed sea of human despair—while the young are sliding away from the church to the world, it is time that those who ought to be keeping the waning light bright should awake to a sense of their neglect My firm conviction is, that at this time the cunning Tempter has thrown an Apple of Discord into the race of Christian runners, and I, for one, am asking of God grace to run onward, convinced more and more, as I am, that the solution of all social problems of ignorance and sin is to be found in Christ alone—in loving Him and all men, and in living to Him by bringing all men the Truth which can alone truly free men from all oppressions—from the oppressions of Ignorance, of Hatred, of Fear, and above all from the chief of all oppressors,—Self—sinful Self.

I could say much, but writing is too clumsy a vehicle for expression and takes more time than I can devote, in defense of the faith that is in me in this matter. Meanwhile, it seems best to keep out altogether, for some time to come, from public expressions on this matter, so far as I am concerned.

The Church of England are holding this as a week of special mission services in and around Sydney, and I am looking with interest to see with what apparent results, though apart from that I feel it must be blessed, when I consider the truly pious men who have to do with it I never was less inclined to Episcopacy and English Churchism; but I never so admired Episcopalians before They compel your admiration by their simplicity and truly evangelical action, and the apparent purity and elevation of their motives Of course there is a ritualistic set, but they are very weak, having both Bishop and Dean against them, and there is a sort of rationalistic element which bitterly opposes the evangelicals, and which is ranged just now under the banners of the Education League

. Ministerial freemasonry, and all other sorts of freemasonry, are abominable to me; and as for the secret jealousies and whisperings you mention, I have some evidence that they exist. But I have learned a lesson it is useless and noxious to follow a polecat into its hole; for the creature, when heated or enraged, emits, it is said, an intolerable stench, while even dogs will not eat their flesh

Neither will I, unless it be absolutely necessary, follow the whisperer and slanderer into their loathsome darkness: for they, too, emit a vile stench. Let them be. Let my life give the lie to the backbiting and insinuating tongues Let my words be sound and timely and loving speech Let my work go on uninterrupted by frivolous defenses against frivolous talkers.

I cannot complain: for I receive honor and rewards enough, even now, in all my poor endeavors; and, if someone does wrong, let me take it patiently, answering softly as far as in me lies God is my judge, and not man. Let me live rightly in God's sight, and then indeed will I find, through loving obedience, the blessed experience that "He doeth all things well".

May God give me grace to remember and do as I now write, and to pity and try to save even the human "polecat".

I am glad you are happy in working for Jesus, the Christ and Lord I am, too, with all my longings and cries and tears on account of sinful self. Surely He will bring us quite through But do not let us be unjust I am afraid, dear father, you were when you wrote "all men are after self". It reminded me of David's words, "I said in mine haste all men are liars" Truly that is our temptation and infirmity, when we, like him, are "greatly afflicted".

But the charge is not true There are multitudes

who have not bowed the knee to the Baal of Self; and many are, just as we, fighting against the enemies of their souls. Why, to many whom you and I meet in our daily paths, we may appear selfish when we are only timid, and, looking back upon my past, I can see that to be clearly true. No, there are many who love us unselfishly.

We are amid many who would gladly respond to that sympathy which foolish timorousness locks up within our breasts, with patent locks of Fear and Mistrust, in iron safes of cold and selfish Isolation By many a bedside, in stately house or lowly cottage, would our sympathy and firm hope in Christ bring hope to the hopeless, and to many a weary muck-rake toiler would we be blessed, if with the hearty tone of blessed cheerfulness, we said, "look up man, look up!" and perhaps he might see "Jesus" written upon our brows, and, looking higher, see Jesus Himself in all His beauty. And oh, if it were so, never again could he see in the muck-rake of commerce, with its sticks and straws of earth, that beauty which he saw in Jesus

Let us be unselfish enough to brave possible misrepresentation in our endeavours to make a way for Jesus to the sinner's heart, and, depend upon it, we shall look more lovingly on all around, and find them look more lovingly on us

You speak of the approaching reopening of our enlarged and improved church. It will take place on Sabbath, December 20th, and 22nd we shall have a tea and public meeting The Rev. John Graham will preach morning and evening on 20th (I supplying Pitt Street,) and the Hon. John Fairfax will preside at the public meeting I wish it were all over A minister never feels the need of a wife so much (ah, I hear you laughing at me, mother,) as when there are tea-meetings and kindred enormities afoot. If I had a fit of nightmare just now, I should expect the "horrors" to assume the shapes of cups and saucers dancing upon attenuated legs and leeringly charging me with an innumerable number of teaspoons, while buns and cakes and sandwiches and plates of butter came flying at my head in every direction, and hissing teapots puffed up and down, while hot water ran in every direction around my feet, and shower baths of tea came from above—while, to crown all, a chorus of mammas and maidens pouted and cried "shame!" in fashionable, musical discord

Oh, tell it not in Gath, else the Philistines will rejoice! If only the dear creatures in Manly, who have "engaged" me, at least six times, to widows and maidens of all sorts, could look over my shoulder now, it would be such fun. But I am like Aesop's frogs, who appealed to the boys who stoned them, calling out, "what is fun to you is death to us!"

There is only one way out of the difficulty,—as the foxes who had tails were told by one who had lost his in a trap but who had convinced them of the superiority of being tailless—"Only one way to be as handsome as I· off with your tails!" "Ah," you say, "just the opposite, it is adding a tail." Well, never mind, if I live I am afraid I will prove the auld maid's saying true, and "gang the way we've a' tae gang"

Seriously, though, I am now feeling that if I am to settle in New South Wales or elsewhere, I ought to marry, and if I do. I mean to. "Now that is plain," you say "But who?" How can I tell? "But do you not know?" No, I do not know; but the Bible tells me that "a good wife is from the Lord," and since I want a good one at all risks, I will ask the Lord to send her to me.

Of course, if one is looking out for the answer, one may see her coming Perhaps, if like Isaac when sitting by the well Lahai-roi (the well of the quickening-vision), I get up, and in the eventide walk out into the fields to meditate, I, too, may on lifting my eyes with their quickened vision (they will need to be washed with the waters of Lahai-roi)—I too, may see "the camels coming," across the lonely fields of my bachelor life   But my Rebekah, alas, is closely veiled, and even if I see the camels I cannot see her   You see, I have been studying Isaac's story.

Strange coincidence, though, that the poor fugitive Hagar should find that God pitied her at probably the same well of quickening as that where Isaac sat meditating or praying just before he arose and found that God had pitied his loneliness and sent him a wife to comfort him for the loss of his mother.   Ah, but Rebekahs and Isaacs are scarce now—even the names are found to be unfashionable

Now are you not—I am—amazed at the length of this letter, all written during twelve hours, of which it has occupied a good part?   The weather was hot in the morning, so I thought I would write, and in the afternoon it rained, so I thought I would keep on, and between the two, I have been at home all day and produced this.   Getting weary towards the end, I see that the end is seriously funny, but the letter as a whole is seriously serious.

Dear parents, pray for me   It is a relief to chat away to you freely with the pen for an hour or two, but it is a joy beyond all to think you ever pray with and for me   Here below I trust we shall yet meet, but hereafter and above we shall, if we truly trust wholly to God in Christ   May that trust deepen, widen and heighten, till it fill all our souls with a glorious confidence of the regenerate children of God, who never die.   .

(Dated at "Devonshire House," Newtown, Sidney, Nov. 25, '75— tells of his love for his cousin Jeanie—makes plea for her—argues against blood relationship being bar to marriage)

Dear Father and Mother:
Since my last I have received one short letter from

you, written in very laconic fashion, but containing some very interesting items and news—one item being of very painful interest.

I sympathize very deeply with H— and A— in their great disappointment, for I had quite looked forward to being an uncle long ago, and my hopes were revived by your information of some months since. It must be a great sorrow to them, and I trust they have carried it to Him who can alone mitigate its bitterness, to Him who bore their sins and carried their sorrows, and who can lead them to dwell forever where sorrow and sighing cannot enter. I, who am alone as to human near ties can feel for them. God has made us not for solitude, but to be set in families, and when by reason of special trials and disappointments we dwell in silent lonelihood in our homes, there are few sorrows heavier to bear. How our hearts long for some perfect, visible love and sympathy ever seemingly denied,—nay, it is only deferred, and its fullness shall be realized hereafter in purer, sweeter forms than was possible to us here.

They still have each other, and though it is a trial to be almost promised a great gift and then lose it, yet love remains and these trials borne together make love stronger and purer.

Not so with me. I am alone as to such a love, and perhaps it is destined by God that I should ever remain so. It may be, yea it is, His way, so far as I can see, to draw me closer to Himself, the Source of Love, and to find in His work objects of love which shall lead me to look forward to the life hereafter for the realization of my longings in pure and perfect scenes of heavenly intercourse. . . Hence my soul strives to enter more into loving, faithful union with God in Christ, and praying for more of His spirit in my heart, I trust to be upheld and led out at last into the light. There are grand and glorious enterprises needed on earth for the reclamation of men in the glory of God, and to these I must· with more entire devotion give myself and all my powers. It may be God may have more comfort here for me even in human love than I can now conceive to be possible

But, however that may be, I must not allow human trials to crush me, and by God's grace I must do my part as bravely as I can. Last night I was greatly comforted and strengthened preaching from the text which has been in my mind with special force all day It is in that glorious Song of Deliverance which Isaiah composed, on the occasion, probably, of the destruction of Sennacherib's army, and the raising of the siege of Jerusalem and the invasion of Judah Doubtless, too, it is a Messianic prophetic song, and, indeed, it was so applied by the Jews themselves in after ages Then we may surely use it

For does it not become us thus to rejoice when God's "anger is turned away" and when He strives to "comfort" us? The words on which I discoursed, and which have given me much comfort are :—

> "Behold, God is my salvation ,
> "I will trust, and not be afraid "

Oh, how God comforts! How good He is to me today ! My heart has been made very sore—yea it is sore now—but amid my tears of sorrow, I see the rainbow of God's eternal love spanning the heavens with brilliant hues of hope, and though dark days may come when the rainbow of promise is not so clear, yet I pray that then I may still be able to say—"I will trust and not be afraid."

Last night after my service three or four persons were waiting to speak to me concerning various matters, and one came home with me for a few minutes. When I had finished my business with him (it was a case requiring much care and has given me a good deal already), the house felt very hot and close.

Outside it was cool and pleasant, so feeling a quiet walk in the starlit night would do me good and help to soothe my troubled mind, I took my hat and walking stick and went out, not intending to call upon any one. The road I happened to take led me by Mr. Clark's house, and seeing the door open and a light burning, I went in. I found Mr. and Mrs. Clark were both out but was welcomed by Mrs Clark's mother—an elderly lady who lives a mile or two from here, and who occasionally has attended my ministry She was quite alone—only a servant being in the back premises I sat down for a minute or two, and spoke to her about her family and then ventured to make some few remarks to her about her spiritual condition, to which she only made at first a very slow response Let me here say I had attended her daughter frequently upon her death bed—a very fine Christian young lady, who died last year. I was about to rise and go, when she suddenly made an observation which induced me to remain, and soon I found she was in a very deeply anxious state of mind She told me she had long wished to see me, for she was deeply concerned about her soul's salvation and longed to realize peace with God. So then we had a long and interesting conversation, and having been myself so comforted by trusting and not fearing, I found that the Word of God was dwelling in me just then with power. I especially impressed upon her the Saviour's own exhortation—"Be not afraid, only believe"— and the effect of our quiet talk was marvelous—verily, it was the Lord's doing She said, "I will trust Him and not be afraid," and we knelt in prayer and told it to God .. I left her, Mr Clark had not then returned, and wended my way home full of heartfelt love and gratitude to God that He had not only comforted me but another who had been long seeking, and with her last words ringing like quiet joybells in my heart, in beautiful harmony with the stillness and the starry sky,—"God sent you, sir! God sent you!" Was it not true? I asked myself. How could I doubt? Every little circumstance surrounding the scene convinced me it was true; and something of the awe of Jacob, the wanderer and lonely, friendless man, came into my heart, which ages ago came into his when he, wakened up from his dream under the eastern sky, exclaimed, "Surely the Lord is in this place, and I knew it not!"

I, too, then shall raise here in a pile my strong griefs and call that pillar an altar of sacrifice in my Bethel. This little incident has cheered me and since it has been much in my mind this morning, I have been impelled to narrate it. God is good.

And now I can imagine you are somewhat surprised to read all that I have written as to my sadness and pain of heart, and wonder why I do not tell you plainly what has happened. Well, I really do not see how I can keep it from you, and yet I do not know how to tell it. Even now I feel strongly tempted to tear up all I have written and not add to your troubles any anxiety about me. But yet you are my nearest and my sorrows are yours, and I will not longer hide my severest trial from you. I do not see how it will help me to tell you, but it will at least relieve you and me from something: you from suspense and surmise, me from bearing the burden quite alone. I know on paper it will look very little, and perhaps you may rejoice, or be inclined to, at things being as they are—but it is a matter great beyond expression to me and a very grievous affliction just now and for I know not how long, perhaps ever. Do try to look at it from my point of view, and give me your sympathy and counsel.

Well, it dates back, in its beginning, to nearly three years ago. I had the—shall I call it misfortune?—to, what the world calls, "fall in love" with my cousin Jeanie, and I must confess it bothered me for not a little—unused as I was to it—until I found out the nature of my complaint.

But what was I to do? I was in a whirl of mind and blamed myself severely. But that did not alter the matter Our relationship, which in theory I had always considered a bar to any marriage, I now found a practical difficulty, and other difficulties—how she thought, how uncle and aunt thought, my unsettled condition, etc etc. Still all these difficulties did not remove the stubborn inward fact, that I had gone and lost all I had to give of true first love to any woman I did not say much, I felt I must wait, indeed, I never told her. But a circumstance occurred where I thought she was running into danger—Henning's Ball—and I spoke and wrote to her about it, in the letter "letting the cat out of the bag"— in plain language, telling her my action proceeded from a very deep and special care for her welfare and herself.

That letter was not well received, I feared it was too plain my affection was not reciprocated, and therefore I pressed on the correspondence with Sydney, and left Adelaide in less than six weeks from that time My hope was, that distance and time and other associations might work a cure, and hence I hurried away, too proud and too pained to try again or to thrust myself upon her, yea, and caring too much for her to wish her to do or say anything not spontaneous, for true happiness must depend upon mutual and equal love. I came here, threw myself into work for God, finding in that my only happiness and care, but as time rolled on and friends increased I did not find, though sometimes I fancied, my thoughts regarding her substantially altered Indeed, my anxiety to absorb myself in work, and to crowd my hours of home solitude with occupation or to find it outside, caused me to neglect my health, and my spirits were often very low. Hence my illness of last year and my sudden trip to Melbourne. This affair was indirectly the cause of that illness, which was much more serious than I was willing to confess to you. Well, I returned, threw

70

myself again into work, pushed on my extension at Manly and cheated myself with a vain illusion of another love at the end of last year (but that soon vanished, a good deal to my pain for a while, but now I see it was for the best, for it was only a beautiful, transient, desert mirage.)

However, I again pressed on in work, concluded that at Manly, accepted Newtown at the beginning of the year, wrought on and on all through these nine months, feeling my home and heart loneliness as to human love more acutely than words can tell, knowing how much better a man and minister I would be could I only get from God that great gift, a good wife, and making it a matter of prayer and frequent thought Of course I was brought into circumstances which led me to see much of many young ladies, any of whom would have made me a good wife. But I need scarcely tell you that in this matter choice is not a mere matter of reason, and that there is reciprocity which must be ascertained, and which one does not care to do until one is stimulated by stronger motives than mere curiosity—a course of conduct which I call heartless trifling, likely to produce much sorrow. Toiling along here, I get from you intelligence that uncle and Jeanie are coming, and when I received a telegram from Andrew telling me they have started and asking me to meet them on arrival, I do not know whether I felt more glad than sorry

Anyway, now they were coming, I felt my only course was that which our relationship and my affection dictated, namely, to invite them to stay with me and to do all I could to make their visit agreeable. One determination I made, that I must in no wise renew my attentions or make any proposal to Jeanie unless I saw plainly some reason for encouragement, and then after the most candid talk with uncle. Most firmly did I keep this resolve until Monday evening last, the night preceding their last full day with me.

Then uncle, being very weary, retired early, and Jeanie, who had been with me to our prayer meeting, sat chatting with me. Now though we had never before spoken a word to each other about our old interesting and painful little episode, yet it was quite apparent to us both that it was in our minds. I, however, wished to act with most scrupulous fidelity to uncle, and though I had ample opportunity, I had until now never used it to ask her how she was disposed toward me. For instance, one whole day—Thursday last—Jeanie and I were away together for the day up the Paramatta River by steamer over the Domain there and back here by train in the evening—uncle keeping at home owing to his suffering from a scorched face. On the particular evening to which I now allude it all came out between Jeanie and I, and that without the slightest premeditation on either side, I am quite certain—indeed almost before we were both aware we had glided into it, and quite as much was she to blame as I, if indeed there were any blame to be attributed in the matter,—if there is, I am willing to bear the whole responsibility. It came out through our comparing notes upon our conditions, and we found we were both free, which was apparently a little surprise on both sides. From that came out a reference to my letter two years ago, which she kindly and frankly acknowledged now was quite right in its advice to her

Then we naturally, and on my part too quickly for my judgment to pass more than a very hasty approval, glided on to the deep question underlying my letter, and as to whether we loved each other   I told her just what I have narrated to you in substance, and she told me that, though she had not thought of it as much as I, yet she knew she cared very much for me, and could wholly, as she ought in such a case as being my wife implied, but for one fact, that we were cousins. This was the substance of what she said

Of course this barrier of relationship has been, throughout, the great one, and yet, is it a real one or only a seeming one? is the question I ask myself. She feels it to be one, and so did I; but that was more the result of nameless fears, owing to feelings which I cannot find such real grounds for in reason and in fact, as I could in many other marriages not open to this charge. This was the one obstacle, and it had evidently been impressed by someone or other upon her mind with an almost superstitious shadowy dread. We found no other difficulty. I believe she loves me, and I do her with a strange intensity, not the growth of a day, or with passion like a beardless boy's or a fool's devotion. We parted for the night, and I do not know which was the most sorrowful—it was a strange wooing—I only know that for some time before and since, sleep has been difficult and, but for God's love and goodness, work would have been impossible.

In the morning I arose early. Uncle and Jeanie and I had promised to go down the harbor in a steam launch for the day and Jeanie was too unwell to come down to breakfast. Uncle had to go in to Sydney, and was to meet us at the wharf; and after he went I found how Jeanie had been crying bitterly about it all. We had a little talk about it again, and I asked her to allow me to speak to uncle, but she asked me not to. Eventually we agreed that she would think over it all, and then when she got home, she would write and tell me whether I should write to uncle asking his consent. Thus deciding, we went with the party for the day, being driven into town in the barouche of one of my deacons whose wife and some of my Newtown folks and others accompanied us. Wednesday— yesterday —morning came and they were to leave at half past four in the afternoon. I stayed here to see the luggage sent off and to attend to some pressing duties, and they left here about eleven o'clock, I arranging to say good-by on board the steamer. I was very sad, and premonition of more sorrow was shading my mind, when I went to see them away. When I got to the steamer, and after having said good-bye to some friends who had come to see them, Jeanie and I went aside, at her request, and had some talk. Then she told me that after leaving me that morning, uncle asked her if I had said anything to her, and said he knew about my old letter.

She told him I had, and what she had promised to do—write when she got home and so forth. Upon this he expressed his disapproval of the matter, as being wrong between cousins, and told her she must write at once and tell me that it could not be. She preferred to tell it to me, and did so in this conversation. That is all.

And now what can I say? So far as I know, this will exercise, now more than ever, a most important influence upon my future, though it would be quite premature to say in what particular ways. One thing has been growing clearer and clearer, that however easy it may be for any person in private life to live singly permanently, it is, as society is at present constituted, a condition full of vexations and difficulties for a minister of the Gospel, and interferes with the thorough discharge of his duties. Now you may say, "There is no reason to realize the supposition, for you may yet marry some one else."

I do not think so, and I think I know myself better than you can.

In almost any other position my condition would be comparatively easy to what it is now, for often it is almost intolerable, and that in ways impossible to express in writing or even in speech. Then at my age, and with my temperament in these matters, it is difficult to conceive any likelihood of a different disposition of my affections.

Had this visit not revived my love, it is possible, and indeed not unlikely, that my strong conviction of what was necessary in my work might have led me to seek, and possibly to secure, a pious and intelligent Christian young lady of my acquaintance, who would have made me a good wife, I am sure. But seeing what I do now more clearly than ever of my own heart's feelings, **that** is now impossible. Hence the question is of vital moment to me.

Now here is the point at which I ask your sympathy and counsel, and, if you could do anything, your help.

When I began this letter to you, it was with the full intention that it should be quite private, and without desire that other eyes shoul look upon it. But now, when I begin to consider how you could aid me in this vitally important matter, it occurs to me that it might best be done by a calm conference with uncle upon its subject, and by showing him this letter, as a candid history and a permanent statement of my feelings regarding Jeanie. You might put before him my views on this matter, and asking him to consider whether her future peace and happiness may not be bound up in my getting her, even as mine appears to be.

I know that he is a reasonable man who loves his child greatly, and he will be ready, I think, calmly to review the whole matter should it be properly laid before him. Unless I am greatly mistaken he is well inclined and friendly toward me, and upon no other ground but that of our relationship has opposed this matter. Let me then address myself as briefly as possible to that subject, and state a few facts and considerations bearing upon the "physical question" to which he very justly attaches considerable importance. I have studied it, and with a full view of all the risks supposed by some to exist, I am quite prepared to face them, since on me they will principally fall should they ever become realities. The stress which he attaches to this view of the subject must be my excuse for going into details which would without that reason be unnecessary and undesirable; and I rely upon his fairly and dispassionately viewing the matter as one of vital moment to me upon whom the future troubles, were there any, would chiefly rest

When uncle was here he spoke to me about an article which he read in my study in "The British Quarterly Review" for July 1st on "Sin and Madness, From a Physician's Point of View".

He referred to that article with approval, and as it did not occur to me at the time as having any lengthened allusion to the question of cousins marrying—for I had read it many weeks ago and considered it altogether a rather weak production which had made no deep impression upon me. He subsequently referred to it conversing with Jeanie, as containing reasons adverse to our wishes.

The only sentence bearing fairly upon cousins marrying therein is as follows: "How far cousins may marry with safety is a disputed point; some maintain that they can do so with perfect safety, provided both families are free from disease, but it is generally acknowledged that there is much risk "

This risk, it is understood, applies only to the offspring of such a union—one doubtless sufficiently great —but one principally affecting the parties themselves, be it observed. But I contend that the "disputed point" of our reviewer must be decided rather in favor of those who contend cousins may marry "with perfect safety," subject to a provision which is, I am sure, true to both families.

My conclusion is based upon the following facts— viz. That throughout the whole record of Jewish law and history this practice was not only permitted but especially permitted and approved in the most illustrious examples; and that no stricter or severer marriage code ever existed than that of the Jews, which moreover was of Divine authority. To take an instance.

Jacob married Rachel and Leah, his full cousins—daughters of his uncle Laban—his mother's brother—and from these were descended the founders of the Jewish nation, and through their line came Christ, according to the flesh. Esau likewise married Mahalath, daughter of Ishmael, his uncle and father's brother The Mosaic law, famous for its model purity, contains no prohibition of the sort, and even after the return from captivity, when ceremonial defilements were innumerable, the Rabbis, we are told by Dr. Ginsburg, held "intermarriages between cousins are quite legitimate." No legislation of modern times in the world except in Roman Catholic countries has proscribed it, and it is sanctioned in England and here by law and custom.

No ill consequences to offspring are traced throughout Scripture or to parties themselves; and I feel certain that the whole affair has only a Middle Age origin, and has some of the superstition yet around it which was imparted to it by the cunning of a Papacy for the purpose of acquiring a more spiritual, or rather superstitious, hold upon the people. Remember the Church of Rome has done much to weaken the marriage tie, and has subordinated it, like every other, to priestly aggrandizement. The prohibition, therefore, of anything by it should be viewed with suspicion. As far as I can trace the objection, it rests upon the prohibition only of the Church of Rome, and was first formulated at the Council of Trent which taught "that the Church hath power to annul any of the impediments mentioned in Leviticus, or by the Apostles, add new ones, or dissolve any now in use." It was this arrogant and blasphemous Council which first enacted the prohibition, and all history proves it was only for the purpose of oppression and gain, as in the case of Indulgences Dr. Croly, a great authority on marriage, remarks: "The Church of Rome also prohibits the marriage of first cousins; but she grants a dispensation (a good round sum of money being first paid) for the marriage, and . . thus relaxes the practice for the sake of **revenue.**" At the same time as this horrid prohibition was made, creating a purely imaginary sin for gain, it also imposed upon Europe, (and Britain was then Romanist,) other impedients to marriage arising from spiritual kindred such as godfathers and godmothers, whilst on the other hand, (for money) it threw wide the door to marriages between uncles and nieces. Dr. Elliot in his "Delineation of Romanism" (1437) remarks:—"It is unlawful for the Church of Rome to restrain other degrees than those which are commanded in Scripture." "To forbid," he continues, "more degrees in marriage than what are either directly or indirectly by necessary consequence prohibited by law, is presumptuous, as the Most High best knew what persons were fit for marriage, and how far the line of marriage was intended to reach" I charge the entire responsibility, for my part, of prohibiting such marriages upon the Church of Rome, and especially in its Decrees at the Council of Trent. I believe there is not an atom of truth against such marriages in Divine law or ancient Christian and Jewish practice I believe the impediment was **invented,** like many others, as a likely pecuniary speculation, and I, for one, repudiate altogether the imposition of such an impediment from such a source as being of any value whatever. Let the light of truth reveal the baseness of its origin, and let the fresh breezes of Divine law drive away the mists of traditionary ignorance from our minds, which only Papal filthiness invented, and which is one of its chains—not the only one by any means—from which we are not yet free

This is my honest conviction as in the sight of God, and I believe the whole weight of reason and truth—as shown in experience and Divine law—will support me in it, whatever the event may be as to Jeanie and I

No, this question of our marrying must now be

considered, altogether apart from the idea that relationship is any bar.

Are we agreed otherwise, and is there no impediment in uncle and your minds such as would prevent my marrying her were I not her cousin? As to your agreement, I think that is a settled matter apart from the "Roman Bogie", which surely we will not fear, and I know I would give to her an undivided heart and loving care such as none can exceed, I care not where; and I am not ashamed to say it boldly, now that I have to plead for her. Then as to any other impediment, what is there? What can there be? I know I am very imperfect, and I know I have to subdue evil tendencies in my disposition, like others. But God has been good to me. I have had many trials, many toils, and need to exercise every Christian grace in self control, and in guiding, teaching and aiding others. I know I have been an eager learner in the school of experience—I wish heartily a more successful one— and I have been taught to exercise patience as well as diligence. These three past years have been severe ones, and had God not sustained me I must have fallen. But here I am, what I am, by His mercy today, and nothing earthly could add to my joy more than the realization of that for which I now plead Allowing for human frailty and my full share of it, is there any special impediment in me? I am not hard to live with, I think—I may say with truth none have ever said so who during these seven years or so have served me; and you know my home life, when grace had not wrought in me what it has now, I trust. I am stronger, taking it on the whole, just now in mind and body than I ever have been in my life, and have done, and am doing, work which none but a strong man could do I have a good, though not a palatial house, and with her it would be a good home I have a fair position and increasing income, a kind, appreciative people, a growing church and congregation, and above all the gracious assurance that God's blessing is with me in my very consciously unworthy endeavors to do His work, to proclaim His will and mercy, and to save many from eternal ruin

Uncle knows a little about all these things Let him give me, as I have hope he will, an indulgent hearing, and see whether he cannot give me "a guard" to all my treasures here, far more precious than the golden one with which his kindness fettered me upon leaving—that "guard" is Jeanie—I need taking care of and she can do it; and if he will, I will promise to value and wear with loving care, and preserve with undimmed brightness that "guard"—yea, hoping that we shall shine brighter in the life beyond for having trod life's pathways here in union, hand and heart together.

Now, why not? I plead as for that most precious to me, and pride or shame are alike cast behind whilst I think of how precious it is to me to succeed, and how bleak and barren and stony will the way through life appear should I fail. Do not think my feelings are running away with my judgment in this matter, for that is not so There is a calm intensity of conviction about my being right in this—and I have sought Divine guidance earnestly to write every word in simple truth without exaggeration, and my reason, my conscience, my will, my love and my judgment (five inward causes) all agree in approving my plea. Indeed, I had almost "given in" and left Melbourne full of gloom and something like despair—Sydney seemed a stony, heartless desert, and every man a floating iceberg on a sea of misery, for the moment—when there rushed into my mind suddenly, while whirling along to Newtown words which seemed to be accompanied by the softest of musical voices thrilling my heart with fresh hope and trust in new determination—"I will trust, and not be afraid." From that time the conviction has steadily grown in my mind to try again, and

Man, in his weakness, needs a stronger stay
 Than fellow-men, the holiest and the best
And yet we turn to them from day to day,
 As if in them our spirits could find rest.

Handwriting of John Alexander Dowie at the age of twenty-four.

Let us believe that : —

" Slow and sure comes up the golden year,
" When wealth no more shall rest in mounded heaps,
" But, emut with freer light, shall slowly melt
" In many streams, to fatten lower lands,
" And light shall spread, and man be liker man,
" Through all the seasons of the golden year.

Ten years later.

not until I lifted my pen and began to write to you, did I begin to see that through you I might make a new appeal and enter the lists with my stammering pen.

Now, father, I constitute **you** my ambassador to uncle, mother will do her part in a loving way, I know, should opportunity offer, and I beg you as early as you can to have a long chat with uncle about it all, presenting this letter as your credentials, and as my plea. One thing do—excuse it's not being shorter and more coherent, but both of you will cover that sin with your charity, seeing how difficult it is for me under the circumstances.

Every word I have written is my most solemn conviction of what is true, and I send this letter on to you wafted by my fervent prayers for its success.

And now this very long "brief" begun on Thursday closes on Saturday; and as I wish to post it in time for the P. and O. mail this afternoon and then proceed with my preparations for tomorrow, I must close without reference to many topics of interest to which we are having our minds directed here, in impending changes, etc. I am very busy, and am glad, for it helps me to get through without fretting. There are many things which are making heavy demands upon every power, and the little lull which existed while uncle and Jeanie were with me, has ended in a great pressure of work of all kinds, involving me in much anxiety and care sometimes—but it is for a gracious Master. I have three sermons for tomorrow and they are all **special,** two or three meetings on Monday, two on Tuesday, two on Wednesday, one on Thursday are already on my list, besides many pastoral duties. Too much, you say. Well, this shows the need for an adviser and reprover as well as a helper. Try to secure me this.

I will write again early, and meanwhile shall look eagerly for your reply to this, which I do hope will

lift me up and not otherwise. Indeed, if you have anything especially good to announce let it come over by
the lightning.

I hope this will find you and mother well. Tell me
all about her Try and get aunt on my side I used
to think she was very kind and friendly to me. Be a
good ambassador, and I will decorate you with another
Star of Love, and send you thanks immeasurable. I
cannot revise this letter. Words may be missing, or
the sense obscure, but I must leave it.

With earnest prayers for you both,
I am
Your affectionate son,
John Alexander Dowie.

<hr>

(June 18, '75—settled in Newtown, N. S. Wales.)

My Dear Friend:

I feel quite ashamed, when I look at my letter book
and see that my last letter to you was written on
August 26th in last year. "Out of sight" you have
been, but never "out of mind"; and I question whether
your name has ever been out of my thoughts and
prayers for a single day. Does it not seem strange
that I have not written for so long, and how can I account for it? These words—procrastination and incessant occupation No man is too busy to write a
few lines, and hence I do not excuse myself on that
account, but you know I do not content myself with
short letters, and put off writing, therefore, until I
could find time to write a long one. Then I have lived
a very busy life since coming to New South Wales, and
my work is now very arduous and important, but I
felt that I could no longer delay, and must find time
to write and tell you how I stand, knowing how glad
you are to hear always about me Pardon, then, my
past shortcomings, and with this assurance at the outset, I shall the more confidently proceed with my let-

ter, which must needs be written in snatches of time between numerous engagements.

About the time I wrote to you, I also wrote to Donald, and mentioned, curiously enough, the expression of the minister who was then here, who telling me that he was possibly going to Queensland, said he was sure that the people of Newtown would call me to the pastoral oversight here, and so it happened, and I accepted

Doubtless you heard from father the details concerning this matter, and the success which God graciously vouchsafed me at Manly I was enabled to build up a church materially and spiritually there, and there are not a few whom God hath brought to Himself under my ministry there. It was hard to part with them after having wrought for them so, and they manifested their love in many tokens of affection, in words and little gifts

I closed my ministry at Manly on the last Sabbath in January and commenced that at Newtown on the first Sabbath in February There were months of negotiation in various ways, before I could feel it my duty to accept the call to Newtown; but the formal call was presented and accepted within a week. Had I wished, there were many who were prepared to guarantee me fully as good a salary as I am getting and build a church in a new district of Sydney, named Woolloomooloo, now one of the most important divisions of the city No doubt it is necessary, and the work of building up a new cause is precisely that which I love, but then Newtown seemed to have still stronger claims. The church was more united in calling me than it had ever been in its history; and there seemed to be no one here or in the other colonies who, being available, would be likely to secure so unanimous a call— at least prominent men here said so. Then the cause was drooping greatly through the vacancy in the pastorate, and no church in this colony is more important to us denominationally, from a variety of reasons.

The population is large—generally considered the largest suburb of Sydney—and there are many educational establishments in the vicinity. The University of Sydney, St. Andrew's (Scotch) College, St John's (Roman Catholic) College, St Paul's (Church of England) College, and our own Congregational College, named "Camden"—are all in and about Newtown.

The students, both lay and clerical, who attend Camden College are attendants upon my ministry, and that is one reason why our church is looked upon as important. Then it is a large church—over 120 members—and seats easily 850 persons—no doubt nearly 1000 persons at a pinch. The building has galleries on three sides; and there is a large, separate building, which we use as a schoolroom. There are about 350 or 450 on the Sabbath School rolls; and a large staff of most efficient teachers. We have also a considerable library for the children

The people are intelligent—a few rich, many middle-class, and a few poor—but the best of all, many godly, earnest and kind, amongst all classes. Indeed, I have received nothing but the greatest kindness from deacons, teachers, church and congregation, and also warm words of welcome from the ministers of other churches here.

This seemed to me the call of God; and not without much anxiety and thought did I accept it. I have never for one moment since regretted doing so. During my stay, the extension and renovation of the church was completed and paid for— between 500 and 600 pounds— a communion roll (now a "church") was formed, many of these members being converted under my ministry; a Sabbath School and library, class rooms built, and a Young Men's Association formed, were also results, with Bible classes, etc., and from a congregation of about 20 it so increased that we were crowded out of the old building, and compelled to extend Have I not reason to thank God for all His goodness to me and others, in thus · blessing my labours, conscious as I am of such great shortcomings and sin, and wholly unworthy of such honour? For it is honour of the highest sort, "which cometh from above", and I would not exchange it for any earthly honour whatever.

The house in which I live is church property and cost about 1800 pounds, without land. In Scotland and elsewhere we would call it "The Manse" But the name given it by the minister for whom it was built was "Devonshire House," which it still bears I have only come to live in it within the last few weeks, for during the vacancy in the pastorate it was let to a doctor, and his term did not expire until May 1st. Then my deacons set to work to prepare it for me and put the house and grounds in thoroughly good order. The furnishing, of course, has devolved upon me and very costly indeed it is. for in the position in which I am placed, I am compelled to furnish in a style corresponding to the house, and my status amongst the people. It is a large, two storied house with a fine, bold front and balcony, not very singular in architecture, but plain and solid looking. You will see how large a house I am living in, and still a bachelor. However, I am not without hope that by and by the Lord may give me that great blessing—a good wife It is a trying thing for a man in my position to be single, I could easily remedy that, people may say Truly they know nothing of it and would not so speak if they did, for I am not a bachelor by choice, but by necessity. I will not marry mere beauty or money bags, and, unless I love truly, not at all. I wish I could report to you that I can see my path in this matter, but I am truly sorry to say, I cannot. May it please God to make it clear is my earnest prayer; and I know in that you will heartily join.

Last year you thought of coming to see me; and now, surely you will come this year. Let me tell you that no one will be more heartily welcomed than you will be, and all that I have is at your disposal. We have money matters to settle between us; and I should hope to be ready then. Hitherto, it has been a hard struggle, and Manly did not really pay my expenses. Newtown gives me 300 pounds per year, but my expenses have been very high indeed, and it will take a very strong pull to get through with the furnishing. However, I have a strong conviction that all will be well ere long and that I am seeing the beginning of an end to all financial troubles

Now, when shall I expect you to come? I have been telling you all about my new home hoping to attract you thither; and I am sure you will prefer this to South Australia in every way . . .

You will, of course, have heard a great deal about the great work of grace going on in the old country, in the doing of which God has so signally owned the labours of Messrs Moody and Sankey In letters which I have received, and still more through newspapers, I learn that the work in Scotland has attained solidity, and permanent blessing has followed.

The work in England is truly wondrous Liverpool, Birmingham, Manchester and London—the greatest city in the world—have all been deeply moved; and still the work goes on, and will I trust We are praying that great wave of revival blessing may cross the mighty deep, and overflow our lands with its blessed influence, and though it seem to tarry, yet I feel often a very strong conviction that times of blessing are coming to us also May we be found ready to make full use of the glorious opportunity.

And now let me ask you about yourself How goes on the work of grace in your own heart? Do you find much closeness to God in prayer and daily life, and more power to speak and act for the Lord? Write to me frankly, as we used to talk to each other, and as we shall yet again I trust   Why should we not write as freely about these things as of less important things? Nothing can be more important to our eternal interest than to know by examination the "state of affairs" in our souls, and men know right well the statement is true in regard to temporal affairs That morbid fear to speak which is often in us, is even more dangerous, in some respects, than an over anxiety to talk of these things   In the latter case, that tendency in every reflective mind is corrected by the necessity for reducing things to practice; and when men begin to **practice** religion, they are careful only to **talk** as much religion as they are prepared to try to put into practice   There is, consequently, little danger of one who is truly Christ's talking too much of Him and his ways; and it is indeed a mark of a true Christian that he is ever ready to talk with a fellow Christian   In the old time we read that "they that feared the Lord spake often one to another," and the Lord hearkened, and heard it, **and a book of remembrance** was written before Him for them that feared the Lord, and that thought upon His name "And they shall be mine, saith the Lord of hosts, in that day when I make up my jewels; and I will spare them, as a man spareth his own son that serveth him." We read, too, that while the two disciples were talking to each other on the way to Emmaus, the Lord Himself drew near, and talked with them, in words that burned within their hearts. So, too, with us, while we write or talk to each other of Him and His work in us, He listens, He records, He comes near, He talks with us, though unseen, and we long to see the face of Him whose voice is to us so sweet

Come, then, let us talk about the King,
    Our great Elder Brother,
As we were used often to speak,
    One to another

The Lord will stand quietly by,
    In the shadows dim,
Smiling, perhaps, in the dark, to hear
    Our sweet, sweet talk of Him

These words I have adapted from a beautiful little poem, of which you may remember me to have been very fond when in South Australia; and they represent what I mean. "Come and hear, all ye that fear the Lord," was the old cry, "and I will tell you what He hath done for my soul" Thus it is that the world will be won for Christ, when we say,

"Now will I tell to sinners round,
"What a dear Saviour I have found;
"I'll point to His redeeming blood,
"And say, 'Behold the way to God.'"

And while we tell others all we know, we shall be increasing our knowledge· for when you clean out and deepen a well, the more does the water flow into it.

Remember me to all Give all the children assurances of my love. I remember all their little faces as it were yesterday, their different dispositions and ways, too I remember the hymns we used to sing together in the little white house on Carter's farm at Alma Plains. It seems only yesterday, since I used to speed along on your "Nellie" under the hills, on my way to Lower Alma preaching station; and meet you or Donald sometimes at the slip panels Our long rides, and talks, and happy hours together come back to me sometimes as memories laden with precious things, wafted though they sometimes are upon sighs

88

of regret—regret that these opportunities were not more valued and improved, and regret that, though years are now past since then, I have lived to so much less purpose than I might.

Write to me soon; but above all come and see me soon. Don't think I am too grand. I am just the same; ay, and more radical than ever. You know I'm not proud God forbid, when I have so much to humble me. And now—"the Lord bless thee, and keep thee; the Lord make His face to shine upon thee, and be gracious unto thee; the Lord lift up His countenance upon thee, and give thee peace"—is the earnest prayer of

Your affectionate friend in Christ Jesus,

John Alexander Dowie.

(Written to his bethrothed—April 1, 1876.)

. . . I know I wish to do all I can to secure your happiness and make you a good husband. Sometimes I fear lest I should even partly fail through lack of power or qualities which many possess, but then I am reassured by remembering that the will to be brings the power to do, in this as in other things. And I know I have the will to be true and loving to you. We shall ask God every day to chase all self-love, and self-will, away from our hearts and lives Shall it not be true? Never until our wills are in accord with God's can we be happy truly and permanently; and it is a joyous thing to live the life God's will appoints My griefs and my trials have all sprung from self-will, which after all is only another name for self-love, or self-worship; and God has found me a dull scholar in learning **practically**, how completely every life must fail in which the first principle is not an entire renunciation of self It is a fearful delusion to imagine that the gladness and beauty of living can be found in a self-pleasing, feverish life of pleasure or ease. To do quietly as may be, cheerfully and with a light footstep, the work to which God has called us must be—and so far as I have experienced it is, the happiest of lives Not knowing, or forgetting this leads many away into worldly by-paths, into meadows which look cool and green, into paths of sin, which bring the soul into dangers or dark Doubt, and into the hands of Giant Despair—as Bunyan would say—into the Highway of Death.

What a blessing that every Christian carries in his bosom the key called Promise! He who pleads that in prayer which God hath promised, shall be delivered, and so get back again to the King's Highway.

You remember the quaint song which Bunyan puts into the mouth of Christian and Hopeful when they were delivered:

"Out of the way we went, and then we found
"What 'twas to tread upon forbidden ground
"And let them that come after have a care,
"Lest heedlessness makes them, as we, to fare;
"Lest they, for tresspassing, his prisoners are,
"Whose castle's Doubting, and whose name's Despair "

And he adds:—"then they went on till they came to the Delectable Mountains   Immanuel's Land, and within sight of His City." And so may we.

. . . Reverse the weaver's beautiful, silken, brilliant and almost perfect fabric. It is all a tangled mass of confused, disorderly threads on the side from which he wrought, very different indeed to the beauty upon which you look So with life—the side from which we work looks tangled indeed, and without plans; but it is not so. Every man's life is a plan of God, in one sense. O that we could rise on the wings of faith and love, and view our lives from the heavenly side, which God looks upon!

If we "wrought out" in our lives with the ever

present consciousness that He was "working in" our souls His own good "will and pleasure," we should not fret or murmur because all the threads did not seem straight, and because we could not quite see His design

It is only to be shown at the Great Exhibition of the Eternity, when the prizes are to be accorded to every man's work; and what wonders will that Exhibition disclose! At a great bazaar once, I saw a great crowd of people pressing eagerly around and loudly praising an object of artistic skill and beauty. After a time, I got close enough to see, and I admired it too—it was the most beautiful object in all the exhibition, and I was told by some one that it had been purchased by a great person for a princely sum

Suddenly I asked "Who did it?" And I was told it was the work of a poor, deformed, unknown man who lived in obscurity and neglect and poverty in a wretched part of the city. But he was a true artist, and a most wonderful genius. 'Twas strange.

It seems to me it will be so at the Great Exhibition of heaven. How many who were obscure and despised on earth, will then be seen to have done great and glorious work of Eternal beauty. Nobody knew them here Or if so they were counted fools and bunglers, mayhap knaves and deceivers, or perhaps they were extended a sickening, tolerating patronage which is as degrading to him who would receive it, as to him who bestows it.

Wonderful lives are being woven by patient submission and love to God on earth. How much we have spoiled by sin and folly! Let us quickly do better together; and we shall be blessed in our doing, and one day God will show us all. To get the spirit and temper, we need much prayer, and retiring from the bustle, need to seek God in the stillness. I find it so amid my many failures and frailties, and I say to you, Jeanie dear, get often alone with God.

Here are a few verses which I wrote some time ago They may tell you better what I mean. But do not think that I am all my words would make you suppose. I am very frail and very faithless, often it seems to me, but the words breathe my desires and hopes and strivings to be what Christ would have me.

How good to leave the world awhile,
How good to seek our Saviour's smile
    And follow in His way,
Oh, could we but our hearts resign
And fully trust God's own design,
    We soon should find it day.

Though night encompass us around,
Though foes despoil our holy ground
    And cause our hearts to fear,
Our Saviour, from the Mount of Prayer,
The feeblest cry doth bend to hear
    And quickly doth appear.

The stormy seas His feet can tread,
They hear the Voice that wakes the dead,
    Commanding, "Peace, be still,"
And guided by our Pilot's hand
Our storm-tossed souls shall reach the land,
    Preserved from every ill

I am so glad you came here, though you did not see us at our best and brightest. You will be heartily welcomed by a people among whom today there is not a jarring note and who are loyal and good to me; and you will feel, I am sure, that this is **home**. I want you to feel that You are leaving, but yet you are going home—to our home   I, too, have a home once more, when you come to make it one,—hitherto it has been "my house."

I was very sorry indeed to read what you wrote

about my mother being ill. As you may suppose, I am very fond of my mother, and it will be hard to see her, and then part from her, perhaps forever on earth I cannot bear to think much of it in that light. She was ever so good and tender to me But I am sure she loves God, and she has in many ways fought a good fight Sometimes I think amongst such as she are found God's heroes and heroines, who, all un-known, meet and overcome great floods of sorrow and trial You must tell her I am looking forward to see-ing her, and she must not have a place for gloomy forebodings "Sufficient unto the day is the evil there-of " If sorrow is to come, we are not called upon to meet it half way

. How often have I wished for the soothing touch of your loving hand, when I have come home weary and sad after scenes of sorrow such as have lain heavy on my heart. But God is very gracious, and I have a bouyancy and strength given, though responsibilities and cares grow And I have a good wife coming home with me, by and by Should I not be grateful to God? And I am. I say with all my heart, "Bless the Lord, O my soul." I do not fear I am doing God's work, and He will take care, if I am faithful and wise My only sorrow is that I have been faithless and foolish too often, alas But I am with Him still, and, I say it with deep and solemn awe and wonder at His condescension and love, **He is with me,** and is giving me most gracious tokens of His presence and blessing When I am ready to faint He gives me some fresh evidence, and every day I seem to see His hand with me, and hear His voice in my heart. Is it not amazing that God should thus use a human soul, and that in work angels might covet?

(April 7, '76—writes of his approaching marriage—religious act first —civil second—marriage favorable occasion for miracle of grace.)

Dear Father and Mother:

It seems quite a long time since I had a letter from you; and I dare say you are thinking the same thing regarding me. Are you not the transgressors this time? I think I wrote you last; and I am sure that I wrote you longest However, if it be God's will, I shall see you soon, and be able to say more in ten minutes than I could write in ten hours. You will have long strings of questions, I expect My catechetical instruction has been entirely suspended since I saw you; and it will be quite a new experience to be questioned largely. Still my letters have kept you so fully informed as to my personal history as to leave little to add; and then—

"There's always something in the heart,
We canna tell to ony"

That which cannot be told, is that, generally, which **words** could not adequately express Indeed which **words** could only darken and becloud. There runs "deep waters" in every soul, which no "sounding line" of human insight has fathomed—not even our own; and there are "quiet under currents" whose existence is often for long years unrecognized These influence, unconsciously, our life in its most momentous issues, but they defy definition and their power defies arithmetical or methaphysical calculation. This is an almost new truth to me

But instead of a letter, I seem to be beginning a discourse. The ruling passion is strong, you see. You have known of me, through Jeanie lately, I daresay As far as I can see now, I will leave here on Friday, May 12, by P. and O branch steamer "Avoca," transhipping into the Galle steamer at Melbourne, and will thus get to Glenely about Thursday, May 18. I suppose the marriage will take place about ten days

94

later. Jeanie fixes the exact date somewhere between 25th (my birthday) and 31st.

I hope there will be no great fuss made over it. Of course it will awaken interest in a few, and some excitement—however mild—is inevitable; but such a quiet and insignificant being as I was amongst you in Adelaide may surely claim immunity from making his private affairs a public spectacle. Jeanie wants it in the church; but whilst I, of course, agree, I have expressed my desire that the day should be kept secret as far as possible

Do not think, however, that I am nervously apprehensive: for, as you know, I am used to being gazed at, and am not likely to lose my self-possession in a ceremony with which I am so practically familiar from the minister's point of view.

I only desire to feel that neither Jeanie nor I are "on exhibition," and every glance and tone under severe scrutiny.

I thoroughly approve of the idea that marriage is a religious act first, and a civil act next. I have no sympathy with those who would degrade it to the level of a "civil contract;" for whilst I admit it is that, and such a contract as the state is bound to record and recognize since it lies at the foundation of all government, yet I contend it is much more. It is a great mystery—a type of the highest mysteries of our spiritual affinity with Christ—and is the only institution which, ordained in man's innocency in Eden, has been perpetuated unbrokenly since. Such being my feeling, you can see that whilst I should like the brightness and joy of Paradise and Cana to ring in sweetest harmony our marriage chimes, yet I want to feel "Christ is here today"—"Christ smiles upon us" —"Christ transforms our insipid earthly water into sweetest, richest heavenly wine"—"Christ sees us take the cup of salvation and call upon the name of the Lord." I am very weak, I am very unworthy the honour, but He has himself encouraged me by His past condescension to do it,—I have invited Christ Jesus, my Lord, to come to the marriage; and I expect, therefore, to "see Jesus" there. I do not want the crowd to shut out my view of Him then—I can see them any day, and besides, I want Jesus to do great things for us then, and "manifest forth His glory," so that the white raiment of Divinest brightness may shine upon Jeanie and I. A marriage is a favorable occasion for a miracle of grace, and since the House of the Lord is to be our marriage place, surely we may expect many bright and cheering tokens of His presence and transforming spiritual power Angels sung Adam's marriage hymn, in the abode of human innocence and love, and all sentient nature, from air, and earth, and sea, joined in grandest orchestral chorus.

Who shall say that Christ's own children's joy shall be less gloriously attended? We are of "the second Adam"—the Lord from heaven—, and claim the sympathy of a more glorious throng than even that which sung the marriage songs of Eden

We know there is an Eden above, and is there not, too, an Eden here?

Thus you see why I object to mere fuss. But perhaps all my warnings are vain and needless, showing too much self-consciousness about that which will create no widespread interest such as would cause people to flock to see. Possibly this severe self-reflection is just and true I will be very glad indeed if it proves so . . . . I must get on quickly now with this letter for there are many interruptions, and the mail closes in an hour at Newtown We have had a terrible time of sickness—since I came here I have buried twenty-five persons—twenty of them from my own church and congregation, and I have been very much exposed daily amongst fevers of every sort. My health is, notwithstanding this and my heavy work, very good—wondrously so, I must admit I am far stronger than I could have expected, and am most grateful to God for such signal blessing. But I am mentally a little weary; and you could scarcely wonder if it were so after such constant mental effort as I have had since I left Adelaide—now over two years and a half But my work never was so interesting and successful from every point of view. My people are kinder and more loyal than ever—many who were idlers, almost, are working for Christ in various ways, with an energy and love as surprising as it is pleasing—many are coming to me as enquirers—my services are increasing in spiritual power, I am sure, and the numbers are steadily increasing. The future opens out into vistas of possible things, should I be spared, which are very attractive and beautiful to my eyes, in the way of extended church effort.

Are there no difficulties? Many. Many are overcome, some still remain, and there are more ahead, no doubt. But I not only do not fear them, but there is a sense in which I positively welcome them. They prove I am on the right track—the way which Christ trod—the path of Life and Peace, even though it be midst death and calamities However. strange though it seems, I have learned to welcome the sight of every obstacle in the way, for I have found they have given me, when enabled to surmount them, a vantage ground and grandeur of view which I would not have missed for far greater toil than were needed in pressing upwards. My only sorrow is that I have sinned so much in giving way to evil temptations, instead of overcoming them by Divine aid .

4

How thankful I feel to God who has protected and preserved me in my journeyings to and fro, and when I think of our passage from Adelaide a few months ago I often wonder we escaped   Had it been just a little rougher the greed of the overloading port agents would have brough us to a watery grave; for as it was the sea was breaking over us, and in weather like the recent hurricane the ship would not have lived three hours.

The correspondence I have referred to arose out of a leader published in the "Herald" and is a case of the pot and the kettle   The "Herald" devotes whole columns of "betting business" at Tattersals, spicy accounts of the stakes and morning canters, etc, with long, sensational accounts of the "sport" at Randwick—where every blackleg and scoundrel who can get from Sydney and Melbourne assembles to indulge in "the noble pastime", which occupies the attention of "the gentlemen of the country" whose names are enrolled in the scroll of sporting fame by the so-called first gentlemen in it.

It was therefore a merited rebuke when our horsey Governor charged upon the "Herald" the chief responsibilities of the impetus given to the operation of the betting ring, who like vultures with a taste for putridity scent a race and its abominations afar off, and hasten to plunge their foul beaks and unclean talons into the hearts of the foolish and greedy throngs of fools. A racing week in Sydney is a carnival of all abominations—it is said 40,000 persons attend—and leaves deadly results. It has been shown that the races are held upon part of our water reserves, and as a gathering area, and that the filth and garbage ad nauseam is carefully carried down into the Botany Dam from whence Sydney is supplied with its water—thus carrying dirt, disease and death into every house, through every tap. And this is the work encouraged by a "wise statesman," and a "Christian philanthropist" The moral results of the race course are like the physical: it carries a moral death into every part of our social system, and is proving the ruin of thoughtless thousands.

And this is the man, whose treasury is swollen by the proceeds of the race course, who is to be elected our chairman for 1877-8, if some can carry out their plans What a spectacle! I am ashamed of the whole affair; and it seems to me quite certain that the Lord Jesus, or Paul, or any New Testament saint would roundly condemn any man who claimed to be a Christian having a business—newspaper or otherwise—the profits of which were derived from advertising operas, theaters, falsehoods about medicinal pills, horse races, betting, etc. etc These are the things that do more to disgrace and hinder the cause of Christ, than any number of infidel attacks upon Divine revelation How can we wonder if the Gospel does not spread, when leading professors are making of God's temple only "a den of thieves"? How can we wonder, when, instead of being living **epistles** known and read of man many are read only too plainly by all men who are not born idiots, to be mere Mammon worshippers? I do not wonder at the spread of secularism and materialism amongst those who do not study Christ's character, but who only judge of Christianity by many of the specimens with whom they come closest into contact I solemnly declare I will never sit under the presidency of John Fairfax—never!

And now I must close this long screed, hoping that I shall hear from you soon good news as to the health of body and spirit May God give you much of His love in your heart to draw you close to His comforts and joy in Christ, of His faith to see and grasp the unseen realities beyond earth's shadowy passions, of His light to make the path of your life all clear, and at eventide clearest of all, and of His peace to keep your heart calm and confident amid all the vicissitudes of all its trials   Yet a little while and we shall rest from earthly toil. 'Tis worth all the agony, a thousand fold, to win a crown more enduring then earthly gold—the Crown of Life will then replace the Crown of Thorns, and the welcome of Christ will far outweigh the rejection of men. May I be faithful unto death, and whoever passes through the portals first, let him or her find that we are each following one by one into heaven's rest . .

(Devonshire House, Newtown, Sidney, N. S Wales, March 16, 1877. This letter was acknowledged by Mr. Gladstone, who expressed his appreciation of the same, and sympathy with the writer's aims)

To the Right Hon. W. E Gladstone, M P.

Right Honorable and Dear Sir:

In this remote portion of the British Dominions, we are not without our share in the great controversies which are profoundly agitating our Fatherland and Europe generally

Not least of these is that concerning the present aspect of Papalism towards the consciences and the liberties of men everywhere, and, since you have taken a foremost place amongst contemporary men in laying bare the real nature of the great conspiracy against all progress and freedom now embodied in the Papacy, I have taken the great liberty of forwarding to you by this mail a pamphlet written by myself, exposing the falacies and the fictions of the champion orator of Papalism in Australia, Dr. Roger B. Vaughan, Roman Catholic Arch Bishop of Sydney

You will see from pages 37 how he has dealt with your late article in the "Contemporary" on "The Courses of Religious Thought," which very effectively illustrates, I think, the truth of your eight charges against Ultramontanism, viz "its tendency to sap veracity in the individual mind."

There are also other aspects in which my pamphlet may prove interesting to you, such as the undoubted aim of this clever, fascinating, and unscrupulous prelate to endeavor, by means of our free institutions, to acquire State sympathy and aid in controlling the education of the Romanist children, which is in danger of slipping from the priest's grasp, and passing into the liberalizing hands of a national and uncertain, though not irreligious System of Education.

The Roman Catholic population of this colony is very large— some estimate it at nearly one-third, and they have great influence in the Legislative, Judicature, and Press, so that we may truly say there are practical dangers connected with their ascendency.

Politicians here are, for the most part, mere office seekers or selfish speculators with very little principle of any sort; and there is room to fear that the Roman Catholic vote and interest is often wielded in such a way as often decides the fate of the Ministers and the power of Parties, according as these may favor or oppose the priestly policy. Dr. Vaughan is welding his church together, with objects like these before him, in a very masterly manner, and thoughtful men are becoming seriously impressed with the possibly grave dangers near, and the need for watchfulness and preparedness

Amongst other things which greatly favor such orators as Dr Vaughan in their influence upon public sentiment, and there fore, upon law and Government, are the following·—first, the extreme general industrial activity, and the avidity with which pleasure is pursued in every form by the mass of the people, to the exclusion of vigorous, thoughtful inquiry regarding religious, moral, and in the highest sense, political, subjects

Second, the fact that History has not been taught in the public schools for a long time past, owing to Romanist influence largely, and that, from similar

105

causes I believe, there are no Chairs either of History, or Metaphysics, or Moral Philosophy in our University, so that Australian born and educated people are very largely a prey to any orator who has impudence or unscrupulousness enough to palm off on them fables for facts, or rhetoric for reasons.

Third, the sorrowful fact that the sine qua non of that mighty power, the Newspaper Press, is here as elsewhere that Pluto shall be propitious, so that "will it pay?" is the primary question in every case, and consequently, the fanaticism of Papalism is skillfully deferred to for purely commercial reasons.

As an illustration, I may state that Dr. Vaughan's address of October 9 last, delivered to little more than 1,000 persons, I am informed, was published in extenso the next day in the "Sunday Morning Herald", our only morning paper, occupying about 13 colums of small type, whilst my lectures, delivered first in this suburb to nearly a thousand persons, and then to audiences which filled the largest public hall in Sydney—say in all to over 3,000 persons—did not receive, in all the paragraph notices, more than half a column

I say this from no feeling of personal annoyance, I trust, but simply as a fact beyond dispute, which arises either from the cause I name, or an even less creditable one. You will, therefore, see the nature and importance of some of the difficulties with which we are surrounded in dealing with such subjects in this colony.

On the other hand, there are many things in this land favorable to the extension of the truth, and there are hundreds of thousands of good men, who in every department of Australian life, are labouring in a hope that true liberty and rightousness may prosper and exalt the rising nations of this continent

Forgive me, if I have trespassed too long upon your attention, but the subject is one in which I feel a deep interest, not only as a citizen but as a Christian, convinced as I am that the Papal system is not only dangerous to true political freedom but is opposed to the extension of the Redeemer's Kingdom in the hearts of men. Knowing that this is also your conviction, I feel sure of your sympathy with me in my imperfect endeavors to follow in a contest where you have so nobly led

May I then hope that you will be pleased to accept my pamphlet as a tribute of my most profound respect, and my admiration for your noble work as a statement and author?

Very sincerely do I regret that it is not more worthy of your acceptance, and I can only hope that you will look upon it as the first effort in this direction of a man still young, and almost without literary experience. Since I am about it, I may as well state, since it may give you even a moment's pleasure, that my first born child, just given to me, is named by us Alexander John Gladstone, as a memorial of my gratitude for your noble services, and that reverent regard for your character, with which your life's work has impressed me

Again I solicit your forgiveness for my long trespass on your attention, and praying that our Almighty God and Father may bless you and yours, for His dear Son's sake, with peace, love and joy of spirit now and forever,

I am, with respectful esteem,

John Alexander Dowie

(*Dated from Camden Street, Newtown, Sidney, N. S W , October* 22, 1877.)

My dear Wife:

Your most welcome letter of 15th reached me this morning and I was glad to know you were stronger, and that our wee pet was well, excepting the slight cold you mentioned, and from which I trust he is wholly recovered now. I thank God for His mercy and care over you in your journey

You know already from my previous letters that the letter you mention as having been written from Scotts' Hotel, Melbourne, never reached me, and that I am quite ignorant of the events which happened up to that time or how it was that you came to be there. Please tell me all about that part of your journey and to whom you gave the letter which never reached me.

I am thankful to the Meadowcrofts for their kindness to you, and sorry that poor M— has such hard times You did right about the money, though I will never ask them for the balance until they seem more able to pay it, but will leave it to their own time. for with so many children it seems to me they must be only one removed from positive need, and though I am poor, I will not verify Solomon's proverb—"A poor man that oppresseth the poor is like a sweeping rain which leaveth no food."

About your question as to how I got on upon the Wednesday evening after you left, the evening upon which the stars, shining out overhead in the sky, seemed to raise your heart to thoughts of God, and by His conscious presence make you to trust Him with a firmer faith and a purer love—a presence which caused your depression to fly—and no wonder, for darkness always flees before Divine Light in the soul

Well, I must thank you for praying for me then: for just about that very time, probably from what you say, a quarter of an hour later, I had an especial blessing at my meeting, where without a single note, I preached a most comforting and strengthening discourse to a very much larger audience than usual. And this is more remarkable still when I mention the text, which came to my mind with much force just about one quarter past seven o'clock, in the second chapter of Matthew, 10th verse—"When they saw the star, they rejoiced with exceeding great joy " I have seldom felt calmer or more thoroughly at ease in preaching than I did on that occasion. Some day I must preach it again, when you are among my hearers. Now is not this an encouragement to us both to pray and believe that God, while we are praying, is answering our requests for each other? I so regard it. And another thing it shows us is the good we may get through writing to each other about these things; for, if you had not mentioned the fact of your so thinking, feeling, and praying, I would not have known that I was specially helped in answer to your special prayer. The Holy Spirit which dwells within us both will often thus reveal to us our union with each other in God, and this is true (to adapt some lines of Tennyson)—

"For thou and I are one in kind,
As moulded light in God's own mint;
And hill and field and wood do print
The same sweet forms in either mind."

But there is one thing, dearest, we must seek to preserve and increase this communion by constant watchfulness over our hearts and life, and by continual looking to Him whose last Name in the Revelation of Himself is given in His own words—"I am. . . the Bright and Morning Star."

We know Him as the Star of Hope when all earthly lights are gone out, and no friendly face seems to look upon us; and seeing Him our soul is anchored

We know Him as the Star of Guidance, the Polar Star, which never changes and to whom the magnet of our love, like a compass, always points; and no matter how dark the night or stormy the Ocean of Life may be, we are safe when He is in sight

We know Him as the Star of Joy, for whilst we are weeping in the night, we are sure when we see Him that the Morning will come, when we weep no more, and when we shall know why we were afflicted in the darkness.

109

Yes, and we shall know Him in many ways yet more beautiful than these when we get nearer to Him, and lose sight of the Star in the consciousness at last that we are in the Presence of the Son of Righteousness, who is the Light unceasing of the home, of life in Heaven itself. Meanwhile, we must journey on, and when clouds and darkness seem to veil the heavens above us so that we cannot see the Star, let us have the Light of it within us which assures that there is a Star behind these clouds. Says one:

"I remember well
One journey, how I feared the track was missed,
So long the City I desired to reach
Lay hid; when suddenly its spires afar
Flashed through the circling clouds; conceive my joy!
For soon the vapours closed o'er it again.
But I had seen the City, and one such glance
No darkness could obscure."

Sometimes, darling, I am ready to say to myself—"You have missed the track—you are going without clear guidance—you will stumble and fall in the darkness, and woe to him that falleth when he is alone—you see everybody thinks so, and even Egypt, though you were bound, was better than the Desert where you are sure to die, for there is meat, flesh and wine, there in abundance, and what though all are slaves there—is it not better to be a slave and fat rather than be free and die?—besides what good can you do going out to conquer armed foes in Canaan (call it Sydney) who are strong and don't care for your Joshua (say Jesus) and can easily beat you who have got no money to carry on a war with, and no big cannons to break down the walls of prejudice in thousands of hearts—go back, go back, before you are ruined!"

And then, to make matters worse, I seem to hear "the elder brethren" add their sneers—I have heard them before—and some Eliab saying—"Why comest thou down hither? and with whom hast thou left these few sheep in the wilderness? I know thy pride and the naughtiness of thine heart, for thou art come down that thou mightest see the battle." To all which I can only say as David said long ago—"What have I now done? Is there not a cause?"

Then turning to my own heart, having first turned my soul to God, I rebuke my faithless fears, and silence the cunning whispers of the Tempter. For I can say—"I know I'm on the right track—I know who guided me to enter upon it, and that it was for His glory I begun to tread it, for His glory I intend to continue in and to finish it—I know I may stumble, but that will be my own fault, and I know at the same time that I am not alone, for God is with me and for me so that even I can say, 'Rejoice not against me, O mine enemy, when I fall I shall arise; when I sit in darkness the Lord will be a light unto me'—I don't care what 'everybody' thinks or says if that is contrary to God's thoughts and ways: for 'I will hear what God the Lord will speak'—I don't believe it would be better to go back to Egypt, I hate its wine and flesh, I don't murmur for 'quails', and there's plenty of manna for today with a promise of plenty tomorrow, I don't believe I shall die in the Desert, and even so I had rather starve and die there where God calls me than live fat and a slave under any Pharoah either in church or state; for I would be sure to get to heaven from the Desert, a more than doubtful matter if I died in Egypt. I can conquer without money in Sydney (Christ and Peter and Paul and all His first followers and many of His best in all ages had none—they 'became poor' yet they conquered Jerusalem, Rome, Athens—the world); and those who don't care now for my Joshua will soon, if I am faithful, for He makes His victorious presence and power felt, and men must listen, even if they are His enemies,

111

for 'Never man spake like this man' is always their verdict now as it was long ago, and as for money to carry on the war with, I have God's Promisory Note payable on demand of faithful Prayer at the Throne, the Treasury of Grace for 'all things' (is it not written 'God shall supply all your need according to His riches in glory in Christ Jesus' and 'who goeth a warfare at any time at his own charges?') and He is my Backer, ay, and He can open the hearts of men to see that all my proper wants are supplied in His service, for all men are His and all they have they hold as stewards on a short lease to be employed for Him—I can get plenty of cannon to batter down the Walls of Prejudice in human hearts, for the whole Armory of Heaven is at my disposal if I am true to God, and I know a Trumpet before the sound of which no Jericho Walls of Pride can stand,—the gospel Trumpet when breathed into by the Spirit of Truth and Love. I know I shall not be killed outright, and I am certain to conquer even if I die in the fight, and I won't, I won't go back an inch, so long as God pleases to say 'go forward' And why? for though 'I am a worm and no man', yet to all who are convenant with Christ, God has said, 'Fear not, thou worm Jacob, and ye men of Israel; I will help thee, saith the Lord, and thy Redeemer, the Holy One of Israel Behold, I will make thee a new sharp threshing instrument having teeth thou shalt thresh the mountains, and beat them small, and shalt make the hills as chaff. Thou shalt fan them, and the wind shall carry them away, and the whirlwind shall scatter them: and thou shalt rejoice in the Lord, and glory in the Holy One of Israel'."

Now this is my strength, these are my resources, these works are my purposes, and in the Lord—the Star that never sets—is my rejoicing, and His victory is my glory With all humility—and prayer for deepening within and all foes without, for knowing from my heart that I neither covet worldly wealth nor hon-

" As the British Constitution is the most subtle organism which has proceeded from progressive history, so the American Constitution is the most wonderful work ever struck off at a given time by the brain + purpose of man."

Handwriting of John Alexander Dowie at the age of forty.

ours, knowing that I am personally content with such things I have, and relying upon Him who has said **"I will never leave thee nor forsake thee"** I, too, may boldly say, "The Lord is my helper, and I will not fear what man shall do unto me."

And, Jeanie, my love, this is my answer to the words of your father's, or my father's who, instead of giving sympathy, sneers at faith. I do not need to be told that my life has been full of sins and errors of judgment, and certainly when I am suffering do not need any of my nearest to join in the cry "He saved others, himself he cannot save," which comes to me now as to many since Christ heard it in His hour of darkness—though then it came from His enemies. I have confessed my sins to a forgiving and gracious God, I have even confessed to man, and I have done, am doing, and shall do, what in me lies, aided by God, to see that no one suffers permanent loss through my errors, and through my overconfidence in men who should have been trustworthy.

But I fail to see any one's right to reproach me, simply because I did not burden them with my troubles; and I now say without any anger but with calm deliberation, if you find yourself and our pet looked upon thus in the slightest degree, you are to come back to me at once, for I will not have that, no, not for a moment. I can keep you here, as you know, and I would a thousand times rather submit to any privation than have you there or anywhere looked upon as one of my "troubles" thrown upon other people, for you two are my greatest earthly comforts, whom it was hard to part with even for a time, whom it is harder still to do without as I daily find, and whom I want back the first day they cease to be happy in Adelaide. Indeed, even more than you know, it was for your sakes I let you go. But come back at once, I charge you, if you are uncomfortable or unwelcome in the smallest degree. Don't think that I

have misread your letter; your father is kind to you
and wants you "to eat well, sleep well, and live out
in the open air"—all very good—and so do I—but you
could have done all that without leaving New South
Wales But that does not make "kindness", if I am to
be sneered at, for surely my sorrow will be yours, and
I am hurt and sad to get these words from him—he
shall yet see that God's people are as richly fed as
ever they were when manna fell from heaven, for every
day He gives them daily bread, and though he is our
father, and I desire to treat him, as you know I have,
with all due respect in word and deed, yet he shall not
sneer at the promises of my Father in Heaven with
impunity, whilst I at least can speak a word or write
a line to protest—for that is really what his words
amount to, in my opinion As for "quails" from
heaven, I never asked for them, never sighed for them,
and don't want them—they are "game" which the
world seeks after, and are emblems of that food which
is desired by the unfaithful Christians who murmur at
the food God provides—Manna and Truth—and get
"quails", but with a curse from the lips of God while
"the flesh" for which they have lusted "is still within
their teeth"—no, I don't want "quails" from heaven,
in case I may get "the plague" too

Now as for writing again and arguing the matter
as you suggest, I will do nothing of the kind. I have
written one letter which contains all the facts and
arguments, which is not answered, and I can add
nothing to it—a letter which, had I thought such comment would be made on the writer, I would never have
written, for as you know, it was painful to write, and
a pain that might have been spared, as I now see. The
absurd telegram for more information pained me too,
because it was sent to me after reading two letters
to which I could scarcely by any possibility add another fact I thought if anything could be full it was

the minute account I gave of everything in these letters.

Please do not let your father imagine that I am asking him to help me, for I have not asked a penny, am glad I have not, and do not intend to. It would hurt me now for him to help. These many years past have I toiled on through all sorts of discouragements, difficulties of every kind and heart breaks, and I have never found God to forsake me in my time of need, and there are many true men around me who will stand by me should I be oppressed beyond my power to endure, if they knew it, for one who knew nothing of these affairs of mine said noble and kind words to me the other day, bidding me to use his purse if I needed it, which declined with warm heart thanks. I will confess to you alone, that I thought then I would go to "my ain folk" for what aid I might need, but after your father's sneers and criticism, I would rather go back for a time into business if it were necessary, than to ask any of them. So you will please let your father know, in your own words, that I am sorry I wrote about my troubles to him, that I did not, and do not, ask him to help me at all in any way, and that I want you to come back at once if there is any more said about me and them such as has been said, for there is fresh air, and food, and a house here for you as well as in South Australia. Indeed I am thoroughly sorry you went back now, and you will remember that I had a half foreboding that something like this would occur. I cannot bear to think of you, even though in your father's home, being anywhere that I am so spoken of, for much of that kind of influence would go far to lessen your love for me, if anything could, and put thoughts of bitterness into the cup of our life which would embitter our happiness for many a year. Neither my father nor your father might do that willingly, but though I love them both, I know that they can both say and do bitter things that can rankle like poisoned arrows for many a year, as they both know to their mutual cost; but I am determined, if possible, that they shall not even thoughtlessly do this to me.

October 23rd.

Looking back this morning over what I wrote yesterday I find a good many things rather more strongly expressed, perhaps, than I would care for any one else to see but you to whom alone I write, and yet there is no substantial alteration in my views therein expressed after a good deal of reflection. So you will please, my love, consider them as expressing my thoughts and wishes in substance, even though were I to rewrite them it might be in a milder form However you know me now too well to imagine that there is anything of personal rancor in my apostrophes, for you know my tendency to forcible expressions regarding what I see to be dangerous things. You will not need that I should say that I don't hate your **father** for what he said, though I very heartily hate and strike at what he did say, as wrong in itself, and not very kindly or tenderly conceived so far as I was concerned, because my present position, viewed from the human standpoint, is not very enviable, and very hazardous, I fully admit. When a man is climbing up the face of a precipitous cliff, with stormy sea and sharp rocks far beneath him, it would scarcely be kind, no matter how strong and sure footed he might be, for any one to shout "Go back! You will fall and kill yourself if you go a single step further!" And though I will not say that is really my position for, viewing it from the Divine side, I would say that even were I, which is likely enough, in a dangerous human position (for I carry my life and all, as every one does, with but a step between me and death) there is no reason to fear.

Psalm XC expresses my highest expectations, and its promises fulfill my highest longings and still my clamorous fears into quiet confidence. I do not intend to cast myself down to prove the 11th and 12th verses, any more than our Lord did in the Temptation, for my aim is to get higher by doing work to which God appoints me, and I know that just so long as I am faithful to God and His work—and that I want to be He knows—just so long may I safely say of disaster or of death "It shall not come nigh me". . . . and He "will be with me in trouble, and deliver me, and honour me."

Did you ever observe a bird—or even a fly—clinging to the face of a precipice?

I am sure, when you did, you were not concerned about the fly's safety, or fear that the rock was giving way, and that the fly was about to be plunged into the gulf. Neither may you fear, if you and I are clinging to the Rock and hiding in some little cleft of Him, for He can keep us where life would seem to be impossible, because He Himself, the Rock of Ages, must be torn away from His everlasting foundations of Omnipotence ere the weakest believer that hangs upon Him can perish. Is not that a firm foundation for us to build upon?

I had rather, though I am myself one of the very weakest of His children, build my house there though it made but a very poor appearance to the sneering fools of earth—yea, I had rather do this, ten thousand times rather, than own all the palaces and treasures of the world built on the shifting sands of Time, for they shall fall, and, with all who cling to them, be swept away into the sea of Divine Wrath whilst the soul on Christ's foundation shall behold with joy the morning of a New Heaven and a New Earth wherein dwelleth righteousness alone.

If I give up that hope, then I should turn to the world, and fight for and enjoy to the full pleasure it affords, and sail with its current, and wear its honours, and win its applause, and cry "Let us eat and drink for tomorrow we die." "Soul, take thine ease, eat, drink, and be merry!" "Come, I will fetch wine, and we will fill ourselves with strong drink, and tomorrow will be as this day, and much more abundant!" Yes, this would be our best alternative—for it would be consistent with the rejection of a Resurrection Life, and if I did that I would not be such a fool as to imagine a middle course preferable, for I know that the attempt to serve 'God and Mammon' is a most miserable failure, for he who tries it will find that he has lost eternal happiness in heaven and even temporary joy on earth—and deserves to, for he is the worst of all sinners—a hypocrite and a sham The most miserable wretches on earth are those who build palaces in and enjoy all the World can give, whilst they vainly imagine that by some money gift, Sunday observance, or lip service, they are going to secure a Palace in Heaven where all is Purity and Love. They are, at heart, despised on earth by man; they are rejected in heaven by God, and they are sneered at even in hell, I should imagine, by the Devil—they are fools as well as knaves.

Well now, dear, I must say, any how, resolved I am to leave Newtown, and though I can see how I could do good work for Christ in Sydney yet I do not feel as if I had yet got the command—"Go forward into that city!" Every day kind friends in all ranks of society, and in all denominations speak regretfully of my leaving Newtown, and the more so because they have got it into their heads, through your going to Adelaide, that I am either going to Melbourne, or Adelaide, or to England—the rumors are many

And when I say that I have not yet decided when I will leave Sydney, there are immediate and hearty responses of "I am glad to hear it," and "I hope you will remain, there's lots of room," and "we want you here," etc. Especially is this the case among city men, and it is strong among many brethren in the ministry of other denominations, but especially strong is it among Temperance and Anti-Liqour Traffic men and pronounced Pretestants.

Does not all this represent some considerable inclination toward me of a general sort? for these are representative men   At the same time I do not shut my eyes to the serious difficulties in the way, and to the necessity for very great care and prudence in all my movements, so that I will not be guilty of neglecting the means while depending upon God for the power.   However, the means must also come from God as well as the power, and the first means which God employs is a thoroughly consecrated man.   At present I feel more than ever resolved to commit myself to no course, but just to consider myself as in the position of a soldier, whose regiment is in barracks but is "under orders" to prepare for "foreign service" on or before a certain day, with a destination which is unknown—it may be Europe, Asia or Africa—though he is ready, nevertheless, to go where ordered.

Thus am I getting ready to go—where?—wherever God appoints, and sure am I that there is clear instruction coming, when it is His time

Now, Jeanie dear, you are not afraid, I am sure, of going with me through life with such a Guide, for you know His name is Jehovah—jireh—"The Lord will provide."   I fear nothing with God for me, and you with me, and our little Gladdy to care for and love, and train up for nobler service far than I can ever render to the Lord now   Oh, for more faith, more prudence, more wisdom, more love, more zeal, more holiness, then I would fear nothing and walk more nearly as God would have me   May our gracious God hear and answer my cry, for Christ's sake, and dismiss me not from His service and presence, but make me a better servant and grant me more of His Holy Spirit's power to do and to suffer all His will ordains

Here, then, I have shown you all my heart's thoughts about the kind of life I want to live with you—I want to walk with God by faith, for that is the purest and happiest life of all—I want to leave it all with Jesus.

Our Congregational meetings began last night with a prayer meeting in Pitt Street school room, and when you think that the ministers and delegates number about a hundred and fifty, and that all our churches were closed, and that the evening was moonlit and very mild you will then understand how much they value united prayer among us when I tell you that the dozen or more churches and delegates could not muster two hundred at the outside Mr. S— has returned from New Zealand looking worse than when he left, in health that is, and delivered a wordy and wearisome address. Yesterday afternoon was the first session, and three-fourths of the time went in twaddle. Mr H— of M— is Chairman—a man who is pastor of a church in one of the most thriving towns out of Sydney, has a building nearly as large as mine, and though more that a dozen years there has only a handful of people, and lives on a stone breaker's wages or less. He delivered the address last night, but I was not there, for several matters demanded my attention here, and could not go, though I don't think I was very sorry Today they continue, and on till Saturday But I do not think much good is coming out of them, for three-fourths of their talk ends in a fog, and the other fourth for the most part in resolutions which effect next to nothing of a practical sort for the extension of Christ's Kingdom, whilst cliqueism is triumphant and that most narrow denominationalism called Congregationalism is much more potent than the interests of Christianity, than the claims of perishing multitudes outside who want "bread" and not theological "stones". True regard for Christ's work should make that the first question I have come to consider that as of the first importance, and everything else as of only auxiliary value—whether Creeds, or Theories, or Balance Sheets. Let us attend to the first thing first, and then we won't find thousands going to certain damnation through the Devil and his wiles, for hundreds who are being saved through Christ and His Church. There is no lack of power in Christ—in Him is "all power" and "all fullness"—the lack is in His people and because there is with them a "mixed multitude" who are strongly numbered among His people and who suppose that gain is godliness. There lies our weakness. But oh, for the purifying and strengthening **power**! It is the Spirit we need.

We need Love and Self-sacrifice, and Courage to look at things as they really are in God's sight, and Strength to go on without fear and do the right. My darling, I am crushed into the very dust of self-abasement to think of how wretchedly unfruitful my life has been, and how fearful and weak my heart is now when I shrink from the Cross, the pain, and the shame which will surely come if I follow Jesus fully—and yet He knows, He knows I want to. My heart is sick and faint when I behold the desolations of sin among men, and the cool self-complacency of those who look upon them, perishing, without apparently one heart pang of grief or thought of relief—who just "pass by on the other side" and leave the robbed and wounded and naked to die in their sins. Oh, my God, fill my heart with more faith in Him, in His word, and in His Son who is "mighty to save," and ready to save! I am empty, sometimes, it seemsfi of all strength, and have only fearful void in my soul, where Doubt and Fear and Sorrow flit like dark specters, and where hated Sin lurks and wants to drag me down in Despair. May God empty me of all evil, fill me with Light, and endow me with Strength, for elsewhere I know not where it is—for "God hath spoken once; twice have I heard this, that **power belongeth unto God.**" I feel so powerless and so empty even with this Omnipotence and Fullness there for me in God, and the ancient myth of Tantalus surrounded by tempting food and water, which yet fled from him when he stooped to take or to drink, seems my case only too often Yet I have better times, though I confess with shame and sadness that today the Star seems veiled in darkness to my soul. O come, Thou Spirit of Love and Light—come to my soul . .

Tell my father and mother I want to hear from them—I seem to be forgotten by them altogether You should all remember that a public man's life is often a very lonely life, for meetings and committees etc etc , no more make a man's happiness than if he were a bus driver or a railway guard—and sometimes in a crowd one is more lonely than in a wilderness

B— and A— seem to have grown much, and I hope they have grown more helpful to our mother, whom I always remember with gratitude for all her goodness to me and mine even though we could not see alike regarding our ideas of alcoholic poisons and their right place Her love to you and our wee pet will more than cover any hard things she ever said to me, and I hope she does not quite look upon me as a hard man or kind of hedge hog—you at any rate did not find me so.

G— and N— are no doubt running their first races in the battle of school life and with success, I hope, and if as a reward for labour, they can only both secure the prize Knife of Knowledge it will be something of great value to them always, for with its corkscrew they will be able to draw the corks out of the bottles (books) which contain the precious Wine of Wisdom and instruction; they will be able with the sharp little blades of Art to trim what they acquire into more beautiful forms, and remove the rough, jagged corners with the file of Care; with the hoof blade of Sympathy they will be able to remove stones of misery from the weary feet of burdened men and women; and with the large blades of Strength they will be able to cut down the plants of Ignorance and Iniquity which flourish around them—and thus make the world the better for their having the Knife of Knowledge. May they not, as many do, hack at every good thing they meet, and destroy in a moment the growth of long years of toil.

But, better still, I want you to tell them where to find the Sword (the Sword of the Spirit, the Word of God) which is more beautiful than King Arthur's "Excalibour", and more powerful, and more mysterious and more precious far than it, which a greater King gives to all who love Him and serve Him.

Tell him I have got that Sword, and you have, and that we hide it in our heart and yet use it every day of our lives, and that with which we fight a good fight, and win the most glorious of Crowns even if we should die in the fight. Tell them we would not part with that Sword for our lives, and that we must never throw it away nor cease to plunge it into our own hearts every day, and the hearts of the King's enemies, too, for if we should die without grasping the Sword, if we should come back from the Battle (of life) without it, no matter if we had another beautiful sword in our hand, the King would never, no never, allow us to enter His Palace (Heaven) without it—because every one who stands around His Throne has that most beautiful Sword on, and it shines more beautiful, and the jewels become more numerous and precious every day, after we get into that beautiful Home of the Great King. Tell them, too, of many who wore it when they were little boys and girls—Samuel, and Joseph, and Moses, and Timothy, and Naaman's captive little maid, and the Virgian Mary, etc. etc.

Tell them of the young men and women who wore it, also, on earth—David and his friend Jonathan, and Daniel, and the three young men who were cast into the fire rather than part with it, and Miriam, the sweet singer, and Mary and Martha, and many more. Tell them of the grand old men and women who wore it and carried it into the Palace when they laid down

their Crowns at the King's feet as they came back from
the Battle more than conquerers—of Abraham and
Noah—who got drunk and lost it for awhile—and the
grand old Prince, Moses, the ancient warrior, Joshua,
the mighty prophets Isaiah, Jeremiah, Elijah, Elisha
and others, the great Apostle Paul—who once laughed
at the Sword and tried to kill those that wore it—Peter,
who once tried another sword which cut off a man's
ear for which the King rebuked him and said it was
the wrong kind of sword altogether, which was never
again to be worn by His servant—John, whom the
King loved so much—James, who was killed by Peter's
old sword at last—Andrew, Apollas, Barnabas and
many more, besides whom you could name Martin
Luther, and John Knox, and the Martyrs of all ages,
and Charles Spurgeon, and DeWitt Talmage, and
Dwight L Moody, and Ira D. Sankey—whose Sword
can sing—and Thomas Guthrie—who took hundreds
of poor starving children from a cruel enemy just with
his Sword—and John B. Gough—who killed a great
many of the King's enemies, destroyed their fortresses
where they put people to a cruel death (Publicans and
Public Houses) and saved more people from death
than there are in all South Australia, and of Robert
Moffat—who saved many poor negroes from despair—
and David Livingstone, who by his Sword cut the
bonds of many thousands of slaves in Africa—and of
all the hundreds of good men and women who are
doing the same kind of glorious fighting every day all
over the world.

Then tell them, last of all, of the beauty of the Great
King, who is the Captain of Salvation, of how He suffered, how He wore the Sword always when a boy, and
when a man, when He fought and conquered His great
enemy and when He saved poor, trembling slaves
whom that enemy had bound for many years; how He
wears the Sword now and leads on His great army
with it; how He is bent upon destroying everything

wicked and wrong everywhere. And tell them what a grand Review He is going to have one day at the end of the world, when "every eye" shall behold Him, when "every ear" shall hear His voice, when "every knee" shall bow before Him, when "every heart" shall adore Him, when all the Royal Guards of His Palace who have always been faithful to Him will be there, when all the Great Heroes of His Army on earth will be there with all their honours, when all the Sweet Singers with Sword Harps will pour forth their glorious music; and, when the whole Assembly throughout all His wide Domain shall break forth into song—first the Army of the Royal Guards, and then the whole Army of "Kings and Priests" who once were the lost souls of this Earth, and perhaps of other worlds where the King's enemy might have gone—the great Harmony will be complete, and the King and His Armies sing the song of Universal Victory. And there will come a voice "from the Throne saying, Praise our God, all ye His servants, and ye that fear Him both small and great!"

And then immediately the Mighty Hosts will reply "as the voice of a great multitude, and as the voice of many waters, and as the voice of mighty thunderings, saying, Alleluia, for the Lord God Omnipotent reigneth." And then the King (Jesus) will marry the Queen (the Church—you will read all about this in the 19th of Revelation), and then the last enemies will be destroyed, and the King's "Great Enemy" and all his servants will be cast into the bottomless pit and Death and Hell, too: for the King's "Sword which goeth forth out of His mouth" will do all these things. After that you will tell them of "the new heaven and the new earth"—the Beautiful City and the Loving King in it—the Pure River of Life—the rich fruits of the Tree of Life—the Day that never ends—the inhabitants who are never sick, nor weary, nor disappointed, nor sad—the glorious occupations of the

King's "servants who serve Him" just as He may desire them, always wearing His Sword that they wore on earth and love more and more in heaven—and thus, my love, you will be a Blessed, Shining One to them, to me, to all around, and to our precious one whom God has given us, so that he may serve the King in this glorious army here, and serve Him in heaven forever

You understand my parable, I am sure. Good-by for a little while. God knows it is the sweetest service of all, to obey His Word, which I covet May He bless you both, and give you all you need, always, for the King's dear sake

Your loving husband,
John Alexander Dowie

(Camden Street, Newtown, Sidney, N. S. Wales, Oct. 29, '77—resents letter from father-in-law criticising his conduct and "endorsed" by his wife—tells of intention to found a Free Christian Church.)

Dear Wife ·

Your letter of 22nd received today

It certainly needed the assurance which you added in a tardy and brief postscript—"Do not think me hard in this: for I do love you so"—because there was no other trace of love anywhere in the letter

I do "think it hard" and more, I think it full of unkindness and injustice to me, and written in quite an impudent manner There is an utter absence of all true sympathy, and a hectoring tone such as you only once before adopted, and that was before we were married—a tone which you will remember caused me to write and leave you free to withdraw from our engagement—a tone which I never could nor would use toward you, and which you will please never again employ to me. It does not become you at all. I won't reply to it—I will ignore it altogether, else my vexation might cause me to say more than would be pleasant for you to read

126

The fact is, you are thoroughly "demoralized", that is, thoroughly cowed with fear and doubt, through your residence among those whose only standard of success seems to be pounds, shillings and dimes, and who utterly ignore every fact except that one great fact that I am not up to that standard. It is a thoroughly faithless letter, showing as little faith in God as it does in me, and but for the certainty that you wrote it, I would maintain you could not have written it. I daresay you thought you were doing a smart thing in writing it, and imparting some very necessary chastisement to a foolish and weak minded fellow who was too fond of you to resent it; but you have missed your aim completely and only fallen in my esteem as a consequence of your ill-timed and ungenerous smartness. No doubt the frequent discourses of your father upon my conduct, which prefaced the writing, doubtless, of the letter which I received by the same post, had their due effect upon your mind, and your intercourse with a few others of my domestic censors also.

You must surely have woefully misread my character if you expect me to be swayed by such reproaches and such reasons, or foolish, nightmare fancies as you may advance, after feasting on numerous dishes of Newtown Horrors, such as I can see have been manufactured in fertile brains at Kenttown. The dishes must have been very strong to have so intoxicated you with terror as to write me such a letter—the kind of letter to drive me to any course, even if it were true, but that of submission to such insulting and degrading terms as are expressed in your father's letter—which he says at the end "I have shown to both your father and your wife and they thoroughly endorse it." You are not the same wife now as when you left me alone in Sydney: for you left me as you had lived with me,— bright and hopeful, believing in God and trusting in me.

Not a single fact has altered, except that I am a

little poorer than we thought, and that now my heart is burdened with a fresh sorrow in you.

How very kind you were in your condescension to my supposed craven spirit when you "throughly endorsed" your father's epithets, which could scarce have been more utterly abusive had I been a low thief, in some parts of his letter, and which are insufferably impertiment throughout! Just look at a few of the things you have "thoroughly endorsed" I am said to have caused you "to go through an ordeal mortifying in the extreme to all concerned but more especially in her who is your wife and who has such a fine, sensitive nature" Don't you think that I was surprised to find you endorsing the sentiment that selling off our furniture was such an ordeal, when you never once expressed pain at our decision, but said you felt we were doing right up to the last hour I saw you? Will you kindly explain how you came to "thoroughly endorse" that "more especially to your wife's mortification"? Surely either you deceived me, or your father utterly misrepresents you Then you "thoroughly endorse" that I have made a "bad beginning"— or rather "she has had such a bad beginning"—(meaning you)— also that "under the circumstances" (I, John Alexander Dowie, your wicked and cruel husband) "you ought to make a clean breast of the matter and show ME a statement of your assets and liabilities". How kind! What a dirty breast it must be that can only be cleansed by this process, and how comforting to know that my wife "thoroughly endorses" such a kindly estimate of all my unceasing devotion and love as to dub it all for a year and a half as a "bad beginning"

Then to follow this request to make "a clean breast", as if I were a monster of iniquity, is it not pleasant to read the very next words, as being "thoroughly endorsed" by you? viz: "and for the future trust your wife with the spending of the money." Don't you think I ought feel honoured, cheered and comforted by all these kind things, so very flattering, are they not? Why, if I were the meanest human cur that ever yelped, I would not submit to such all round kicking without one last dying bark of protest. But, being such as I am, I am conscious that I would be only foolish to regard such a mixture of misrepresentation and low bounce. How dare any man so insult me—if I have wronged anyone, to them am I responsible and to my offended God; but to this man I owe nothing but a forbearing love, which he is trying to its utmost. I had rather break stones tomorrow on the highway than even turn a thought to him as my helper.

And I feel I would indeed be a distruster of God to think that I should ever be left to his tender mercies. Remember that I thought it only a duty to tell him my affairs, as your father, and that I never asked him for any help at any time, nor gave him any warrant for thus abusing me. And what right or reason have you to endorse these sentiments? Is it likely that this will strengthen our bonds of love or fit us to train up our child for God?

But come, there are other things which you have "thoroughly endorsed", which it may be well for you to look upon again, and reflect upon my happy thoughts of you tonight in my utter loneliness here— worse now than ever before in my life, perhaps: for I feel as if I had not a single one on earth who loved me, as I want, aye and as you should love me. May God in His mercy keep me from falling in this dark hour, for I am sorely tempted to feel all my hopes to be but desert mirages.

Here are some of the things you have "thoroughly endorsed". I will put them in the order they come in the letter of your father.

1. You say I am a deceiver: for I am charged with "concealing the matter from us all, even from your own wife, until you were obliged". Is this a true and fair way to write? Did I conceal like a guilty thief,

5

or did I simply withhold, what I had a perfect right, if I chose, to withhold, a statement of my affairs from one who never asked for it, and who certainly would have got it had he asked me either at my marriage or afterward?

When did I refuse to reveal that which I am charged with concealing, and how could I imagine his interest in my money affairs to be so keen when he almost never spoke of them?

Then as to you—did you not know only when faith was broken with me by others in money matters, which had it been kept would have never necessitated my speaking of such matters as would only have needlessly troubled you? And surely your subsequent, and I mean especially your present conduct, justifies my thoughts that you could not bear much. Besides, I must remind you that very shortly after we were married, I offered to tell you all if you really wished.

Does all this prove me to be the deceiver you "endorse" me? Who is the deceiver, or rather who is the traducer?

2. You call me a cheat: for I am charged not only with having "managed my financial affairs badly" (which is possibly true enough, for money getting does not, and please God never will, occupy my whole energies as it does some folks) but I am also charged that "knowing I was heavily in debt I had it in my power during that time to put myself right",—out of my salary, that is. Now, if a man can pay and does not—he is a cheat. How dare you endorse that false charge?

No one knows better than you how, when I found how it was, I scraped and saved and paid, so far as I could consistent with living where I was and with our position.

You know I spent nothing almost for eighteen months on my clothes, and that I had no expensive habits to squander money upon. The charge is utterly false and you must know it. For I paid off much—and if you must know the whole truth, in a word you shall have it now—and it is this: if I had the money I spent in marrying you in my pocket now, I would not owe any one on earth a single penny. You have brought this upon yourself; but it is true, as I can prove any day. No one shall call me a cheat with impunity: for my character is all the cruelty of the world has left me, and **that** even my friends would seek to damage or destroy, it would seem. I shall fight hard to keep it, depend upon it, for if I can leave no more, I shall by God's mercy strive to leave my son "a good name," and that, a Book which I believe far more in than I do in your father's boasted ledger, says "is better than riches". Will you "endorse" me cheat any more?

I won't reply to your father's letter at all, and so I may as well add here that the analogy between him and ourselves, when he was a poor shoemaker earning two pounds per week, and saving one pound out of that weekly, does not apply to our position at Newtown, where it would be sheer idiocy to say a Congregational minister could live like a cobbler, whose whole stock in trade and furniture would not equal the cost of two or three of my necessary books.

Besides, I claim that I did no wrong in my living or personal spending, and that a very little common sense, let alone Christian charity, would see that my losses are due not to my own fault but to my justifiable faith in others—some day yet he may live to know there is truth in such a case as mine. I care not, then, for his sneers about "men and women of that stamp" (that means my stamp) "who declare, 'the fault was not mine, circumstances were against me'." Possibly the logic which confounds the position of a shoemaker and a minister (though the first is a perfectly honourable occupation, I admit,) may still fail to see that it may be possible for a perfectly honest man to make sad mistakes and yet neither be a deceiver nor a cheat. Possibly you will learn the lesson, too.

3   You say I am guilty of that worst of human crimes, ingratitude: for you "endorse" the charge—"You appear to have not been thankful enough for your mercies".

Now if ever you "endorsed" a falsehood against anyone, you did it then against me · for you know that, unless my whole life and words have been a living lie, my thankfulness to God for all His Mercies is expressed every day in fervent prayer and in grateful praise to Him, and that I do not value even my life itself as an adequate return to my Saviour and my God, for all His mercies to me

You know that my habit is to take even afflictions and wrongs as being filled with goodness and mercy. I wonder if your father is as thankful to God as I am for all His mercy? I should rejoice to think it, but I can scarcely believe it, when I read his unmerciful and cruel charges against me. God knows how much I love Him for all His goodness and mercy which have followed me all my life, and which sustains me now in as dark an hour as ever I saw—but I believe it is a dark cloud full of mercy.

Tell me how you came to call me an embodiment of shameful ingratitude?

But I am tired out with the enumeration and exposure of your endorsements, though I have by no means exhausted the list   Yet there is one I must notice. It is one which has cut deeply into my heart

4.   You say I have left you destitute: for you endorse the charge your father makes in these words ·—"You have no other place to go to, and you have nothing whatever to provide for your wife and child, which is your first duty as a Christian man, and there are no miracles performed to provide for ministers' wives and children"

Now how can you grieve my heart with such a cruel, unwifely, and untrue charge as this is? Am I, then, that lowest of all wretches, a worthless, heartless deserter of my wife and child? How do you think I sleep with such charges for my pillows? Why, I can't sleep at all. I sat down after a long, exhausting day, and yet could not think of rest, till I had answered these charges. It was half past eleven o'clock on Monday night when I began to write, and now it is past five o'clock on Tuesday morning—I have sat the whole time at my desk writing this most painful letter and feel, now that I throw myself upon my bed, that I never felt more sadly about you than I do now. Yet may God bless you and my boy, and make you happier than I can be.

October 30th, 11 a. m.

To continue regarding "endorsement" number four:
It is asserted I have "no place to go to".

What do you and your father mean? Am I, then, indeed a homeless wanderer? Where do I live? Why, my present quarters are as convenient as ever my quarters were anywhere, and I could take you to a score of homes where they would esteem it an honour to have me live with them.

Never yet have I been without a home, and I do not believe God will fail me now: for I have a mind to work, and God has given to such a faithful promise to provide. And, if you were here tomorrow, I could take as good care of you as ever I did, aye and better: for the cankerworms which ate into my peace will soon trouble me no more.

"Oh yes," you say, "but what is meant is, that you have no church you could go to; there is no certain prospect of your getting an income anywhere, and in that sense you have no where to go to." Now to bring the case quite within the logical powers of my accusers, let me put an illustration:

133

Suppose a good workman in a boot factory, earning good wages, in a time when work is plentiful and good workmen scarce, resolves to leave his employer, who worries him terribly; is it an awful prospect for him when he leaves the factory and goes out to seek work at factories where they will be glad to get him?

Would not the workman, if he was sober and a good hand, laugh at you if you told him that he had "no place to go to"? Do you see the point?

When I left South Australia, an unknown—and almost, by my "friends", despised—young minister, four years ago, I had "no place to go to", and when I came here they said there was "no place" for me—all the open spheres of work had just been filled

Men laughed when God led me to Manly; but with His good hand upon me they changed their tune in less than a month. for unknown and unpraised, I opened my mouth to speak for Christ in a place where there were only a handful of dispirited people, who had no money and no hope, and the place filled and overflowed and was extended and flourished, many sinners were awakened, many hearts were comforted, many souls were everlastingly saved, and—though I say it, it is true,—there was not a more popular minister in our body in less than a year from the day that I entered Manly, an unknown, weak, and sad-hearted man—a popularity for which I cared little in itself, but which is not less strong today even in our own body, among the people especially, (I never was popular anywhere with our ministers, as a whole,) and which is certainly not less powerful but far more so among the Christian community generally, as is proved by the many flattering enquiries which I have received from eminent leading men in the Church of England and Presbyterian churches as to whether there is any prospect of my joining their ranks. Then when I determined to leave Manly—where I could have got 300 pounds a year, at least, and a house, if I had cared to stay—I say that then it was said by some of my "friends", "oh, don't say you will leave, for you see you have 'no place to go to'." But I did say it, and what was the consequence?

Why, I could have gone to Pitt Street as Graham's colleague, I could have built and established a new church in Sydney, at Woolloomooloo I could have founded a new church, at Ashfield, where one lady alone was willing to lay down a large sum of money, and I had Newtown offered to me with a unanimity never before expressed regarding any minister. Did that look like having "no place to go to?" "Aye, but these things are all past," say my friends, who are very much like those of Job, and even my wife begins to act like his did; and now that they fancy I am on the dunghill and in misery they seem to oppress and belie me.

"Yes," I reply, "these things are all past;" but I am not a worse or less devoted man than I was then, and, if I have erred, as I have, yet my life has not been without many tokens that I have not lived in vain, and my sins God forgives, if man does not.

Yes, and that is my confidence; God has not changed. Yes, and I know Him better, and I love Him more and more entirely, and I love His service more, and I trust Him more, and I want more and more to serve His Blessed Son and my Lord in the ministry of reconciling love, which He has committed to me amongst and for my fellow men. Yes, God is not "past," He is with me and for me "though friends should all fail and foes all unite," and I am sure He has "a place for me to go to."

"But how do you know that you are not in the place where God would have you," my friends say. Well, I have told you and them both, and if you don't see now, it is not my fault, certainly, and moreover I have a "Witness" within my heart which has never yet deceived me, and that Holy Witness never more

135

approved a step than He now does every day this step of leaving Newtown Can you understand me, or are you without that Spirit of God which I have believed dwells in your heart? The Witness is the same where hearts are alike open to hear His Voice, and if you can't see with me, then I fear for our happiness in the future, for either you or I must in that event be wholly wrong, and our hearts will be speedily wide as the poles asunder.

Yet there are outward evidences as well as an inward Witness that I am in the right course, and that the hearts of many men are prepared to receive me in the city of Sydney, though I have by no means decided to go there yet; for unless God guide me clearly to the very "place to go to" I shall not go—and it might be even yet that He should guide me to the City of London, and, if so, I shall just as gladly go there as stay here Don't be afraid, you need not go with me unless you choose. I have never forced and never will force you inclinations I will reason with you, and show you the way so far as I can, and if you wont do a thing heartily because it is right, I am sure you will never be able to love, to live with, and to aid and comfort me; nor shall I be of any good to you. I will provide for you as largely as I can, if you elect to stay where you are, and I'll have my boy as soon as I think right, but I won't have you destroy my life—no, not if it costs me my earthly life. I married a "helpmeet," not a hinderer nor an endorser of cruelly false accusations; and I say this not loving you less, but so far as I can, as much as ever, though I have set my heart supremely upon God, as I have always told you, and I will not allow even you to keep me back from the right, or cause me to pluck "the forbidden fruit," to me, of worldly conformity to which you and your father's words would lead me, if I followed your course I will die rather than violate my conscience again by cringing in fear of any consequences the world can inflict.

But what evidences are there of an outward sort?

Simply three will I mention, though I might many more, and remember that as yet my intentions are only dimly guessed at, and even the fact of my resignation—for I made it last night practically a **resignation** at our deacons' meeting when I was asked if I had in any degree changed my mind and replied "no, I will leave on the first Sabbath in February, at the latest," —I say, even my actual resignation is not known so very widely yet: for of course the "Herald" ignores it altogether. Well, the three are, first, I was asked to allow my name to be put before a church in Brisbane by the Rev. E. Robinson (I declined); second, my intimation that I might come into Sydney has been hailed with delight by scores; and, third, last night after my deacons' meeting there was a deputation of three gentlemen waiting to see me who said they came—and I know them well—from the Congregational church at Waterloo to say that, if I would give them but the slightest hope of a favorable reception, the deacons of that church were sure that I should receive a cordial and unanimous call—and a position at least equal to that I hold at Newtown could easily be guaranteed, so far as money was concerned.

Do you not see that it is not true that I have "no place to go to" when I leave Newtown?

I must tell you, though, that I declined Waterloo at once; and after explaining why in the frankest manner possible to the deputation, they not only saw the force of my reasoning but applauded my intentions, and in no roundabout way one said, "The day you begin in Sydney my five guineas are ready to put into your treasury, although I am not rich, and as much more as I can give to carry out your aims;" another said, "If I am within five miles of you, sir, I will come to hear you," and the third, "Its the noblest resolution I ever knew any minister holding your

position to make" And what did I say in declining
their intended call, or whatever you may care to term
it? I told them that, if I remained in the colony, Sydney was "the place I had to go to," I told them the
light in which I regarded its claims upon me; I told
them that on the day I left Newtown would be the
day on which I should leave the denomination to all
practical purpose—for I intended to found, by God's
help, a FREE CHRISTIAN CHURCH either in
Sydney, or elsewhere; I told them that it was therefore my intention never again to accept the pastorate
of any church now in existence in any denomination;
I told them that my views upon fundamental Christian truth were not only unchanged but more assured
than ever, so that whilst I would plead for freedom
in interpretation I would more firmly than ever proclaim the infallibility of the Bible as the Word of God;
I told them that my views upon fundamental church
policy were quite unchanged and that in leaving and
disowning allegiance to "**Congregationalism**" I would
not cease to be an "Independent", nor cease to teach
the independent rights and responsibilities of the
churches, but that I was determined to be independent
in every way of the "Congregational Union", which
was in its corporate capacity an aggregation of ciphers
so far as spiritual power was concerned, because Mammon seemed to be President, and mean Cliqueism
seemed to be the standing Committee, which managed
its affairs; I told them that I held in high esteem and
loving sympathy very many whom the denomination
contained, and that my withdrawal was not on account
of want of confidence in the men—though I had no
confidence in many—so much as a radical want of
confidence in a **System** which asserted liberty of creed,
but fettered men in the bondage of tradition and dom-
inant Customs, a system which asserted the liberty
of members, ministers, and churches, but which really killed individual energy, made denominational tools

138

of many ministers, or worse, made them rich and worldly minded mens' flunkies, and which separated the churches more than it united them, and then tying them in a heartless Union together left them high and dry and useless for the most part—good ships, but badly steered, and terribly overladen with worldliness and apathy; I told them, therefore, that as a man's life was a very short one at longest on earth, and that as I wanted to do all I could for Christ and men whilst life and powers were spared, **I came out**, not from any love of being singular, or from any love of the inevitable sneers of the incredulous or the contemptuous, but because my heart was filled with a holy passion for the misguided, ignorant, uncared for, and perishing thousands who are in the bondage of Satan in our cities. This is what I told them, and then I sketched the possibilities of my gathering together many of these from all classes to hear the Gospel and truth of God, and how a church might be formed which should work night and day in various ways for the reclamation, and elevation, and restoration to God of the perishing thousands, first in Sydney, and then around it; and then I asked them from what they now knew whether they thought I was right in my reasonings and determinations, their answer was direct and hearty that I was right; and that they could no longer think of urging their claims, believing that the work which I had sketched out and the way to do it had been laid upon me by God, and with enthusiasm they declared that they believed the heart of Sydney was "the place for me to go to", and that there would be no difficulty in the means necessary to found this Free Christian Church in Sydney.

Now that is all I have to say in answer to endorsement number four; and I will not further advert to the sneers about "miracles" and "the first duty of the Christian man" which I am falsely charged with neglecting, except to say that I have never neglected it yet, that, probably, I provide for you better and have the power to do so even temporally better than he did or could do for your mother when he was my age, that God's promises cover my family as well as myself and they have never been known to fail a faithful man, and that though I depend upon no unnatural interventions with established laws I believe that "miracles" are wrought every day by the operation of supernatural laws, and that God would, if I were to die tonight—and I am not afraid to die—He would, if necessary, raise up from the very stoniest hearts means for my wife and child, even if a miracle was needed, for weak and unworthy as I am, yet I am His minister, and go forth to His services at His charges.

There are other of your endorsements which I might mention, which are equally obnoxious and wrong, but I will pass them by: for I have dealt with no small force, you will see, with the principal ones, and, as I said before, I cannot trust myself to examine your own letter. You say at the end, "Do you think me hard in this letter for I do love you so"—you might have added "little": for so little love and sympathy, and so much blame and distrust is in it that I almost wonder whether you can possibly love me so very much after all. I know that I never felt any doubt about it until now, and you know how precious the thought of at least one heart being wholly mine was, and wholly I gave you mine, but when I see distrust, fear and reproach wrongfully, how can I but question whether your heart is wholly mine?—for such things exist generally only where love is selfish and weak. How different from all this were you when we were together; but you have never during the last two years, I have noticed, been the same to me when some home influence has been brought to bear upon you, and your conduct now is a crowning illustration of the truth of that observation Not a single material fact is altered since you left full of confidence in me and my action; and yet your opinion and confidence seem entirely to have gone against everything which you before approved. You will see from my last letter that I had feared this would take place from what your father was pouring into your heart against me—for it is against me that he has spoken and written. But my letter came too late, the deed was done even while I was writing, the blow had fallen; and you who had stood up for me against an unjust father and an untrue brother, write me a letter to please the one, and tell me you are going on a visit to please the other. No doubt you will disobey me also, and not leave where you have allied yourself to my censors; and if you do, what am I to do?

I will never be a tyrant, and I will not allow you to make me a slave.

If you do not fulfill my request at once, do not be surprised if my letters are brief and few: for I shall not feel justified in writing much, nor shall I expect you to care to hear much from me. In the event of your refusing to come to me in Sydney, I may feel that it is my duty to think of going home to London— either with or without you as you may decide. You say, "how can you go?" I answer, "the Lord will provide" if He wants me to go; and I have never yet been finally kept back from attaining an object on which my heart has been fully set. Go to London I will, if the Lord so wills it, and you know I speak what I believe. On the other hand, please understand you are not to return to me unwillingly and with fear and distrust and reproach in your heart towards me: for if you do that, I say plainly that I would rather never see your face again, much as I love you, than that I should receive you estranged and cold in heart —if you can only come thus, by all means stay where you are amongst those who have succeeded so well in changing your heart toward me. But, if you can come back to me right willingly and with true love, confidence, and sympathy, then you are coming back—and come at once—to one whose heart is most willing to receive you, and who has never distrusted or reproached you until now, but from whose heart every trace of distrust and reproach will flee the moment he knows you are once more wholly true to him in heart

It is for you to decide I have expressed myself fully, and I should hope quite unmistakably, and much as it may pain you to hear or read these words, yet it would be wrong for me to trifle with so vast a question as our true relations to each other and my solemn responsibility to Almighty God. You know I cannot content myself with half measures when eternal issues are at stake, and you must choose between me and my principles of action, and your father and his principles of action.

O Jeanie, you don't know how deeply you have wounded my heart, and when I read first your letter bristling with its unkindness, and then your father's false accusations and abuse with your "thoroughly endorsed" appended to it, I felt for a few hours that the world was empty of all love, and was hard and cruel indeed; for, from the beginning of that letter to the end, there was not a line or word of encouragement or sympathy with me, nor the slightest gleam of kind expression in it toward me, and if ever a man needed a little love and tenderness from his friends, I did

God is good in sustaining me, for my first thoughts were very bitter, and "my feet were almost gone;" "my steps had well nigh slipped" for the time; but blessed be God, I have overcome the dark thoughts which tempted me.

It will take time to heal a wound like this; and it will need love, too, of unmistakable genuineness.

When I think of the sweet face of our little darling amid all this sad trouble which has come between us

142

I am sad indeed and uncomforted, strange as that may seem; for though I love him as I do my life, and cannot bear without a pang of unutterable woe the thought of parting from him, I had rather he would die in his infancy than that he should ever live to see his father and mother separated, or live to know that she could "thoroughly endorse" such mean thoughts of his father as she has endorsed.

This must never be. You must bring back my darling to me from the scene where, though his mother may be cared for, the very sources of her true love are being defiled. These are strongs words, but they are true.

I will have no more such letters—I have not slept three hours since I received them—and, if anything can keep me from the work which lies before me, it will be a widening of this breach; and I will be satisfied with nothing less than your return at once to me with the same love with which you left. If you will not, then a dark cloud which only death can remove will hang over my life until it ends. The saddest day for me you ever lived was that in which you reentered your father's house; for it has separated in sympathy two hearts that had always been true to each other till the poison of distrust, fear, and reproach was instilled.

There are many things happening here which under other circumstances I might care to write concerning. I am overwhelmed with work, and it is such toil when one's heart is sick with sorrow. I really cannot go into any other matter just now.

I shall wait to hear from you either by telegram or letter immediately after you receive this letter; but I feel so ill that it seems to me possible that I may suffer more from all this cruelty than I thought; and perhaps I may be nearer to the end of all pain than I think; but oh, it is so sad to go to bed this Wednesday morning feeling as if there were a dark cloud

hiding from my eyes my two beloved ones, who are
so constantly in my thoughts and prayers Yet again
I pray may God bless you and my boy and make you
happier than I can be

October 31st, 10 a m

Dear Wife

I have just re-read all that I have written and,
though I feel that no mere words ever can correctly
or fully convey what one wishes to say, yet I have
nothing to alter or withdraw, stern though it may
seem to be in some parts, and imperfect in expression
in others. I have prayed these last two days, during
which I have had many duties to attend to, that God
would guide me to write as I should, a faithful husband's letter to you—and you have it. Never in our
life have we had such a determined attempt of the
Great Enemy to put a great gulf of estrangement between us, and it is all the more painful when the means
used are the bitter words which have been written and
endorsed by those who are nearest to me It is a singular coincidence that I have almost never taken any
step forward in my life, but I have had to walk alone
either with scant sympathy or positive hindrance on
the part of "friends," who have forgotten that fact
conveniently when I have succeeded. But I did think
that the days of walking alone had passed when you
promised to "love, honour and obey me" before God,
and when I took you "to love and to cherish" until
death should part us for "better or worse " We are
yoked together now, but it will be awful if it shall
turn out for "worse "

Will you not right heartily stand by me now and
always? Why not trust me until I have proved un-
trustworthy, and have the faith that still trusts and
loves even where the eye cannot pierce and the mind
cannot fully comprehend? Therein consists the true
love which binds true hearts forever Why make it

144

Grave of John Alexander Dowie in Lake County, Illinois, within the boundary of the city he founded. The cemetery plot is owned by the county.

necessary for me to remind you that "perfect love casteth out fear?" Do you not know yet that "there is NO FEAR IN LOVE?" At this time I only doubt your love because I see your fear; and oh, I do pray that the Spirit of perfect Love may cast out the vile spirit of fear: for that spirit is the root of all trouble and contention everywhere, for you see my authority is the highest that there is "NO FEAR IN LOVE" and, how can I help doubting, if fear has so large a place in your heart—God grant that it may be cast out ere it destroys your love.

Have you not proved, since you yielded to the thoughts which dictated your cruel letter, and which have caused you to still more cruelly endorse your father's—I say, have you not proved that "fear hath torment?" Yes, the spirit of fear in the heart produces at once as its first born child a monster called "Torment" because the Word of God says it, and all experience proves it; and unless these two, Fear and its firstborn, Torment, be cast out of the heart then they will produce between them a horrid progeny of devils in the heart—a perfect legion such as dwells now in tens of thousands of hearts, destroying all that is fairest and most beautiful in man, and on the earth wrecking family life in its best forms, and leading men to lose all hope of a Heaven of Love on earth or above.

Do you not see, then, that the conclusion of the whole matter is that "He that feareth is not made perfect in love?" What, then, can we do but go to Him who is Love and its Giver, and seek from Him that perfect Love which casts out this horrid Fear which would doubt His power, limit His mercy and distrust His care?

I did think you were proof against fear in whatever disguise it might come to you, even in the guise of Worldly Prudence, one of its commonest masks; but it has tricked you and got in, and now that you know that, get it out by God's help and keep it out. I go to Him who alone can help this very moment and pray that you may receive this power, and many have His perfect Love in your heart to purify, strengthen and comfort you   . I have prayed· may I be answered now.

The text for the middle of the day in my book is "Receive my instruction, and not silver, and know-ledge rather than choice gold" Does it not seem appropriate to us at a time when we are sorely tempted to prefer the silver and gold we so much require, to the Truth which seems to bring with the love of it such painful sacrifices of all worldly goods sometimes? Yes, but Truth is the "good part" and whatever else we may lose it shall not be taken away from us, for it is "the one thing needful" which must be our guide and strength on earth and our passport to Heaven We shall not be allowed to tread the Way, unless we possess the Truth; but with the Truth we shall, by infinite Love, be permitted to enter into the Life.

My text this morning contains, I trust, what will be our motto and aim in life. It is "Nay, but we WILL serve the Lord!"

Need I say more? Are you willing to render with me a loving service to God? Can any service have joy so pure, or reward so great, or a Master so gracious? No! Then let us turn neither to the right hand nor to the left in the way wherein God is leading us, unse-duced by sin and unawed by man.

> "What well advised ear regards
>   What earth can say?
> Her words are gold, but her rewards
>   Are painted clay."

Is it not so? I am sure Christ and His inspired ones were right, and they declare that everything earthly will fade, decay, and pass away—'tis but painted clay.

"'Tis to my Saviour I would live;
　To Him who for my ransom died;
Nor could untainted Eden give
　Such bliss as blossoms at His side."

With more scrupulous care than ever in my temporal concerns; with stricter care to keep in a condition, the moment I attain it, where I shall owe no man anything but to love him; with economy without parsimony, and careful prevision without dishonoring anxiety; and with a more entire consecration of myself and you, and our precious one, and all our talents and energies—I desire to go on in the noblest service known to men or angels—the service of God in the glorious Gospel ministry of His Son, among men for whom he died, and for whom He lives, an Eternal Friend.

Though I ought to close this letter, still I linger over it, and feel I do not know how to write the last words, though justice to myself, and the work which must be done today and tonight, would warrant me in closing it at once.

But I must add this: There are two things I wish to leave quite clearly upon your mind concerning this letter.

The first is, it conveys my wish that you should return to me as speedily as possible; but that such return must be quite a willing one on your part, and with at least as true a love and trust toward me as was in your heart when you left.

The second is, that whilst it conveys in most emphatic, and on the whole unregretted, language, my most stern repudiation of your father's right to treat me in the way and spirit in which he has written; that whilst I deny the charges which he has made, and which you and my father have most unkindly "thoroughly endorsed;" that whilst I trample upon the sentiments which seem to me to be the staple of the letter

147

—especially as I had myself done and said all that man could in reversing my impolicy and errors, and confessing (quite needlessly to him) my folly, and stating my heartfelt anguish and regret; that whilst I blame him, therefore, as doing me a great wrong in writing thus, and a far greater wrong in putting assunder you and I whom God had joined together—which I feel more than all the rest—yet, notwithstanding all, I can say from my heart that though I was angry, I cherish no anger regarding or against him, that I am ready to forgive and would like to forget his words, and that I pray as heartily for him and all his today, and more so, as I have done for many long years of my life every day. And what I say regarding him, I say regarding you, and my own father, whose kind letter is in strange contradiction and of opposite spirit to the unkind one he "endorsed."

I will write, if spared, a short letter to you next Monday, in case you may not leave Adelaide as I wish you to do, and under any circumstances my letters must be few and short now, if you stay longer away from me, for two reasons: first, because you wont do what is right if you so stay, and therefore can have little real love for or interest in me; and second, you know that long letters are a very great toil, and take too much time, and are never, at the very best, satisfactory

Now good by, good by. May God be with you and lead you in His own right way. May He bless our innocent and unconscious little lamb, who is always in my heart—kiss him now for me May He bring good out of all this, and keep me from sin in my thoughts and deeds, and open up the way, and give me strength to pursue it, enabling me to work humbly for Him, and to maintain and comfort you and our darling

148

May He breathe the spirit of perfect love, purity, and peace upon you, me, and all our relatives. I am,

Your affectionate husband,

John Alexander Dowie.

———

(Written three weeks later.)

Dear Wife:

Your letter of November 5 duly reached me this morning. It is a very loving and nice letter in many ways, and I was not a little comforted by it. I am glad to see that our darling little pet is so well and such a little sunbeam of love to you from God. I seem to want a little of that sunshine here, for I must confess to being in a sadly gloomy condition of heart for the most part, and am only brightened up for short intervals by the necessity of fulfilling my engagements, which always help me to get nearer to God—and there is perfect love and joy there, you know. Meanwhile, it gives me pleasure to know that you seem to be enjoying yourself among your friends in and around Adelaide, and I trust you are getting stronger every day. There are large portions of your letter, though, which give me pain.

I will not enter at present into any examination of your arguments and illustrations in favor of your father's views of myself and my action. They are very well put, and on the whole I must congratulate you upon your skill in making out a plausible case against your husband, especially as that is done by suppressing every mitigating circumstance in my favor.

But your premises are almost wholly unsound, your reasonings are inapplicable, and your conclusions are unjustifiable. You are looking at all my life, and all my work, and all my prospects from a radically wrong standpoint, viz, the mere standpoint of worldly success. That is a very good standpoint for worldlings;

149

but it was left behind by me many years ago—ten
years fully—when I took a new departure for my life
If I go back to that—then my whole life since has been
a huge, a miserable, failure—then I must throw up the
plow and go back

Do you wish it? No. Then what do your com-
parisons and arguments amount to?

Just this—you want me to try a judicious mixture
of serving God and Mammon— and I won't—I can't—
I will serve God or Mammon—nay, **I will serve God
alone,** though I be as poor as the Lord Jesus who had
no home, or Paul who had not a second coat and was
out of writing paper, or many other of the heroes of
God's Kingdom who now inherit the promised riches
of heaven   But, if fall from that service is possible,
then it will be when I fail to believe in God, in Jesus
Christ, in the Bible, in a heaven of Eternal Blessed-
ness—and, on that day, **I will serve Mammon,** and
throw into that service all my energy, and perseverance, and brains, heart, body, and soul, with unceasing toil, to gain the smile of the world, to ensure its
honors and rewards, and enjoy them to the full   I
won't be a fool, to think that I can combine such services, for if the God of the Bible, the God and Father
of our Lord Jesus be not God alone, then I can see
no reason why every natural desire should not be
gratified, for there are no guarantees for another existence and a nobler life either here or hereafter.

But if He be—as He is—God alone, then nothing
can be clearer than that "Love not the world, neither
the things that are in the world" is a Divine command,
illustrated by Divine example, to be obeyed upon peril
of being shut out of His love, for "If any man love the
world, the love of the Father is not in him." No, no,
my darling, let us remember "the world passeth away,
and the lust thereof"—thank our God for that, for it
has a desire to possess my heart—"but he that doeth
the will of God abideth forever."

But all these thoughts of mine are now before you in my letter of October 31 which you had received, I suppose, before you sent the telegram which reached me on Thursday eve. It may be you did right to send that telegram and to stay where you are until you and your father wrote to me in reply; but none the less clear is it that you have disobeyed me, and my desires as to your actions are thwarted by your father's desires and your own. You have broken your marriage vow —you promised to love, honour, and **to obey** me. The threefold cord is not easily broken; but if you untwine one cord you destroy union. I care not what threats were held out, I care not what hopes were held out, I care not what gifts were held out before your eyes— you should have **obeyed me** and left at once. God made you dependent and you assert independence. It matters not that you promised to "do whatever I may desire," after I read what your father writes and considers it; you are meanwhile divorced—self divorced— from me in one of the essentials of true marriage—and your father, not me, is your head. He has "put us asunder" thus far—money won't mend that breach, for the links that bind hearts are not of gold. He gave you to me—God, I believed, gave you to me—and now he keeps you from me. He has sinned, for he had no right to come between us; and you have sinned, for you had no right to allow him to do that. Again I say, money, or advice, or rebukes, or anything he can do, will never mend that breach. Only God can mend it, but God would have been better pleased, I am sure, had it never been made—and I am sure I would.

It does not mend matters to tell me it is only a breach for a week or two—how can we tell whether it is not forever—the breach is made, the cord is untwisted, obedience as a principle is broken between you and I, the vow is broken. Love and Honor are now disunited from that Obedience which can alone preserve them from destruction and give them permanence.

How long, do you think, will our Father in Heaven look upon us as loving and honouring Him, when we disobey His expressed desires? Not a moment after, it seems to me, for our love and honour depends upon our obedience to His will as expressed to us by His Son and Spirit "If ye love me, keep my commandments" are His words again and again. We may be, and are still His children, though we often disobey, but we are none the less sinful—yea, all the more sinful because inexcusable—when we thus trample upon His love, and most plainly dishonour His, by a disobedience, no mattter how short or in what matter. Christ is our Pattern and His life was a life of obedience to His Father's will, and thus He showed His love and honour of that Father whom a false friend had traduced, and a rebel world has scorned.

And Christ and His Church are our pattern in our marriage bond—"as the church is subject unto Christ, so let the wives be to their own husbands in everything" This is a loving and a willing subjection to a wise and loving Director, and a true Church obeys at once, like the true wife.

I have expressed no desire that can possibly be considered oppressive, and I desire never to be obeyed wherein what I wish is contrary to God's Word in principle; but if you are to be really my wife you must show me your love by your obedience, or else we shall be miserable and in a state of spiritual divorce —the sense, by the way, in which I use that word on the previous page.

God knows I have striven—no, not **striven**—have done willingly, from my heart, from my great love for you, my part of the bond, so far as I could, "to love, honour, and comfort" you since our marriage. And you are still my wife, if you will have it so, in the fullest sense of that term, but you must not break

any of the cords, and you must ask God—aye, and I
do not say it harsly—me to forgive you for your breaking one of them, and **that** will mend the breach—for
my heart yearns to mend it rightly, and infinitely more
does God's, I am sure. Do you think me too stern, or
that I overrate the importance of what has happened?
All I say is, I do not love you less that I am stern, but
rather prove my love to be yet more strong and true
that I will let nothing and no one break it if I can
prevent it, and thus fulfill my vow to protect and
cherish you; and as to the great spiritual importance
of what has happened, the fact itself that my wish that
you should return to me as speedily as possible is
deliberately disregarded and disobeyed, and God's
Word as to your duty towards me—these two shall be
our judges, and I leave you to decide what their judgment proves, that I have not overrated the real character of the breach. It is because "the points" are not attended to that a railway smash happens—for the train
gets off the line; and it is because God's Word is not
obeyed that families and kingdoms alike are wrecked
for time and eternity.

Now Jeanie, my wife, before I married you I sought
God's guidance and direction, for I wanted a wife of
God's choosing if I were to get one at all; and you
know I wooed and won you fairly, for yourself alone.
Did you marry me for myself alone? I believe you
did. If so, then circumstances won't alter our case,
and come riches or poverty, honour or shame, we shall
be true to each other. But why do you then fail me
in my hour of need?—do you not think I need some
one with me now who really loves me?—I think I
understand now a little more of what Christ felt in
His last temptation when His "soul was exceeding
sorrowful even unto death". He took three of His
loved ones with Him into the garden and said "Tarry
here, and watch with me." But twice He found "they
fell asleep" and in the great crisis of His agony He had

153

to pray **alone**; and when it was past **He did not need them,** for He had overcome   Yet was not the Cup of Suffering more bitter that He drank it without the sweet, sympathetic love for which even He craved? How much more a sinner like me needs that, then. And yet, when I say "Come with me—tarry with me— watch with me—" I am answered, "Listen to what this one whom I trust, and think over it—perhaps you will see that it will be better for me not to come—but, well—if you should think it—well, then, when you ask me again, I'll come then." Ask you again? No. You have been told what I wish, and no letter from any one can alter it, and you must act upon that. And yet "ask you again?" I shall not, so long as you have that word of mine, "Come at once", in your hands and memory.

If you are really, wholly mine in your heart you will come without delay. This is a test of your love which I had never designed; but you don't bear it well, it seems to me, thus far. Depend upon it, no letter will alter my opinion as to your duty.

Amongst the many portions of God's Word which claimed my attention before I asked you to be my wife was 1st Corinthians, chapter 7. It is one which is, in its way, a most mysterious utterance—and seems to be in parts only semi-inspired (see verses 6, 25, 40) and in other parts fully inspired, (see verses 10, 17 etc.) therefore it must be read with care and applied with caution   Anyway, it kept me from caring for marriage for a long time, and made me rather afraid of it   But I got over it, rightly, as I thought, when I found you had such a place in my heart; and the three verses, (3 to 5,) have acquired since that time for me a meaning which they could not, and did not, have before. When I see how Satan has tempted and destroyed many around me thus, then I desire the wish I have expressed to be obeyed

And do not misunderstand me—I do not say I am

so tempted, but I am very human, and Satan is not dead, as I find to my sorrow every day. The exhortation at the same time has its meaning and lesson and those who are wise will learn it. Verses 29 to 31 are very serious and needed words, for who can say how short the time may be for our life here at all— I always seem to have the thought that my time may be very, very short; and but for Christ's work and you and my darling boy, I really do not care how short it may be for my own part. My life seems to be so out of gear with things around, and it is so hard to fight on alone for truth and purity as sometimes I seem to be doing, that I could sometimes wish

"I could see Christ's face in the City
    Of everlasting strength;
And sit down under the shadow
    Of His smile,
With great delight and thanksgiving,
    To rest awhile."

Yes, only for that sense of an unfulfilled mission, sometimes I think an un-begun mission, I could say "Make room for me and take me home"; but remembering the poor day's work my life would show, I am filled with shame and sorrow, almost with despair, and

. . . . . ."So at times
The thought of my shortcomings in this life
Falls, like a shadow, on the life to come."

Scarcely a word of cheer seems to come just now to help me onward in my path from anywhere; yet I have laboured hard for others' good, but it is a toil which has almost no reward but suffering and weariness here—loss and pain, neglect and contempt.

And yet, right certain am I it is the noblest of services, with the best of Masters, and richest reward.

But yet I seem to cry in vain, "Have pity upon me, have pity upon me, O ye my friends, for the hand of God hath touched me!" But I am wrong to cry thus at all—I turn to God whose hand hath touched me—He is my Friend, were there none other, and there is love in all His ways. The hand that permitted affliction to come, can send consolation—that touch is life and peace.

I shall wait with such patience as God can give me, an intimation of your intention to obey me at once or not. I expect it at once to be given, and for your sake, for our child's sake, for—perhaps, since I know not what is best—my own sake—I say more, for the sake of the work Christ the Lord hath given me—for all these reasons, I expect to hear from you at once that you have taken your passage for Melbourne, unless you have any request from me to the contrary by telegram. It may be that your father's letter, which will reach me I suppose either this week or on Monday next, will cause me to alter my desires; but if so, it will be because I see from it that your heart is changed still more, and that some other cord is broken, in which case you had better stay where you are until your heart is right, for I could not wish you back again if that were so.

My perplexities are many, but the greatest one of all is yourself. I can bear anything but the continuance of your absence; and I will not write one word to you concerning my prospects or intentions while you are under your father's roof, unless something totally unforeseen should happen, and this letter is only as long as it is by reason of the importance I attach to your course of action, and the actual consequences of it already Your place is here now. I can bear no more of this strain upon my heart, and mind, for it will render me entirely useless should it last long.

Remember me to my father and mother. You say that I do not understand my father, and that he loves

156

me. I never doubted his love; but I do not understand him, though you know I love him—and yet more sure am I that he does not understand me. But I do not, certainly, want quarrel with either him or your father —I only want to take care in the future never again to give either of them occasion to say bitter things to me. It is the first time in his life your father ever had a chance of doing me a kind action in my affairs—I did not ask him even to do it, when he pounces upon me like a nasty bulldog, and jumps straight at my throat, as if I were a ragged beggar at his kitchen door. Do you think that is likely to enable me to honour him more? Do you think I am likely to turn out my pockets, to show him how poor I am, in answer to his growling demand? Do you think I am particularly delighted with the sight of you and my father stand-ing patting him on the back, and bidding him to go at me, till I cry for mercy and lie down with his paw upon me, whilst he examines the contents of my pock-ets, and then, if I am a very submissive beggar, he will share with me some of his bones? No, no, 'tis all a mistake, I Iam not a beggar at your gate—no, nor at any man's—and even if I am to lose all I have, and even were that not enough to pay my debts—yet will I not beg, for I can work, will work, ay, and am working. I can go out of the ministry altogether if need be—but I will be free; and I do not fear I shall die in debt, if God spares my life, and maintains me in strength. Nor do I fear that I can keep you and train my boy by my own honest labour. Never was debt incurred with less design to be debt at all. I have been a miserably foolish man to trust in men at all, he says; but does not your father trust in them every day and have not they trusted him—or where would he be today? But I won't go back to the matter—ex-cepting to say this: bid him to leave me alone and growl away no more. If I were even to be compelled to become an insolvent (you first used the ugly word to me) I would not ask him to come between me and that—I would drink my cup to its deepest dregs rather —and I would rise again with an untarnished name · for if I lived no man should suffer loss through me Please keep him back from me if you can I want no more letters from him of the last kind.

And if you are coming to me, come at once; and bring nothing but what you took back with you again, for I won't have his gifts at all, and I do not want to have any controversy with him. I have never cringed before any man and never will I love all men (I don't love all their ways, by any means) but I fear none.

Bitterly as I have felt what it is to be poor, I have never had the worse, infinitely worse, bitterness which consists in the meanness of soul which dwells in many who are called rich (poor, poor indeed are they) and can kick and trample upon a man because he is poor, or delight to see him grateful for their wasted crumbs as he lies at their gates full of sores

Often and often have I given my last shilling to the hungry and needy during many years, (and if ever I gave what was not mine it was unconsciously) and I never regret that I did, for even I can say "I delivered the poor that cried, and the fatherless, and him that had none to help him The blessing of him that was ready to perish came upon me, and I caused the widow's heart to sing for joy" I have not lived for self, and never will, by God's help And whilst I exercise more care and wisdom in my money matters, yet I will not cease to live for God, and to live for men, and to live for the Blessed Inheritance above

Need I ask you to acquit me of self-righteous boasting in all this? Surely not, for you know I trust not in my works for any acceptance with God, but it is well at this time of reproach to remind one's self that the past has not been all "a bad beginning", and to feel that I may say with that grand old man, Dr. Guthrie, that

> "I live for those that love me,
>   For those that know me true,
> For the heaven that smiles above me,
>   And waits my coming, too;
> For the cause that needs assistance,
>   For the wrongs that need resistance,
> For the future in the distance,
>   For the good that I can do."

And I will not surrender an atom of my independence to your father in the slightest degree. I have never received a word of encouragement from him when I have been in a conflict and sorely need sympathy, and I have no confidence in the love that is simply represented by a pair of taws, or, as you have called it, "a tonic". It is a farce to treat a man and Christian minister of over thirty years of age, who has been fighting the battle of life alone for ten years of no ordinary temptation, trial, and toil, and who fought it very much alone in many ways for a good many years before—I say it is a perfect farce to treat him as a naughty child, or bully him as a compound of fool and knave and ne'er-do-well.

The fact that I have got on thus far, with at least some measure of success, and with as bright prospects as ever in some respects, and certainly with larger powers than ever before, augurs something different, and deserves better treatment. My life is far from what I could wish it to be; but I would not fear to leave the judgment of its usefulness to compare with that of my self-constituted inquisitor and judge. He is your father and I do not forget it; but the time has come for me to say that in becoming his son-in-law I did not give him the control of myself or of my affairs, and I accepted a solemn trust in receiving you as my wife which I have not in the slightest degree consciously failed to perform. If he interferes any more with that trust by your acquiescence, then he has no sense of his true position towards God and us in this matter, and you will place me in a most serious position toward you.

Oh, my love, do not place me, by your action, in that position—for who can tell what may follow?

My hands are still very full of work, and yesterday was a very trying day for me to preach Ever since receiving your telegram I had much depression of heart, and my mind reverted to the words of the Lord to Peter—"Simon, Simon, behold Satan hath desired to have you that he might sift you as wheat, but **I have prayed for thee, that thy faith fail not,** and when thou art converted strengthen thy brethren " "Out of the abundance of the heart the mouth speaketh," and I find I comforted others with the precious thoughts which are contained in these deeply mysterious and yet assuring words—thoughts which had comforted me not a little

There is much sickness. Altogether, it seems to be setting in very much as it did about two years ago, and from similar causes I fear—a defective water supply, and the want of drainage, etc Newtown is by no means earning a good name for its healthfulness— we are higher sometimes in our death rate than any other suburb. I dread a time of fever again amongst us—though it may be that the symptoms will pass away All this adds to my work and anxiety

Kiss again and again my little darling for me. He and you are ever in my heart, and many times every day in my prayers, that God will bless you and keep you, and bring you to me soon in safety again. Do not fail me this time

I am,

Ever your affectionate husband,

John Alexander Dowie.

(*Dated at Camden Street, Newtown, Sidney, N. S. Wales, Nov. 19, '77—wife restored to his heart—expresses contrition for letter sent —complains of state of body and mind—tells of dream.*)

My Beloved Wife:

Your two long and loving and satisfactory letters of 10th and 12th are now before me, and I thank God that I can once more feel that there is no fear in your love for me, and no doubt in my heart as to your being wholly and truly my own trustful and beloved wife. Surely then I may praise God for this token of good, and be grateful to Him that He so directed my thoughts and guided my pen that I was enabled to break the horrid spell of the Enchanter, Fear, who had well nigh alienated us in heart, under the most specious of pretenses. I fear this victory may lead me, if I do not take care, in the toils of an Enchantress named Vanity: for I cannot help remembering that twice I have won you to my heart by my pen, which has stretched across the lands and seas, and gained each time "a famous victory."

But I must say that I not only give God the glory, since, so far as I was right, He gave me the thoughts and the power to express them, but I have no desire to fight such battles again—especially the last—or gain any more such costly victories. Madame Vanity cannot make me forget that she is a full sister to that villianous scoundrel Fear, nor can I forget the hard knocks and deep wounds and many heart agonies I suffered in the fight, and the danger which I felt there was lest I should injure you, my beloved, whilst fighting to get you out of the hand of your enemy— a man had need to be a good marksman who would shoot a lion as it was bounding off into the forest in triumph with his "one little ewe lamb." It is the sort of experiment, Madame Vanity, which one does not care to repeat; and I trust that my darling "ewe lamb" which I have given of "my own meat," which has drunk of "my own cup," and which lies "in my

6

bosom"—my own dear wife—will not be enticed away again either by cunning foxes or roaring lions.

Nothing could be more complete than your restoration to my heart after receiving your letters; and my only regrets were, first, that there was ever any cloud between us—though even that we shall yet see was overruled for good—, and second, that there was a letter of mine upon the way, which was written and sent before I received either of yours, that might pain you needlessly.

However, I dispatched a telegram ahead of it, which has, I trust, taken away its sting. I only wish it could have brought it back to me unknown to you · for it is the letter I least like in all I have written, in some parts at least, which I need not now particularize. Just look upon it as another shot fired by me into the body of the aforesaid lion, which my first shot had killed outright, though I knew it not; and forgive me, if I have borne too hardly upon you, as fully and freely as I forgive you.

When I wrote that letter I was very weary in heart and in body, and had to begin late on Monday night after a heavy day's work. The shadow of death, too, seemed to rest upon me, and I finished it, you saw, after leaving a death bed.

Your letters have driven my weariness of heart away, as the sun drives away the mists of the night —and proved a true comforter from God To see you so truly one with me again, and to know that even your father had been so favorably affected by what was, I must confess, rather stern handling in some parts, was so unexpected and complete a change of the whole situation of affairs, that it seemed too good to be true, and my heart found relief in what you women call "a good cry," and a very grateful tribute of praise and prayer to God.

Thus strengthened I wrote my notes, and went off to the Convention and made what Dr. S— called a "first class speech," and at the end of the day, when we all left the Exhibition Building together, he took my arm and walked down the street with me, telling me that my little address was "the most finished and able speech at the Convention."

So you see your letter helped me greatly—it was a Love Cordial, and that is a million times better than all the Critical Tonic that was ever manufactured.

I had been drooping very, very much. I was strengthened, and filled to overflowing with suitable thought for my speech—wifely love and obedience and trustfulness and prayer was rewarded by God, and I just struck a few notes of truth of which more will be heard . . . . .

At the same time I cannot help feeling very sorry to see this spirit among the brethren; and while I am quite conscious that I was saying the thing which was right and true, and trying to say it in a right way, as I am quite sure I was saying it with a loving spirit and the highest motives, yet I often question my own heart sharply as to why I never seem to get along with some classes of minds—and these not a few in the Christian Church—to whom my words seem to act like a red rag does upon a bull which, until it sees the color, is feeding quietly in the meadow. Nothing could have been further from my desire than to give needless personal offense—there was no personal antagonism in my mind at all—but yet the application seemed to be made.

I hate "strife amongst the herdsmen," for I know the enemy rejoices; and I make none, so far as I can prevent it or avoid it without sacrificing principle; but that I cannot and dare not do: for every good principle is just a Divine truth, and it is not mine to surrender, if I would, but God's gift, which I must use as a talent and account for, when the Lord and Chief Shepherd of all the shepherds shall appear—for when He cometh "He reckoneth with them." Still, I am

163

but human and would fain avoid wounds like these, even though I may be quite right, if only I could without sin; and I am sorry most of all to think that those whom God has sent to bring in the outcast, weary wanderers, or foolish prodigals, or defiant rebels—who are yet God's children though far away— I say, I am sorry to think that those who go out to seek or bring them in seem to be so careless in their mission, and so angry, should one of their number show how very far it is from being accomplished.

What will the Lord say to you and I, if we leave undone the great work He has given us to do—work which, so far as we shall be concerned in the doing of it, will remain forever undone? Only think of what God would do by us if we were wholly consecrated to Him, and when I think what a wasted life so much of mine has been, and how poor and miserable is its best, I am overwhelmed with shame and almost filled with heart sickening despair. Very far am I from feeling holier than others, even though I point out wherein we have erred and should now labour.

But really my digression has carried me quite far enough and I must return to the subject from whence these remarks about my work has sprung—and that is your last letters.

I have already said how much they have cheered me, and especially the first of the two, and how fully your frank admission and loving, trustful expressions have won my heart and comforted it. But no words can express how much I needed that comfort· for I had an awful fear sometimes tempting me to doubt what the issue would be; and the picture of our wrecked lives would force itself upon my imagination in unrefreshing sleep at night, and interfere with me in every engagement by day. My nerves seem to have been a good deal shaken during the past month, and I have felt that until I could see exactly how your heart stood that I could determine nothing concerning

164

my affairs, for everything hung upon that. And now that I do know how you stand, now that you are ready to do whatever I wish, and that I see from your letters that your delay to come at once did not arise from any spirit of resistance to my wishes—I am yet still unable to state my desires or form my plans, until I receive your father's letter for which you have asked me to wait and give consideration.

Meanwhile, I am in a very weak, nervous frame of body and mind—my brain seems to be sometimes charged with blood to bursting point, and I do not eat or sleep very well,—and though my judgment and actions are pretty cool—I am resting at home for a day or two except in the evenings—yet I am conscious that the agitation of the past few weeks has shaken, **not** my resolutions, but my powers to carry them out; and I must confess that I feel less able to face the work that lies before me, and the arrangement of my affairs, now, than I did a month ago. I feel that after your loving conduct towards me, I should be stronger; but I am only a man, and a very weak one after all, you are far away, and I am very lonely in the midst of my busy life, and seem to want some of that Cordial every day which helped me so much last week—in short, there's no question about it, you want me, and I want you and my little darling—it is not good for me to be alone.

I feel that I can do nothing, meanwhile, having determined to await your father's letter, and especially after the way—so much better than I at all expected he would, in which he received my perhaps too vigorously worded letter to you.

I am sincerely sorry that he expresses himself so unfortunately; but of course I could see nothing beyond what he had written to me, what you reported of his sayings to you, their manifest effect upon you, and now the confirmation of my conjectures as to his influence upon your mind and direction of your attitude towards me, in your confession that your letters, and especially the one accompanying his, was written at his distinct command—for you say, "He told me to write more decidedly upon the matter, and I just sat down and wrote that letter without thinking a bit what it was about or how you would take it, and in fact I do not know what was in it;"—surely a most foolish thing to do, and a wrong thing to require Candidly, then, you must admit, and you do, that I put upon his letter its apparently correct interpretation; and desirous as I am not to bear too hardly upon him —for I do love him and them all very dearly—are they not my nearest, next to you, to whom I owe and feel respect and love?—I say, that though I wish to spare him, you must permit me to say that he not only failed in a correct conception of my whole position (for which my imperfect letter to him may be in some degree to blame) and, worse still, he failed to realize his changed position towards you, now that you are my wife; for though he can never change in his relation to you as your father, yet his power to direct you has passed away by his own consent and God's ordination into other hands That is the cardinal mistake which he made, and now that he sees something of these mistakes—from what you have written I infer that—surely I can overlook them: for after all they sprung from his great love for you, his child, and he evidently thinks with me, and there we fully agree, that we cannot love you too much

We, too, may one day need to take care that we do not interfere with the prerogative of some fire-eater of a son-in-law; and, looking forward to that extremely questionable future occasion, had better not sow regrets that we were not more considerate. In short, you know me too well to think I would wilfully pain anyone, much less our father and mother who love you, even if they do not me, with so true and strong a love, and I only wanted to preserve my prerogatives without infringing upon theirs, and my right to dispose of my life as God might direct, without wishing to refuse their right to advise in a proper way—not in the way of the man who had "a donkey that wouldn't go."

Then, they must not think that they are not respected because their advice is not always taken: for if I were to take a tithe of the contradictory advice which has been given me during the last ten years, I should come to a dead stop and do nothing. I would be like the captain of a steamer who stopped his engines because one passenger was sick and could not bear the vibration of the screws; or reversed them because some one wanted to go back to port; or send at high pressure all the way to please another passenger who wanted to see what could be done without bursting; or pulled up and lowered a boat, because a child demanded that his toy which had gone overboard should be got back for him.

When, do you think, that captain would accomplish his voyage? Never!

And even so it is with every man's life. The path each man has to tread is before unknown and untrodden: for the time that lies in the future no eye but the Eternal God's hath seen; the circumstances of every man differs from every other and from all that ever preceded him, in many important matters; and though the experience of the past and present must be studied and not ignored, for it is of very great value, yet it can never be a guide for any man's future or for another man's path entirely—only God who knows all can be a safe Guide into the unknown (and that is life), and His Word is the Chart, and the Spirit is the Guide, which leads us into the path which Christ has trod before us—the only safe and true Way of Life. Therefore, with all love let me say it, I will take no advice from any one which differs from the Chart; and I desire to give none but what agrees with that. This is my one answer regarding advice.

God is too loving to leave us without sailing directions. They differ, doubtless, from those of the god of this evil world, just in the same way that the "Trinity House" charts differ from unauthorized and erroneous maps; and if we want to be God-directed we shall go by the Bible, and if we want to be Devil-directed we shall go by the world 'Tis a most serious matter to give or receive advice from any man; and 'tis a yet more serious matter to follow or to reject it—I never do either lightly. But seeing I have been left so much with God and His Chart for my only advisers during many years, I have become accustomed not to commune with flesh and blood, but to go straight to God with every difficulty and trust Him in every danger. Then, when I get into the world, I do not run about asking every one to advise me—I go right on with the thing that seems to me to be right, and that is by no means always or often the thing which seems pleasantest or safest. I find it comes out right always, and if ever it does not come out so, it is because I have allowed men's opinions and advice to over-rule my serious convictions This habit of mine no doubt makes it sometimes appear that I am impulsive, when I am only earnestly working out previously matured decisions—and gives a color to the charge of egoistic isolation (I do not think it is a general charge against me though), when I am only deeply conscious of my individual responsibility to obey clear, Divine direction.

Explain this to your father, and tell him that though I am deeply conscious of being but a poor exponent of my "sailing directions", and make many very stupid mistakes, yet I am determined to sail more closely by them in future, and that all the trouble which I now have in earthly matters is of my own making to a certain extent, and arises from my following human advice rather than the Trinity House Chart of the Bible.

One think I must just at once say in the frankest way before it comes, that from what you and my father have said, I acquit you both of "thoroughly endorsing" his letter—though it was less his fault than yours that he so wrote because you both acquiesced; and, further, your statements have proved to me most conclusively that he did not intend either to insult or injure me, and I am very sorry if I have seemed to insult him in any way by my expressions, some of which I would be prepared to greatly modify—and I say this hoping for nothing, but simply because it is right to express my regret, even though none of you have said that he complained. Indeed, it seems very generous of him to praise the "ability and talent" of a letter which dealt so severely with his letter to me; and I respect him all the more for the remark, which is, I fear, more flattering than it is deserved—for my letter was simply an honest examination of his, to a large extent, and made no claim to anything of a "masterly" sort, since literary achievement was not in all my thoughts. Please tell him what I say, and that I will wait for his letter before writing to him.

Now, my darling, there is but one thing in your letters that I do not like. I fear you are in danger of rushing now to the other extreme and thinking far too highly of me. I thank you for the true, wifely love which makes you to say so heartily that you will do anything and go with me anywhere, to prove your love for me; and I did long to have you near me when I read these words. You know I will never take advantage of such love to ask you to do aught that is wrong; and, indeed, you know that such love as this is the surest of safeguards to our happiness: for I would give my life to bless you.

But I did fear, when I read that you had seemed to make me your interpreter with God instead of going to Him direct yourself, for "when you left me you fell." And no wonder, my darling, when you rested and relied upon so puny a creature as I am—so poor an interpreter of God's love and power. But I am sure you exaggerate and wrong yourself.

Our union was indeed sweet and unbroken, and I did try to sustain you, but you greatly helped me, my love, and by your patient gentleness bound me more than ever to you, and especially from the time when we first knew God was going to send us our little Sunbeam Yet, dear, we must take care of idolatry: for God will give us sorrow if we place any creature before Him. Let us both love Him more, and we shall love each other more purely; let us lean on Him for strength, and we shall be strong to help each other; let us seek His Spirit to be our interpreter, and we shall be wise to instruct each other—and our darling one too— and so shall we walk aright, and walk in the light, trusting in Him who is our life

"Help us, O Lord, with patient love to bear
Each other's faults, to suffer with true meekness,
Help us each other's joys and griefs to share,
But let us turn to **Thee alone** in weakness "

Some day,—who can tell how soon it may be—I may be taken from you, and oh, it would be dreadful if I were your only guide and strength; yea, and I might fall—may God forbid it in His mercy, and how awful to have only a broken reed as your stay—no; let us trust in Him whom neither Death nor Sin can affect; and then we shall be strong to help each other, and our love will be sweeter and purer, and our child will live to bless the world yet, and we shall meet again in the Beautiful City of our Beloved King. I am sure, my dearest love, that at bottom you and I see alike in this matter, only I thought it was right for me to refer to the only thing I did not like in your loving letters, because it would offend God for me to even seem to rob Him of His glory.

170

At the same time I will always give you, and you know it, all the help I can; and when we come together again, if the Lord spares us, we must pray more together and read God's Word more together, and talk over it at regular times. But, my love, when I think of how imperfectly I have discharged my duties to you in many ways, and when I know how weak and foolish and sinful I so often am and have been, I can only wonder at God's mercy in giving me so comforting a love as yours is to me. My heart longs for the time when we shall prove to each other how true it is that our love never was broken, and that now it is stronger than ever. May we live so good and pure a life that we shall not fail to get through all our difficulties, see the work of the Lord prospering in our hands, and leave to our children the legacy of a good name and the memory of a good life—I have no higher wish, and no other, except to see them well cared for so far as I can in worldly things, if God pleases.

Oh, how poor all speech is to express one's thoughts, and how especially poor is written speech! There are a thousand things I want to say to you, there is nothing which I would withhold from you, were you only here to look in my face and hear my words, and ask me what you needed to understand. How it would give relief to my full heart and weary head! But I cannot attempt to express some things at all: especially some things which I am greatly tempted to be anxious about, and indeed concerning which there is room for reasonable anxiety, in one sense. Troubles shared are half solved, I believe; and a lonely man's heart has a terrible tendency to feed upon itself, and in unsatisfied hunger to gnaw and wear itself away to ease its pain—thereby only increasing it.

I had the other night a half waking dream—I can't recall it all, but it was something like this: A lion from the jungle, through which we were traveling, rushed

forth and with a roar, seizing you in its mouth, dashed
back again into the dense forest, ere I could even raise
my hand or utter a sound   Immediately I grasped a
rifle and followed on, but lost sight of you soon. However, I toiled on and on to reach the lion's den through
the damp, slimy bog and thick undergrowth, until at
last I came to a place where I was told by some one
that the lion would have to pass that way to reach its
den. There I stood and carefully laid my gun across
a little withered branch and placed it to my shoulder
prepared to fire as the lion passed. Soon it came,
walking slowly, carrying you along in its teeth. I fired
—it fell dead—and you came towards me with a cry
of joy   But just at that moment, when I would have
run to meet you, I felt myself held back and at the
same time a pressure upon my breast and a choking
sensation in my throat. The gun fell from my hands
as I looked, and **saw that a great serpent had coiled
itself around my legs and body**; and there was its horrid head raised to strike, and the coils were tightened
around me—with a shriek I grasped the monster
around the neck just beneath its head with both my
hands—and awoke!

'Twas not a pleasant dream, and it abides with me
despite my self-childings—at least at times   But I just
feel the best way to interpret it is that the lion was
your fear, from which you are now, thank God, free,
and that the serpent is my cares which have been coil-
ing around me while I was anxious about you; and
now I just ask God for strength to grasp them firmly
and crush them by as prompt action as I can. When
I get your father's letter I will act at once to settle
the best I can at the bank and with others— anything
rather than that serpent, even were I left with bare
life; but God will see me through, I believe, and then
you must come back as soon as you can, and we shall
live in Sydney quietly with our pet whilst I begin
the new work in the city to which I feel more and more

every day that God calls me. Now, darling, even the telling you this queer dream has eased my heart, and I earnestly beg you will not let it trouble yours— but pray for me, pray for me, and believe that God is hearing and answering you. It will grieve me to think you should fear again.

You told me, dearest love, that you had prayed and felt answered on Wednesday week, about 11 at night, seeking God to forgive you and to comfort me. Well, it is very strange, but that night I was very much comforted by God. After the service Mr. A— came home with me and we had a nice, comforting chat; he left me about 11 o'clock, and I went out with him to the gate. The sky was a glorious sight, all tremulous with countless stars in the cloudless midnight. I stood there for a few minutes after he left, and a great peace came into my heart whilst I gazed upon all that infinite glory of creation and thought how sinful it was to doubt the love of the Creator, the infinite pity of my Heavenly Father for His foolish child. Then that night you prayed for me in Melbourne, and its answer, came to my mind; and another night in May of last year when we were betrothed and we walked home from my father's together; and another, our starlight drive to Alma. My heart was full of you then, and these lines which I repeated to you then came into my mind with peculiar force and meaning:

> "The sun is the eye of day,
> Yet its light conceals
> The sight of a thousand suns
> Which night reveals.
>
> And love is the sun of life,
> Yet its light conceals
> The vision of ampler love
> Which death reveals."

And thinking thus, I felt comforted with this thought, that the darkness of death would only be the introduction to the revelation for us both of that ampler love which we long for now—and I felt I could wait, if need were, till then for you to love me fully. Comforted with God's peace I went to sleep—as I do now at the midnight hour, praying that He whose watchful care never slumbers may guard and bless you both through the night. . .

I feel rather better today, and a good deal more hopeful in spirit; but yet I am not what I ought to be with so many precious promises. My passage for noonday is · "Thine expectation shall not be cut off."

"Though thy sky be over clouded
Though thy path be dark and drear,
Though thy soul with doubt be shrouded,
Oh, let Faith still conquer Fear "

And really it is so with me I trust—only that when one is not over well one is apt to look at the darkest side of things, especially when much alone. No doubt days of darkness have their good side, but I can get along best with spiritual sunshine—and I know I shall get it soon again. Let your heart be at perfect rest concerning our future, for it is in the best of hands, come what may. I can see that future far more clearly than I can solve the mysteries of the immediate present.

I seem like a man who has his goal in sight on some mountain side, but there lies between a misty valley, where the fogs cover all from his eyes, as he passes through them, across the little river from whence they rise. Going on, going on, watching, praying and working, is all I can do, certain that whatever happens I shall get out on the right side; but I won't turn back because I can't see all I would like of the road before me. . .

174

Dearest love, there have been so many interruptions to this letter, and it is so incoherent and such a thing of shreds and patches that I am ashamed of it.

Writing is so cumbrous and unsatisfactory a mode of expression, and I do so long to have you so near me that you can see what I mean, as you used to, without roundabout speech. I have quite lost all conceit of my powers as a letter writer to you: for what I have written is so imperfect an expression of what I mean. "Language is slow. . . Yet there's a lore,
Simple and sure—the language of the soul,
Told through the eye—for oft the stammering lip
Marreth the perfect thought. . .
But the heart's lightning hath no obstacle;
Quick glances, like the thrilling wires, transfuse
The telegraphic look!"

For instance, all through these letters I seem to have said very little about our darling little boy; and yet he has such a large place in my heart and thought. I would find speech here very inadequate; and yet I read all you say about him—as indeed I do all your letters—over and over, and over and over again.

You must tell him that father does love him, oh, so much; and that when he comes back I will sing to him, and make all sorts of speeches to him, and play bopeep, and give him rides upon my head, and laugh until he laughs again, and steal him from mother for ever so long. And oh, I do so long that he may be a good, noble hearted man if he lives—free from all pride, and meanness, and self-seeking, and filled with gentleness and generosity, and coveting earnestly the best gifts, above all the gift of Divine love, the greatest of God's gifts.

Sometimes I feel that God has given to us a very especial mark of His favor in our darling, whose future will be a blessing to thousands and tens of thousands; and I pray that even now the foundation of that light

175

may be wisely laid by us. You have, my darling, a glorious work in hand—to you God has given the implanting of those first principles which affect the whole formation of character and conduct—and let your eye, my love, be clear and without cloud or doubt—for his will reflect yours; and let your heart go out, as I believe it does, in all your looks and acts to our dear son.

There are three songs, my love, which I think every mother who wants to see how God's Spirit can fill a mother's heart with joy and strength and hope should sing. Just look them up and sing them in your soul today. The first is Hannah's song (1 Samuel 2: 1—10); the second, Elizabeth's song (Luke 1: 41 —45); and the third is Mary's song (Luke 1 46—55). You will see in all these many beautiful thoughts of inspired motherly hope and expectation that will act like guiding stars to you in your wishes and efforts for our little gift from God.

And now, even while writing this page, I have received quite an unexpected joy—a letter from you; and I am delighted, my darling, with a picture which it gives me of the little scene you describe when you gathered the little ones around you, with our darling listening on your knee, and read to them the parable of the Sword and the King and the Palace. I fear it was rather deep for them; but I feel we often err in thinking of the capacity of children, who, because they fail to develop when young, often grow up with all their "chambers of imagery" closed up, darkened, contracted and empty

And this reminds me of a little poem which you and I have read together, but which I will copy out here for you I feel it is in season now: for I see many beautiful and most lovable girls spoiled through their foolish pride and affectation.

At the brook, a maiden glancing,
  Saw a form divine:
Said she, all her heart exulting,
  "That fair form is mine."

As she spoke, an angel whispered
  "Maiden, heaven is fair;"
Said the maiden to the angel:
  "Angel, take me there."

"Maiden," said the angel sadly,
  "Heaven is **for the fair.**"
"Therefore," said the maiden proudly,
  "Angel, take me there."

At the Gates, the glory burning,
  Smote her soul with dread.
"Angel, from that awful glory
"Hide me," said the maid.

Then the angel, gently soothing,
  Drew His robe aside,
"Maiden, in this wounded Bosom,
  Wounded souls may hide."

"O my Saviour, pierced and wounded,
  Heaven is for the fair;
I have sinned, but Thou art holy,
  Cleanse me, bring me there."

And the loving Saviour gently
  Drew her to His breast,
Made her fair, and at the gateway,
  Thro' the glory pressed.

You can't think how I am wearying for you, since
I got these **three** nice letters which I read so often and
feel so happy over, now that I know you are all my

own again. Dearest, I want home comfort and love
to strengthen for the public service to which I am
called, and it is a service which will tax every power
I possess There is only one thing lacking to make
my life when you are with me the happiest on earth—
and that is enough money to set me free from care,
but God sees best, I doubt not, and if I have only faith
to "cast on Him my every care", and go on wisely
doing His work, then I have the happiest lot on earth.
I believe all will be well—the happiest days are yet in
store, and I feel that if spared there is better work by
far in me than has ever come out of me. I am young
yet, ay and on the whole a strong man; and with you
perfectly trusting and loving God and me—why I
shall feel fit for anything, my darling love.

Tell M— I was very glad to hear she was "well and
keeping well," and I hope the new arrival is also well
(is it the seventh or eighth? I really forget) Why,
what a thriving family tree we are getting! Perhaps
centuries hence we shall be looked upon as the stem
of a noble race. May God grant that every generation
shall become better and purer and nobler than its
predecessor Who would have thought that those
two poor Alloa boys, and that quiet, calm, almost
mythical man, our grandfather, who died so young—
I say, who would have thought, seeing them, that they
would have been the roots of this fair family tree,
which seems to be entering upon a far spreading life?
I have often thought of that grandfather of whom so
little is known,—except just one thing I now remember nothing:—It is that of a calm, quiet faced, rather
tall, fair young man, walking on a Sabbath morning
with a little boy's hand in his around the works where
he was employed, to see that all was safe ere he went
to worship in God's house,—reverently, I doubt not
That was all my father remembered.

But do you not think of that grandfather's father
and mother, and think "How did you look with your

178

little boy, and how did you train him?" I expect they were a thoughtful pair, and if our family crest, a dove with an olive leaf flying across a dark sea and "Patience" as the motto, had meaning to those of our race who first chose it—then the dove means Purity or Holiness—the olive leaf means Peace and Victory— and the motto, Patientia, means Patience or Perseverance. Did they not hope—these first Dowies long ago in auld Scotia—that all their race would be pure messengers, patiently bearing the Gospel of peace across the troubled sea of life to sinking hearts, and did they not hope that they would be victorious over all ill? I do not, and no one, knows, but I like to think it sometimes; and what a glorious thing it will be for us to find in heaven some of them who can tell about it, and show how we fulfilled in this Australian land the thoughts God put in their hearts long ago. Better is the Olive of Peace than the Emblem of War.

Remember me with love to all and be especially good to my dear, dear old mother. Kiss her for me, and tell her how sorry I am that she is not stronger. Assure her of my love and constant prayer for her; and tell her that I have been often tempted to think I would like to be rich, if it were only to make her more comfortable. I wish I had been more of a comfort and help than I have been. She was always good to me, and I fear I was sometimes impatient and fretful—for which I know she has long ago forgiven me. During the last nine years from home my life has been very busy, but I have never forgotten her and my father for a single day in prayer and loving thought. Tell her so, and say, too, that I am glad my little boy has been folded in his grandmother's arms, and that she has seen his face and blessed the child. I hope to see her yet again on earth, but I feel sure by God's mercy I shall see her in heaven—not old, but young for ever—where no hearts ache, where no tears dim the eye, where the inhabitant is not sick, and where

sin and death cannot enter. Kiss her for me, my darling, and tell her I love her more than ever   May the
Lord sustain her, and when heart and flesh fail, be her
strength and her portion forever

And now good-by, love; for a little time only, I
hope. I feel as if we cannot do without each other
for much longer I pray God to comfort and strengthen
you, my dearest love. And as for our little gift from
God, just give him father's love in ever so many kisses
and show him my portrait when you do it. Let us
pray, and believe God answers   Let us watch and
pray. And may our loving God fill us with His peace
and love.   .   .

---

*(Written in answer to a personal letter from the Secretary of the
Ministerial Association, of date Nov. 28, 1877.)*

My Dear Sir .

Yours of 7th with its enclosure duly reached me.

As to the resolution of the Association I have
nothing to say at present

But as to your letter, there are several observa-
tions upon that extraordinary production which I now
feel myself compelled to make: not that I deem any
defense of my actions to be due to you in the slightest
degree, but that you may see what your letter really
amounts to, and to what extremely absurd results
the principles set forth in it must inevitably lead you.
And since perfect candor of expression is your evident
motto, I will not waste words in useless apology for
adopting a similar mode of writing, but shall deal at
once with your letter in the plainest and most candid
fashion. At the same time, I very deeply regret that
such a task is forced upon me; but my longer silence
might be misinterpreted to my damage, and, what I
care infinitely more about, to the damage of the Lord's
work.

Your letter is meaningless, or pernicious nonsense

in some parts, utter folly in others, and quite presumptituous in tone throughout.

I begin by dealing with the last of these three assertions.

It is presumptuous because you and I have never been on such intimate terms of private friendship as to warrant the adoption of your tone of writing; nor can you possibly have a knowledge of my private feelings, or thoughts, or ministerial and other life as could in the slightest degree fit you to take upon yourself the role of the candid friend. When I know that I never made a single important personal confidential communication to you in my life; when I cannot recall a half an hour of private intercourse, or any conversation of that length with you, except in the presence of one or more other persons, for fully three years —a period which covers the whole of my ministry in Newtown; when I remember the treacherous whisperings, concerning which I was only too well informed— of which you and others were guilty at the time I left Manly to come here, or rather when the church here were considering the desirability of calling me to be pastor; and when I reflect for how long a time I have ceased to respect your judgment or to regard your opinion upon most matters—for your inflated conceit in your general conduct most effectually repelled me—I cay, when I remember all this, and much more, then your impudence in attempting to play the part of the well informed, trusted and confidential friend does seem to me to be a piece of unjustifiable presumption.

It is not to be wondered at, therefore, if it be scarcely possible for me to find anything like a wise or fair view of my conduct or capacity in your letter; and to call the miserable scarecrow sketch of myself a correct portrait is indeed "utter folly". But it is very much more than that, it is a miserable, spiteful estimate of my career—a career of which, whilst I have

181

no reason to be ashamed, comparing it by human standard, I yet feel very much ashamed of when judged as in God's sight. Yet more, your letter is contrary to fact

There can be no facts within your knowledge enabling you to speak and write—for you do both— of my conduct in resigning the pastorate of this church as if it were the unavoidable result of some pressure of some concealed external or internal kind, for the very conclusive reason that there are no such facts as you insinuate Your insinuation is veiled in cloudy verbiage in many places, and is almost expressed when you write of my being in a "present apparently painful position, surrounded by difficulties," etc., and. when you demand to know whether I "have not in great measure" brought myself into that alleged position, you seem clearly to presuppose the fact that my position was brought about, or that I was compelled in some way to resign, by other means than my own voluntary act, or through some failure to fulfill my office

Now such suggestions are, in every sense of the words, wholly false · for my position in this church was never stronger than when I intimated my intention to resign, and that intimation was wholly unexpected, was made at a time when various inherited difficulties and difficulty creators had been most completely, or very largely overcome, and was, I venture to say, a source of real regret of nineteen-twentieth's of those under my ministry, of which I had many touching proofs. Whatever such persons as you, who are almost wholly ignorant of me or my position, may imagine—and ignorance is the parent of credulity, and, notwithstanding what you may have heard from three or four miserable "dead flies" who have caused the church here to be very offensive for years, there is not an atom of foundation for such insinuations—and my hope for the Church in future days is very low unless these said "dead flies" are got out. And the spiteful character of these unfounded and offensive remarks is very apparent, when you inquire from me, with all the bumptiousness of a pedantic "Sir Oracle" whether it is not "your extraordinary self-confidence, always willing to give advice and never to take it" which has brought me to this position—my only remark upon which is, that I have no confidence in myself whatever, and that I am only confident when consciously trusting in God, and I hope you are not judging me in this matter by your own measure. Then, apparently unsatisfied with this flight of genius, you soar to prophetic heights, and from the giddy summit of your self-conceit, you behold my future misery, and warn me that I shall "bitterly rue it," if I "plunge into fresh schemes and fresh expenditure". And then you meekly descend to communicate to me the interesting results of your profound inquiries concerning that awful question, in your sight, of my "dispensing" with your sympathy and support—I never had it, by the way, and never missed it—for of course you were doubtless, in your opinion, one of the charmed of "right minded men with whom I have been publicly associated."

Summarizing, therefore, your own sum total of gifts and graces, as well as mine, you find yourself in a position to announce with an air of final certainty all the depths and even the possibilities of our respective ministerial powers—wondrous being! And linking me to yourself, with quite a touching humility in so profound a creature, assumed no doubt, to let me down a little more easily from my supposed over-ambitious aspirations, you say that it is "only men of rare talents, and who to a remarkable degree command the popular ear", who can afford to stand alone; and—oh marvelous condesension—you add these words: "neither you nor I can, I am sure, boast of such gifts as to make headway against the opinions of the men of piety, zeal, and learning about us". Amazing discovery! Worthy of the days when the Pharisaic concluded that unlearned and impious fools like Jesus and His followers must fail because they were none of them—who were all properly submissive and learned—who would go with Him How awful, then, must be our fate if these tremendous "men of piety", etc., should turn their formidable artillery against us. Does your timorous little soul tremble before even the thought of such a catastrophe? Well, if so, I must pray you to slip your imaginary cable, and sheer off, and leave me to my doom: for, even if it should happen that these awful, ecclesiastical great guns should fire away their broadsides at poor me—surely now they could scarcely be so cruel—yet I shall very certainly dispense with their "sympathy" if I am to pay your price for it, and without fear incur their "antipathy"—which you prophesy will surely follow—since my mind is wholly resolved to assert my liberty by going out of the Congregational Union.

And I can do all that the more easily that with very brief and unsatisfactory intervals, I have had to "dispense" with that "sympathy" throughout my whole connection with the said Union, and have, during that period, developed a very profound contempt for their antipathy, which did its poor best to keep me out of Newtown when the people were unanimously for me That antipathy, also, did its poor best to damn me with a faint praise and hinder me with open sneers in most of my public efforts. That same antipathy did its poor best, for over four years, in keeping me out of all public position, so far as was in the power of the clique who managed the Union—and you were a specially active offender in that matter, for you are the Mercury of that ecclesiastical Olympus. That antipathy did its poor best in the efforts of a deceased leader, who like a modern Jove, tried to crush with the lightnings of his fierce anger and the thunderous rattle of his awe-inspiring money bags—but he failed ignominiously. That antipathy did its poor best in suppressing my solemn protest against an iniquitous appointment to the Chairmanship of the Union, the truth of which—and the document has been for a year in the hands of the Union Committee—has never once been disputed; but in those days, alas, I was not wholly freed from the apparent enough delusion, as I now see it is, that **truth** was the **first** consideration with the Congregational Union and not Mammon or other cognate powers. That antipathy, to pass over to one of its last manifestations, did its poor best in the unmanly, unprovoked, and most anti-Christian attack of the editor of the denominational "little candle" (you know I am not joking, for that is your approved title of it on its very front) at the Christian Convention in Sydney, when that faint luminary of Congregational darkness was promptly put under a bushel by the very distinguished Christian minister who presided, and whose repeated expressions of loving sympathy with me, and of entire approval of my speech, more than compensate for any pain which that ponderous "little candle" holder's conduct had momentarily caused me. Yes, I now fear nothing which these "men of piety, zeal", etc., can do to me; and, if they are true servants of the Great Master, they will pause ere they enter the lists against any of His servants and see good reason to retrace their steps with shamed faces; but, if they are not, then it will be seen and known of all men what they really are in spirit—persecutors, and unfaithful will they be—no matter what their Mercury may call them, no matter how their "candle holder" may illumine their characters.

From numerous ministers and members of leading position in every section of the Christian Church, and from large numbers of the people in the Congregational churches generally, I have received a large and an increasing amount of warm sympathy, and by their kind appreciation of my services, I have been placed, almost since my entrance, a lone stranger into New South Wales, in positions where I have taken, and still take, a fair share of work in religious and philanthropic affairs, and in public questions of great importance—for all which I give grateful thanks to God who permits me to labour in the Gospel ministry of His Son But to the support of Congregational ministers in my work I owe next to nothing, to the funds of Congregational organizations I never was indebted one penny, and my work has been blessed in proportion to my efforts being apart from them in a spiritual sense Indeed, I may fairly say, that instead of being "publicly associated" in labour with "Congregationalism" (what is that "ism", I wonder?) my connection therewith has been largely a nominal one, as I now see, and my real association has been with men of earnest, catholic, Christian sentiment in every denomination—whose kind sympathy I hope to preserve and do highly value.

Then as to my third assertion concerning the meaningless and also pernicious nonsense you write in your letter, about "the wrong" which you say I am about to inflict upon myself, upon my wife, and upon the church, by not fleeing for refuge to the only hope you can see for me, which is found in "the many brethren who are willing to help you if you will but only trust them", and also the further farrago of nonsense which you have scribbled in support of this—why, to answer these would be to accomplish the feat of proving the existence of the non-existent.

Utterly ignorant, as you cannot but be, of my intentions or resources, your impudence in building such painful charges upon the basis of your fancies, is only excelled by the audacity with which you transform your imaginations into facts—and looked at thus you are an interesting and curious psychological study. I have, in short, made such a study of you, in return for the candor you have shown, and I am sorry, sincerely sorry, the result is not very flattering to you.

It is quite apparent to me that, all through your ministerial life, the folly of your Gawler escapade—when your were nearly frightened out of your wits, and frantically sought advice from Dan to Beersheba of Congregationalism in South Australia,—I say it appears to me, that has haunted you till this day. The ghost of that or some other affair, still manifestly exerts a very potent influence over your mental conceptions, and you are evidently accustomed to obey its mandates with much devotion—the first of which is "Look always first to the brethren!" And the second, it utters in mournful tones, under the very shadow of the ecclesiastical gallows tree—"Obey always the brethren!" Such, night and day, and year by year, with sad cadence, and ghostly accompaniments, is the cry which your ghost utters in your ears.

And indeed, this seems to be rather a serious ghost for you, my poor, deluded brother, because this wretched Gawler and Burwood spectre or ghost, seems to interfere with your confidence in the direction and promised helper of God, the Holy Ghost, in answer to the prayers of believers. This is beyond question, when you counsel me not to place reliance upon the fact that I "have prayed over the matter and that God has shown me the plain path of duty"; and further, inspired by this said ghost, you utter this sublime dictum for my guidance: "I say do not trust your own impression for answers to prayer." And then you go on by a puerile illustration, to assure me, with your usual modesty, that my "judgment" as exemplified by my "whole career"—how much do you know of that—is quite unsound, just as your ear is unmusical; and, upon this most redoubtable piece of assumption, you arrive at the astounding conclusion, for my special guidance at this and all future times—

viz "No prayer will give you the right conclusion on which to take important steps in life." Conseqently, it follows that being in this awfully helpless condition I "must recognize my need and trust those who can supply the want". And, in case I or anyone should ask, "Oh, wondrous being, do reveal to my ignorance and woe where these glorious guides are to be found?" The answer is with prophetic instinct provided by you in the very next words: "There are men, whose long, useful, and peaceful career in the churches (Congregational of course you mean) should encourage you to seek from them (wonderful!) the counsel they are willing to give". What a stupid creature I must have been to think my brother ministers were mortal creatures like myself!

Here is ghostly counsel and ghostly conclusions with a vengeance, but, my poor, haunted friend, before I can believe **that** is the direction of the Holy Ghost, you will require to produce another Revelation as well attested as the Bible's—nay, it must be a Revelation of higher authority which shall expose the falsehoods of, and wholly supersede, the Bible as the rule of faith and practice, for such principles of prayer and practice as you have laid down are not only not to be found there, but hundreds of passages prove such principles to be wholly opposed to it, and the whole teaching of Christ as well as the whole experience of the Church is exactly contrary to your directions It is rather too much—I hope you will allow that—for me to set your miserable dicta before God's inspired Word.

But further, permit me to say, that if you will only logically carry out your convictions you will either require to proclaim the discovery of infallibility in the persons of the "pious" etc. etc. "brethren" you have decided upon; or, will it not be easier and quite as logical, for you to find your infallibility where Papalism places it, in the Infallible Pope at Rome?

188

Beware, my poor friend, and take great care that you "tell it not in Gath, lest the daughters of the Philistines rejoice": for Dr. Vaughan would hail you as a convert if this were known, and that harlot Church of Rome would rejoice in the fall of such a soul as the Secretary of the Congregational Union. Honestly have I feared, for some time past, that the spirit of Popery was at work in the Union in New South Wales; but little did I expect to hear the Secretary of that headless, soulless, because wholly mythical, body proclaim the Vatican Decree in essence as being practicable to the **ekycktoi** of that Union. There is no need for you to regret my secession from that strange way: for I am a deadly foe to all humanly concocted infallibilities in Papalism, Congregationalism or elsewhere; for they have cursed, and are now cursing, the Church and the world—defiling, weakening and making despicable the one, and letting the other go on unchecked in sin and perdition.

I only wish I could destroy this creation of your Gawler or other ghosts: for I would certainly free you from an awful horror, a bogie, too, with which you try to frighten others.

And now in closing, I beg leave to draw your attention to the breach of confidence committed by the premature and unauthorized announcement in the "Independent", which, arises from the fact that my private letter to you, as the Secretary of a private Association, is, by a gross violation of all good usage, therein publicly used. I thought that I was at least dealing with gentlemen, and I trust that such an **amende** will be made as will show that I was not wholly wrong in that conjecture. I reserve, however, now my right to publish this and other correspondence I have had with those whom you warned me are against me, should I deem it necessary.

When the time comes for me to retire from Newtown, I shall myself announce my withdrawal from the Union, and either then or later I shall probably state the reasons why, though I had hoped to have found that to be unnecessary, because my whole heart's desire is to work with all my powers, in the most direct and constant manner possible, for the salvation of the perishing thousands in this city for whom Christ died and for whom His Church is doing so little And I shall only strike a blow at your Union if it stands between me and that work   I hope, for many reasons, that may not be required, but, if it is, I shall do my best to make the blow a destructive one; for I shall regard the Union with as little reverence, in that case, as I do the Roman Curia, and count it only another tyranny and anti-Christian imposture which ought to be swept away without hesitation by every honest Christian man.

I am,

Very truly yours,

John Alexander Dowie.

(Addressed to the Editor of the "Sidney Morning Herald," and published by him in that paper, July 27, 1878, as a protest against a proposed address to the Earl of Beaconsfield.)

Sir

As one of many I desire to raise an emphatic protest against the design of the promoters of the meeting convened by the Acting-Mayor for Monday next.

At that meeting it is intended to adopt an address to the Earl of Beaconsfield, congratulating him upon the wisdom and success of his foreign policy.

There are many reasons why no such meeting should be held, and why no such address should be adopted. The whole of the facts are not before us regarding the recent Congress at Berlin, and it will form an inconvenient and dangerous precedent, should an irresponsible public meeting in Sydney express itself rashly upon any act of British foreign policy, and presume to forward that expression as the deliberate judgment of the Colony of New South Wales, as seems to be the intention. Moreover, the act would not only be presumptuous, but I am convinced it would be entirely opposed to the views held by very large numbers of most thoughtful colonists. And I will venture to lay respectfully before the public my reasons for so thinking, with some proofs that these reasons rest upon a solid foundation of facts.

My objections to this proposal are three.

First—the Earl of Beaconsfield's personal and political antecedents do not justify such an expression of admiration.

Second—the facts alleged to be the fruits of his labors are not facts but illusions, resting upon a misconception, or mispresentation, of recent events in Europe and the East.

Third—instead of approval, the Earl of Beaconsfield's policy merits our severest censure, since it has largely caused the recent horrible Russo-Turkish war, since it has sown the dragon's teeth of future international strife by the Treaty of Berlin and the Turkish Convention, since it has seriously injured the constitutional rights of the British Parliament, and created a precedent full of danger to every province of the British Empire.

These are very grave charges, I am aware, and they are not lightly made. I shall endeavor to justify their accuracy and the necessity for making them.

As to the first of my assertions, a really candid and careful investigation of Benjamin D'Israeli's political life will most certainly prove its soundness.

From the day (June 3, 1832) when he deceived Joseph Hume and Daniel O'Connel into the writing of letters approving and recommending him to the electors as a Radical candidate for the representation of High Wycombe, until the last general election in 1875, when "Beer and the Bible" was practically the

watchword which he gave as Tory leader, there
streches an uninterrupted record of political charlat-
anry, impudent imposture, and unscrupulous procedure,
such as is quite unexampled in modern times. History
has constructed for this man a pillory, although at
present he stands rewarded with a trumpery Coronet
and a lady's Garter O'Connel's brand, placed there in
1835, still stands, for those who have eyes to see, upon
D'Israeli's brow—"His life is a living lie". And when
the Irish orator's hand went to nail him to "The cross
of the impenitent thief, whose name," he said, "I verily
believe must have been D'Israeli", he expressed in
terms, perhaps coarse, but not too strong, the detestation which such a character and career inspires The
treachery with which he ever stung the hand that fed
him, the persistency with which he repeated unfounded
charges, the fulsome flattery with which he besmeared
the English Tory squires, the skill with which he hoodwinked the Bentincks, and all that genus, until he com-
passed, by their aid, the downfall in his leader and
benefactor, Sir Robert Peel, are they not all recorded
in his speeches of that memorable time, preserved in
that Parliamentary record which is D'Israeli's pillory?

His subsequent abuse and misrepresentation of
Earl Russell, Mr. Gladstone, and a host of noble men
who have led the van in all the great measures of reform and progress, is too well known to require more
than this allusion, whilst the recent retirement from his
Cabinet of high minded and able Tory statesmen like
the Earls of Carnamon and Derby, with their public
statements of his political untrustworthiness, show
that he is still unchanged.

The numberless instances in which, with most be-
wildering audacity, he has stolen the policy of the
Liberals, after denouncing it for years, and has then
paraded it dressed up in "true blue" in quite an original style, declaring that the little dear was his own
legitimate offspring, proves him to be a habitual and

incorrigible political thief—and though often convicted and punished for his larcenies, he still remains an "impenitent thief," and will to the end, it is to be feared. And this is the man we are summoned to praise!

Let it be shown, if it can, by his admirers, that these facts are distorted or exaggerated, and that he is worthy of the tribute they propose the colony should give him. Historical whitewashing has been somewhat largely practiced of late, and there may be some who are getting the said whitewash ready for Monday evening. Let all such have a care, for they have an ugly task,—the white rubs off sooner or later, and the artist is apt to spoil his clothes, with no other reward than his stupid sycophancy for his fruitless toil.

But I would now turn to my second objection to the address—viz., that the facts alleged as the fruits of his labors are not facts but illusions.

I will state some of the more important grounds for this as concisely as possible, and if they are not expressed more fully it is not because I am unable but because neither my time, nor your space, nor the public patience are unlimited.

1. The promoters of this address declare that Lord Beaconsfield's policy has "maintained the public law of Europe and treaty rights." But the opposite is the fact. There would have been really maintained, had Lord Beaconsfield more firmly and forcibly impressed it upon his friend, the Turk, that Great Britain would not interfere for his deliverance, if he persisted in setting at naught the decisions of the Conference of Constantinople held at the beginning of 1877. These decisions were part of the so-called "public law of Europe", which Turkey was allowed by Beaconsfield to reject. They were intended to force upon the Ottoman Porte essential reforms in its administration, and especially to provide protection for

7

its Christian subjects whom Turkish troops has oppressed and massacred in Rosnia, Bulgaria, Armenia, and the Greek provinces with impunity, as they were fully warranted in doing by the Koran, the brutal Pachas, the pecuniary necessities of the Sultan's harem, and other "sublime" things Russia stepped in to enforce the said "public law" by declaring war, and Great Britain did not then protest, nor has she since, that the Czar was without justification, seeing that the oppressed Bulgarians and others undoubtedly regarded him as the head of the Slavonic Race, upon whom the Turks had exercised their skill in fiendish activity.

It matters not to the question that the Russians had an eye to their own aggrandizement in what they undertook—though Britain had set them many examples—for the matter before us is one of "law", and, on the face of it, it is clear that not Beaconsfield but the Czar was the only one of the lawyers brave enough to serve the writ of "public law" decreed at Constantinople, acting therein as a kind of Inspector of Turkish Nuisances. Personally, I am against war in every form, but since war is recognized by "the public law of Europe" as a legitimate thing, no one can say that, looked at from the legal aspect of the case, Deputy Inspector Nicholas did an illegal thing in pressing on to Constantinople at the head of the Allied Armies, or in doing his utmost to reap the fruits of victory by the Preliminary Treaty of San Stefano. And then as to the question of "Treaty Rights" Why, if the expression has reference, as I suppose it must, to the Treaty of Paris, then Great Britain has so modified that Treaty, for example by the Black Sea concessions to Russia a few years ago, and Turkey had by her violation of "public law" so forfeited the protection which that Treaty guaranteed her, that it is a screaming farce to talk of her Treaty Rights, and no other were endangered To put it plainly, if an adulteress has still a wife's rights and a thief an honest man's rights, and a murderer a philanthropist's rights, then Turkey has also still intact her "Treaty Rights", though her crimes have been greater far.

2. Then we are further to assure the Earl of Beaconsfield that he has won for us by his diplomacy, "the blessings of peace, whilst resolutely maintaining the interests and honor of the British Empire, in which the Australian Colonies as integral portions of the Empire are deeply interested". The mantle of Disraelitish style fell upon the writer of that magniloquent sentence, I am sure. And before dragging down his piece of empty rhetorical rubbish, I wish to draw attention to the fact that here we have a fair specimen of modern idolatrous worship—for therein there is no god but Disraeli.

This is now known in England as "the worship of Jingoe." It seems to flourish here in some minds. In my simplicity, I had thanked the Almighty God and Father of all men for securing "the blessings of peace" so far as we have them. But He did not seem to be in the thoughts of the Jingoes, and so they ascribed it all to Disraeli; or, perhaps they are more ashamed to own God as the peace-maker, than they are to own this successful trickster.

But let us examine these idolatrous ascriptions more closely.

Is it not rather too soon to speak of the blessings of peace as being "secured"? Perhaps Lord Beaconsfield will find that to sign a Treaty of Peace at Berlin is one thing, and to get everyone concerned to accept its provisions is quite another, as Duke Nicholas and General Ignatieff found it to be at San Stefano. Even already our meagre cablegram information proves that scarce anyone seems satisfied except Disraeli and his kinsman, the Turk. We have overwhelming proof that the whole of South-eastern Europe and Asia Minor are greatly agitated by the proposed territorial changes, and for this very good reason, among others, that the populations of these countries have never been consulted by the diplomatic persons who at Berlin coolly handed them over like sheep or cattle, to whatever power their august personages pleased. This kind of work does not last.

With Italy dissatisfied, with Greece indignant at being cheated with fair words and empty performances, with Austria gloomy and troubled with the chaotic disorder of its "mixed multitude", with Russia humiliated but full of pride and passionate desires for revenge, and with all the difficulties and dangers which Britain has incurred by practical Turkish protectorate, does it not seem a farce, with such a mass of combustible elements, and such a political Lucifer sporting amongst them, to talk of peace as being "secured"? If I lock up a very mischievous boy in a gunpowder store with a plentiful supply of matches at his disposal, I would be a fool indeed to go about flourishing the key in my hand, and telling everyone of how "secure" things were in that store. I expect that there would be a very general stampede at once from that vicinity, by all who valued their lives.

Europe is that store, Disraeli is that boy, and the key is the Treaty of Berlin

But we must yet further examine the assurances in question, and see how the Earl of Beaconsfield has maintained "the interests and honor of the British Empire in which the Australian Colonies as an integral portion of that Empire are deeply interested." Every one of these assurances, except the last, I will venture to dispute as entirely contrary to fact.

"British interests" have never been threatened by Russia, and let those who assert that they have prove their assertion by facts, if they can Neither the moral nor material interests of Great Britain would have been entirely broken up, and Russian influence become supreme upon the Bosphorus, for there is not a single inch of British territory to which that famous channel is the waterway. And as to the supposed danger to our possession of India should Turkish Armenia become a part of the Russian Empire, surely that wretched bogie is scared out of all sensible men's minds. But, if there be any who still suffer from that Disraelian ghost "Russian designs upon British India", let them read Colonel George Chesney's article in the Nineteenth Century Review for April last, and they will see how absurd fears are, even from a military point of view. However, we shall still be told that British "honour" if not "interests" demanded the line of policy which Lord Beaconsfield has adopted. But what is "honour"? True honour is a sacred thing, and rightly understood, "the noble mind's distinguishing perfection."

But false honour is a seducer and a tyrant which disgraces and oppresses all its votaries, and such an honor is

"a fine imaginary notion,
"That draws in raw and inexperienced men
"To real mischiefs, while they hunt a shadow."

It is such "honour" as this which is the boast of prize fighters, gamblers, military bullies, and political adventurers. It is a gory Moloch, which ever demands human blood for its satisfaction. Accordingly, bloody battlefields are baptized "beds of honour", and the destruction, outrage, famine, vice, disease and death which follow are all happy nymphs attendant upon that virgin of "honour"—glorious war. Is it not time that this shameless imposture should cease?

There is as much "honour" in any war as there is in a prize fight, a duel, a game of dice, or a cock fight, and a nation which goes to war for "honour's" sake can claim as much "honour" as the individual who engages in these dishonourable games. Lord Beaconsfield has peculiar ideas upon this subject, and he has contrived to make them temporarily popular.

But now I proceed to deal with my third objection, that instead of approval, the Earl of Beaconsfield's policy merits our severest censure

1 "It has largely caused the recent Russo-Turkish War"

Can any one doubt that war would have been averted if Great Britain had made a tithe of the naval and military display employed to coerce Russia, enforcing Turkey to carry out righteous measures of internal reform—reforms upon which all Europe was agreed?

Facts prove that Lord Beaconsfield's selfish policy is more largely the cause of the present miseries of Turkey and the late horrors, than any other known influence. In 1875, serious insurrections against Turkish oppression arose in Bosnia and Herzegovnia. When Germany, France, Austria, Italy and Russia drew up the Berlin memorandum of May, 1876, pledging themselves "to support their diplomatic action by the sanction of an agreement with a view to such efficacious measures as might be demanded in the interests of general peace to check the evil and prevent its development", it was Britain alone which stood aloof, and broke up the concerted action of the Great Powers, which might have led to a peaceful issue The immediate effect of the British rejection of these peaceful proposals was the extension of the rebellion in the Turkish provinces, the declaration of war by Servia and Montenegro, and the infamous atrocities by the Turks in the then peaceful capital, Bulgaria Then, once more, proposals of intervention were made by European powers, and rejected by Britain, until at last the famous capital conference at Constantinople, to which I have already referred, was held at the end of 1876 In the decisions of that Conference Great Britain was not only a consenting party, but one responsible for their execution to a larger degree than almost any of the other capital powers And for a

time it would seem as if Beaconsfield did intend to
prevent Turkey from further violation of the "public
law of Europe", and Lord Salisbury warned the
Turks that "the very existence of the Ottoman Empire" was threatened, if these decisions were not carried out, and he added this significant expression,
"the responsibility will rest solely with the Sultan
and his advisers". But the Porte did reject them almost with contempt, and encouraged by the protection
which Disraeli had hitherto always extended to them,
they went boldly into the war with Russia believing
that even if they were beaten he would not see them
greatly suffer. Turkey was deceived, or miscalculated.
Beaconsfield dared not attempt to draw the sword on
her behalf, for the grand efforts of Gladstone, Bright,
Freeman, Richards and a host of our noblest men, had
thoroughly aroused and instructed the Empire as to
the iniquitous misrule of the foul and cruel Mahom-
medan tyranny which has for centuries disgraced
Europe.

Yet, though Turkey had defied "the public law of
Europe", had trodden beneath her feet in wholesale
murder the common rights of mankind, and had
broken her "treaty engagements", Beaconsfield refused to take any steps to act with the other powers
and prevent war. The proposal which was made by
Russia and backed by all the other powers, to send
a united fleet up the Constantinople and demand the
reforms in Turkey upon which all were agreed, was
rejected by Beaconsfield; although doubtless, without
firing a shot, such intervention would have accomplished its object and **preserved** the blessings of peace.
No, it did not suit this Jewish statesman, who, in one
of his novels, has dwelt pathetically upon the affinity
of race and even religion between the Moslem and the
Jew—a thought which dominates his policy toward
Turkey, it would seem.

He preferred the chances of war, and, with true

Disraelitish cunning he calculated that he could deal more effectually with that Russia whom he has always hated, when it was enfeebled by terribly exhausting, even if successful, war. However that may be, when the presence of half a dozen British ironclads at the Golden Horn would have averted war, he would not so much as lift his finger. Before the bar of human justice and of Divine, I verily believe that Lord Beaconsfield stands today more guilty than any other statesman in Europe of the half a million lives which have been sacrificed in battle, by famine, and by exposure on the desolated land and ruined towns of Bulgaria and Roumelia—and of the awful miseries which still afflict the homeless, starving thousands of refugees. And shall we praise him then? As soon would I chant the praises of Juggernaut or Moloch.

2. I have asserted further that Earl of Beaconsfield's policy "has sown the dragon's teeth of future international strife by the Treaty of Berlin and the Turkish Convention."

The details of neither document have had time to reach us, but already we hear an angry tide of discontent, indignation and alarm. Passing over all the dangers which that Treaty has created in Europe, to which I have already briefly alluded, it must be evident that the British occupation of Cyprus, the exposure by the Earl of Derby of the unscrupulous design upon Egypt meditated by Beaconsfield, and the awful responsibility which Britain undertakes by the semiprotectorate of Turkey in general, and Armenia in particular, constitute unavoidable dangers of a most serious nature. It brings Great Britain, for the first time in its history, face to face with Russia upon a frontier line in Asia at a period when both nations are greatly irritated, to say the least, and when there is at the head of affairs in England a man whose persistent hatred of Russia has been the most consistent thing in his crooked career. Such a position is altogether untenable for any length of time without war—a war which Disraeli has looked forward to for many years, and which he has done his utmost to provoke. The only hope of escape lies in the return of that great British Achilles—William Ewart Gladstone, and his party to power, and an entire reversal of present British foreign policy, by a policy of noble conciliation, which will have a stronger regard for the rights and happiness of peoples, than for the passions of the rulers. A general election might bring this very much nearer than many of us think—and that may not be far off.

3. But the gravest, perhaps, of my charges against the Beaconsfield policy is the last, and that which more "deeply interests the Australian colonies as integral portions of the British Empire," than any of those with which I have been dealing.

I have said that this policy has seriously injured the constitutional rights of the British Parliament and created a precedent full of danger to every province of the British Empire.

In proof of these serious assertions, I will refer to one crowning act of audacity, which Lord Beaconsfield perpetrated in a secret and deceitful manner, just after the Easter recess of the House of Commons—the removal of several thousands of native East Indian soldiers to the neighborhood of the late scene of war.

The masterly speeches of Lord Selborne and others on May 20th in the House of Lords, and the still grander display of eloquence, fact and logic by the Liberal leaders in the House of Commons on the 20th and 23rd have made it clear to all but prejudiced minds that the rights of Parliament have been seriously infringed. If, as the Tories agree, it is quite needless for the Government to ask the consent of the legislature to the spending of the people's money until after it has been spent, then it will be quite as reasonable to suppose that the taxation of the people does not need the prior consent of the House of Commons, until after the taxes have been decreed and collected by Royal authority—a thing which was once tried, which ended in civil war, and in the loss to a foolish King, not only of his throne and crown, but of his head There can be no doubt that specific law has been violated by Beaconsfield, and a most dangerous precedent has been established. Nor has it been justified, except by a mere assertion of the necessity for the action This is in every age the tyrant's plea— "necessity "

But this precedent is especially dangerous to the most sacred liberties of every province of the Empire

Let it be remembered that those native troops which have been sent into the Mediterranean from India were raised for the defense of British India and that they have been maintained by means of taxes levied upon the people of that territory Now it is for a similar purpose that our Permanent Defense Forces have been raised, and they are maintained precisely in the same way Then, if the British Cabinet can by a stroke of the pen remove the Indian Army to fight Great Britain's battles in Europe, what is to hinder them from overriding all local authorities here, and removing our Defense Force to fight in China or any where else? And, if the reply is, that such an attempt would not be tolerated here for a moment, I ask— and have not Indians equal rights with Australians?

But a still more serious case may be presented as possible

If this absolute power continues to be exercised, what is to hinder Lord Beaconsfield, should these colonies displease his victorious party—for example by a peaceful and constitutional agitation for separation and independence—I say, what is to hinder him from sending 10,000 Sepoys and several ironclads down from India, to bring us back again to obedience to British rule? Some may answer that the ill success of a similar attempt of an English Tory Government a century ago, with the then United Colonies of America, might prove a hindrance. But this is by no means certain: for the Tories are like the Bourbons, "They forget nothing and learn nothing;" and Lord Beaconsfield or Salisbury may prove as wicked as Lord North did, whilst Albert Edward, Prince of Wales, on the Throne, might prove as foolish as George III, who was undoubtedly the best man of the two, so far as we can yet see. But suppose all these dangers to be merely, and always, imaginary—are we, as an "integral part of the Empire," to allow such a claim to be asserted without challenge?

Assuredly we would not, if the attempt to enforce it were made: for twenty-four hours would not pass ere the cry would ring throughout the whole continent of Australia—"Cut the cable: send back the Governors: at all risks let us be free!" And Lord Beaconsfield knows this.

Yet this claim is enforced on India, and we raise no voice against it. We are foolishly, guiltily silent, and we may live to repent our silence, aye, our want of brotherhood.

The fire which is burning my neighbor's house a few doors off concerns me: for, if I go not to his help the flames may destroy my dwelling. And what is India's case today may be our own ere long. But some may say that the cases are not alike, for India is not a self-governing dependence such as Australia is. I admit the fact, the cases are different; but the difference aggravates Lord Beaconsfield's offense.

Because much enduring India is gagged, and her people cannot speak in free assemblies through their representatives, she is to be wronged with impunity; and because, on the other hand, Australia is free to speak, aye and if need be to act, she is not to be touched, her rights are not to be violated, for she has the power to make them inviolable. How does that view of the matter look? Not very favorable for the cowardly policy of Lord Beaconsfield Is it for this that Britain rules India, for this that the poor toiling millions of India labor?

Shall their poverty be made yet harder to bear, when they are told to pay taxes to create an army of their sons and brethren who shall shed their blood in foreign lands, in quarrels which are not theirs, but their conquerors? Verily, nay: for the question comes to be as Mr. Gladstone has eloquently expressed it in the "Nineteenth Century" for June: "Is it possible that this can work? Will India be content? Can India be content? Ought India to be content?

In distant, and to her children uncongenial climes, in lands of usage, tongue, religion, wholly alien, the flower of her youth are to bleed and die for us, and she will have no part but to suffer and obey. This is injustice, gross and monstrous injustice; and those who are parties to its preparation, must prepare for the results to which injustice leads."

These are momentous and true words, which will fly far, and be heard of again Some brewer of beer who has, as is fit, a place among the Disraelites in the House of Commons, named Hanbury, is about to distinguish himself by calling the attention of Parliament to these words in censure of Mr. Gladstone. It is well: for the stupid act will make them yet more widely known, and the justification which the debate, if it comes on, will supply, will make their truth and generous brotherhood more apparent to the world It will also preserve the brewer's name from an otherwise inevitable oblivion, and make it notorious, if not famous.

No, India cannot bear her wrongs always in silence. We seem almost to hear her speaking to us by the voice of her brave defender, saying:

"And shall I reverence pride, and lust, and rapine?
"No! when oppression stains the robe of state,
"And power's a whip of scorpions in the hands
"Of heartless knaves, to lash the o'er burthened back
"Of honest Industry, the loyal blood
"Will turn to bitterest gall, and the o'er charged heart
"Explode in execration."

And woe to British power in India if another wide-spread mutiny arise!

It will be far more dangerous than that of twenty years ago, for the missionary has been abroad, and the schoolmaster, and the merchant, and the drill instructor, and the vernacular press is now a power in the land.

Perhaps the trumpery title of Empress of India, which Disraeli invented to please the Court, may then be won, which Queen Victoria may be the first to bear. Could that day ever come, history will record that it was the fatal policy of Benjamin Disraeli, first and only Earl of Beaconsfield, which alienated India, and deluged that fair land with the blood and tears of thousands, which must flow, I fear, if this policy is persisted in, and she to fight for her right to be free. And to sum up, I believe one thing, at least, to be certain, that history will indorse the severe but true characterization of Lord Beaconsfield which a distinguished writer lately expressed: "He is a political juggler, to whom England is a gambling table, not a country, for the purposes of his gain."

Every consideration of eternal Justice and Righteousness calls upon every good citizen to do what he can to let the truth go forth, with no uncertain sound, in this great crisis through which our Empire and the world is passing, and, therefore, I will not take refuge in a nom de plume, but feeling that what I have written is for the public good, and in full accordance with my duty as a Christian minister and citizen, I shall sign myself,

Yours Very Respectfully,
John Alexander Dowie

(Dated Nov. 2, 1878, in which work as an Independent Minister of the Gospel is reviewed.)

My Dear Father

It is just six months since I last wrote you, and so quickly has the time passed that it scarcely seems to me to be as many weeks. But when I strive to recall in detail the many things which have happened, and the work in which I have been engaged it seems to be fully that time That period, too, has been one of severe trial, but God has brought us through, and today we are stronger in body and more truly prosperous than ever before Jeanie thinks she is better now than ever she was in her life before, and works away steadily and cheerfully in a way that would surprise you, whilst our dear little Gladdy grows stronger and more intelligent every day

And as for our work, I feel sure of one thing, that it has been far more largely blessed, in the highest aspects of it, during the past eight or nine months, than ever before in New South Wales. No minister in this city has around him a more loyal and devoted people than around me at the Masonic Hall, nearly three-fourths of whom are the fruits of my own ministry under God, and the large number of men, from twenty to forty years old, especially is a striking and rare feature in our audiences

I often feel myself as one who is being led onward step by step in an utterly unknown way, and were it not for my confidence in my unerring Leader in this path of faith, and the strength which He gives, I could no more face the Present and the Future, than I could without His grace have come through the

206

Past. There can be no doubt that He has concealed purposes—and it is His glory "to conceal a matter" as well as to reveal it—which I do not dream of. This I am sure of, I am where He would have me to be, so far as I can honestly judge, and the proofs of that conviction lie in the facts wrought out already in the work.

At the outset, remember that, humanly speaking, I stood alone. When I stood forth to preach my first sermon in this city in the Theatre Royal, I knew not who would gather around me,nor what the result would be. But in a month I had in the evening considerably over one thousand to hear the Word of Life from my lips—and it was cheering indeed to see the rapt earnestness with which it was received—a Jew, the lessee of the Theatre, listening eagerly night after night in his private box is a sight not often seen. A choir gathered rapidly, and many of the young men from Newtown helped at the doors. But the cost was too much for me in money, and we made what I now think was a mistake—we removed out services to the Protestant Hall. At first we carried our congregations, it seemed, with us, and at our first service that Hall was filled.

About the middle of April we began to think of more permanent work, and after many conferences I expressed my ideas as to the formation of a Free Christian Church, which were unanimously approved, and it was determined to go on with the work with the view of ultimately forming a church. It was towards the end of April that a Committee was formed, and the sum of 10 pounds a week guaranteed for all expenses.

The month of May went on fairly prosperously but my Committee, after a good deal of consideration, with my concurrance, unanimously resolved that it would be better to transfer our work to the Masonic Hall, which was taken accordingly for six months and we hope to find a resting place there of a more permanent kind. Every one was hopeful, apparently; but we little knew what a trial was in store.

We entered into our new home, from whence I write this, on the day before my birthday and I preached on the next day for the first time in the Masonic Hall. We were waiting daily to hear that you had concluded the arrangement with the bank, and were keeping our expenditure well within our income, from the time that we had a regular income.

But the Sunday was one of the stormiest and darkest days of the past winter; and for three or four more it was almost incessantly wet—during more than one of which there were no services in many churches at night.

In the midst of these dark days, without a word of warning the guarantee totally failed me; at the very time when we needed it most. But I felt that I dared not go back, and relying upon the collection, I determined, after receiving your telegram of June 10th with your most kind draft for 100 pounds advanced for our furniture, to go on and depend upon the Lord to revive the work, and enable me to reorganize my fainting and sorrowing little band; for they were sorry indeed, and once more, in the depth of an unusually dark and wet winter went right on. I paid at once over 90 pounds for the furnishings, and had paid about eight or ten pounds of it before your draft came—it cost me over 115—and it is all paid, but a balance of about eight pounds And then came the struggle to live, and yet go on with the work I never passed through a darker time, and light came back very slowly, indeed I was tempted at last almost to give up the struggle. The wet Sundays at the beginning had greatly checked our progress, and the continuance of winter weather, joined to the disheartening effect upon those who knew of the failure of the Committee's guarantee, affected our audiences, and our collections, too, as you may suppose, upon which I entirely depended. But I kept on, and during July earned over 12 pounds by lecturing, my entire income for June and July being under 40 pounds—out of which, say for nine weeks, I had to live and pay rent of house, besides the rent of Hall, etc.—fully three pounds per week. However, I would not incur debt for my living expenses, nor did I one penny, but paid these, and struggled on till I could see an opportunity to rally my people. I called them together at the beginning of August, and asked them to see what they could do, saying at the same time that I should decide speedily as to going on or not.

At first it seemed as if they could not do what was needed, but rapidly the work gathered strength, most mysterious providential aid was received by new conversions, and at last on August 17th a strong Committee was again formed, a capital business man as Secretary and an able young man as Treasurer, took the reins, and a well founded guarantee of a minimum sum of at least 10 pounds per week was given to me— I to pay for Hall, etc.—for at least six months. From that date—now about 11 weeks—the sum has been paid with unfailing regularity, and the Committee inform me that the prospects financially never were brighter than they are at present. We have no monied men among them, but we have, what is better, men who are kind, courteous and faithful to me and to each other, for they are, I believe, faithful to me and to Lord We shall go on, with tried and true fellow helpers, to nobler victories than we have ever yet conceived—we shall go on in the Lord's strength alone, for "The battle is the Lord's "

Did you ever study the life of Gideon and the way in which the Lord prepared him to lead, and selected 300 men to follow him to glorious victory— leaving 22,000, who were "fearful and afraid", to go home, and rejecting 9,700 braver men, that the glory might be given to the 300 whose battle cry was "the sword of the Lord and of Gideon"? 'Tis worth reading closely. I have been struck with it quite lately, and its applicability, comparing a small man with a great one, to my own circumstances We have all been tried in many ways, and may yet be tried more severely, but we are really stronger now with the few hundred earnest working people around us in the Masonic Hall than we were with the great audiences in the Theatre Royal. I am stronger far than I was then, and steadily we advance on a surer line than we could with a "mixed multitude", many of whom might grumble and want me to lead them back into the Egypt of Denominationalism and the grinding tyranny of the Pharaohs of Mammon.

With them I am done forever, come what may. I had rather learn tent making, like Paul, and preach and work as freely as he, than fill the Bishop of Sydney's seat, or the pastorate of the fattest, sleepiest, richest and most self-complacent church of the other sections of "the Laodiceans", whom I see thriving in their own eyes, though I believe in God's sight many of them are "wretched and miserable and poor and blind and naked" The vast majority of the 200,000 souls are utterly untouched by the "lukewarm" churches around, who seem to return indifference by taking care for the most part not to touch them, and very gingerly do they gather their robes together, close their eyes and their ears—their hearts being closed already—and "pass by" the dying, miserable thousands in all classes

Oh, it is pitiful to see how the name of the Lord Jesus has become a shame in many quarters through the poles-asunder inconsistency between the profession and the practice of the members of Christian churches. I feel my own life to be far from the standard, but I do not in the lives of thousands of professors see any endeavour made to fulfill the blessed will of the Lord who loved them and gave Himself for them in pain, in poverty, in toiling, in dying

But considerable as these pecuniary difficulties have been, they are really less trying than many others which are more difficult to express in words.

The city is one proverbially unimpressible in things which are not of what I might call a spectacular order The people are greatly taken by big "shows" of any kind, and objects interest them generally much more than subjects.

People who are pursuing a round of sensuous pleasures with their leisure time, money and strength, are not drawn at first by the mere announcement of one minister more in the city, of whom they know comparatively little, seeing that there are already so many in the city of whom they, alas, know too much in many cases An old Greek saying was, "Against stupidity even the gods are powerless." It is this dullness and insensibility which is the most formidable barrier to the faithful preachers of the Gospel, and I have felt its disheartening unconcern, and its tendency is to stupefy and deaden one's mental and spiritual sensibility.

. . And do not think I am murmuring at these difficulties and oppositions, as if I were specially hardly dealt with, for I do not think any such thing. I only state facts as they stand I believe the trials are good for me in every way; and that they are among the "all things" which "work together for good for them that love God"

The work exists, is a real power, despite all hindrances, and surely that is a proof which appeals to reason and to faith alike. Therefore, I will look upon these very hindrances as proofs of my being in the right place The Great Adversary does not waste ammunition upon those whom he thinks are too contemptible for him to bother greatly about. I know

211

many ministers who are occupying positions so thoroughly to the advantage of the Kingdom of Darkness that Satan would be a fool to disturb them: for they are just as Isaiah described them twenty-five centuries ago—they are "blind watchmen"—"ignorant, dumb dogs, they cannot bark, sleeping, lying down, loving to slumber, yea, they are greedy dogs which can never have enough, they are shepherds that cannot understand, they all look to their own way, every one for his gain, from his quarter".

Aye, and the last verse of that chapter (56) is true to the letter of many of them who are around us in this city. Do you think the "Roaring Lion" growls at them?

Oh no, they are on friendly terms with him, and under their very noses he drives a thriving trade, he dovours the lambs and sheep with perfect impunity from among their very flocks. Paul found his ministry for Christ a very different kind of thing—and every faithful man since has found the same. I can say truly that fear has never influenced me largely at any time; and I will not allow it just now. Paul once wrote to his friends at Corinth: "But I will tarry at Ephesus until pentecost, for a great door and effectual is opened unto me, and there are many adversaries "

And I will, by God's gracious help, tarry here as long as the Lord wills it; and since I may like Paul measure my opportunity by my difficulty, as a high tower may be measured by its shadow, then I can truly say "a great door and effectual is opened unto me", for no one can doubt the fact that "there are many adversaries".

And now, what other reasons are needed to prove my conviction well founded? No other than that given, so far as I am concerned, and yet God in love has given me many more. Instead of one key to open my lock of Difficulty, He has given me many. True, the one just alluded to looks uncommonly intricate in its construction, and it needs Faith to grasp the key called Trial, and fit it in, when one is weak and tempted. But 'tis a good key, indeed I find Trial to be a kind of Master Key—you know Trial is one of the Promises, and they are Divinely made keys. And I must not shrink when God shows me that there is no way through but a right use of Trials—so do not let any of us doubt His wisdom and love in permitting us to be severely tried—tried even in the fire

But He has given me, to carry on the simile, the keys of Blessing—many souls have been comforted, dying beds been lighted up with peace and joy, the wanderer has been restored, the young man awakened from the sleep of sin and death, the widow's tears dried, and the lonely have been brought in and are happy in the family of God. What a key that is!

Often when I have been nearest despair by reason of foolish doubts, there has come to me news of good effected of which I knew nothing before, by some words spoken, or deed done, which I had almost forgotten And then the door of my Difficulty has been flung wide open, and I have entered into the Grand Concert Hall of Heaven and by Faith's eye and ear, I have heard the song of rejoicing over a sinner restored, and have caught a Saviour's smile upon me of approval. Ah, that is indeed a splendid key

Then I have the key of Beautiful Prospect.

That key opens to me a door into the future, and shows me a wide harvest field, and many earnest reapers who are reaping mighty sheaves of the golden grain, which we are sowing now only too often in tears, and I hear a great multitude rejoicing with me. And sure as God is, these eyes shall see it "in due season". Beautiful Prospect is another name for Faith and Hope.

Then I have quite a bunch of keys called Love

There is first of all God's Eternal Love to me, and

when I am ready to give up the conflict—for my natural heart is just that of an arrant coward's—I use this key, and, behold, all is changed within, around, above me. In my heart there is Peace, the storm is at once a calm, and as I meditate on the unchanging Love I am at rest and strong again On things around, 'tis just as when the mists which sometimes enwrap all the beauties of our Harbour and its surroundings are lifted up in the mighty arms of the wind and carried away out to the ocean and dissolved. Then the sunlight streams over rocks and trees and blue dancing waters, and all the city on its many hills stands out as in a picture of Divine and imperishable beauty So, around me I see all things in new lights, and even on the darkest scenes of sin and sorrow, and on my darkest paths, I see that the Sun of Love is shining.

And to crown all, there is the Sun itself always shining by day, and when it is night I know "His banner over me is love": for streaming over the whole sky there are ten thousand suns, which the daylight concealed, that are now shining on me in the Cross, and the White Way, and endless galaxies Are not these emblems of the ever shining works of Divine Love in Redemption and in Restoration to God, whose inspired Word specially bids the weary one to look up and know that He made them by His hands, that He preserved them by His "strong power", and that "not one faileth?"

And then there is another which I shall call Brotherly Love

God never gave a man kinder friends, I sometimes think, than He has given me in those around me in my work They are not "golden" keys, perhaps, beautifully ornamented to men's eyes; but to mine, their hearts are like gold tried in the fire, bright as shining silver, and true as finest steel

They are good keys indeed. May the Lord increase

214

their number, and graciously use them to unlock many hearts now closed to the Redeemer! It is beyond telling what they have been to me, and often they have cheered me by the sight of their pleasant faces—and especially the kind, faithful, manly look which shines with confidence and love in the faces of my young men—who count it an honour to bear a name which semi-jocularly is given to them of "Dowieites"—a name which I want to see hidden behind the One Great Name of Christian, which alone God's people should bear. Yes, this key of Brotherly Love is very pleasant in its effects, for it opens up the way for me to be useful in many places, and to many persons

And besides the keys above named there are yet others

There is a key of Generous Human Confidence, which I sometimes find very useful. I find that there are in all parts of the city, and among all classes, some at least who know little of me personally, who yet confide in me very generously—of which I have lately had various proofs. This is shown at general public meetings, where I am always well received, and I find this key enables me at once to get into sympathy with my audiences and therefore I can speak more effectively. Indeed, this key opens sometimes for me the door of a very dark gate of Difficulty and that is Unpopularity, for as long as there are some in every class who confide in me, I do not fear yet through them to find a way to the hearts of many more who know nothing of me, or who are prejudiced by false rumors or mistaken impressions, such as are sure to gather around those whom it is to the interest of many to misrepresent. But this key of Generous Human Confidence will work wonders yet; and time is the great destroyer of those lies, which are born like blow flies to live but for a day, and to die forever.

With such a splendid collection of keys of all sorts and sizes, do you not think that despite the adversaries there is a "great door and effectual" opened for me in this Ephesus of Sydney, which it only needs patience, experience, faith, hope and love to rightly use?

Success is certain, unless I faint and grow weary, which I do earnestly pray the Lord to hinder: And I long for the success of winning for the Lord thousands who are perishing in sin. This is the "one thing" I want to do, and to make all else subserve this great aim. The Lord has said, and I believe, that He will provide all that is needful. I often think there is true Christian philosophy in the words of a simple hymn which says.

"At some time or other the Lord will provide:
    It may not be my time,
    It may not be thy time,
    And yet in His own time
    The Lord will provide.

Despond, then, no longer, the Lord will provide
    And this be the token—
    No word He hath spoken
    Was ever yet broken.
    The Lord will provide.

March on, then, right boldly, the sea shall divide:
    The pathway made glorious
    With shoutings victorious,
    We'll join in the chorus
    'The Lord will provide'."

. . If leaving the denomination should be a cause of offense, I can only say, is there not a cause? I am sure that is a step I am never likely to regret, and it is one I shall never retrace: for it was taken after more than a year's meditation and prayer, and has been confirmed daily since in every way. I am free to preach what I was prohibited from doing by my covenants, and I am freed from participation in the work of a body of men from whom, as a people, the Lord is withholding blessing, because of the spiritual uncleanness which is cherished in their midst. Let me give one proof, which appeals to common sense, and it will suffice to show the state of affairs: The annual meetings of the Union have just been held in Sydney, and in the report, or appended to it, there are statistics given which show that **during the last five years only 535 persons have been added to the whole membership of the churches, which number 43**   That is 107 annually for the whole denomination, or **less than three persons annually added, on the average, to each church.**   Do you think that is not a cause for humiliation and shame?

All the machinery of sabbath schools, churches, deacons, ministers, services, sermons, prayer meetings, etc. etc , and yet whilst thousands are dying and living in sin, less than three persons of net increase annually is the result

Now I do not wish to boast, but I will state a fact:

I believe there are out of that 535 of net increase at least 100 who are the direct result of my own ministry at Manly, Newtown, and elsewhere, as I could prove, I believe, had I the rolls of the churches before me. Deducting deaths and removals (who of this last of course were added to the rolls of other churches) the net increase to the church at Newtown during my ministry was about 70%, and about 20 to 30 at Manly, besides others. This, I say, was the Lord's doing; but I was the instrument, and it is a fact which still further shows what the Lord thinks of the churches. "By their fruits ye shall know them." I could say more of what these fruits are, but I forbear just now, as it would lead me away from the point I used the above facts to illustrate. Let me add here another fact which I think should be stated, namely, that if the Lord bless my ministry at the same rate as He has since last

February then my first year's work in Sydney will be more blessed than were the previous four and a half years, so far as man can judge   Surely this alone ought to prevent your making my leaving the denomination a cause of offense, else you may be otherwise fighting against the Lord. . .

The work is His. He knows I do fully consecrate myself to His service.

He knows I did not incur this heavy financial burden by my own wilful extravagance, and that much, if not all of it, is a fair charge against the work.

He will not suffer me to be put to shame, nor do I feel He desires the matter longer now to rest upon my heart and cripple my energies. This is His matter, and I leave Him to deal with you, my dear father, convinced that He will guide you, however it may be, or will permit what happens. But it must be arranged now   These delays are great hindrances to me, for I need not tell you that the incessant toil of brain and heart in my work are quite as much as I can well bear, without the added burden of this confused   money matter.

For over two and three-quarter years I have toiled on without a pause, and thank God I am in fairly good health. But I cannot tamper with myself, just now especially. Occasionally, when worried, I suffer from a peculiar and painful sickness, which Dr Neild tells me is cerebro-spinal, and caused by an undue exitement of the brain, and I vomit a pure and sometimes frothy water at such times, with all the feelings of seasickness   I do not get over it for an hour or two at least. But I never have it with mere work to any extent. It is the product of anxiety. I want to stop it: for sometimes it makes me feel a little apprehensive of worse. And for this and my dear ones' sake, and the work's sake, I am dtermined to do what I can to get this money matter into manageable shape

Therefore, I earnestly press you kindly to write me,

a candid, clear letter, telling me definitely what you think, and will or will not do. I hope you will not think me rude, if I urge you to write within two or three days of receiving this. You will confer a real favor on us both, whatever your determination is, if you will kindly do this.

Now let me again thank you for your most kind deeds towards us and please tell our mother that though I seem by some misdeeds to have been placed in her black books for awhile, that I hope she will rest assured I never can forget her many acts of goodness, and that I have not a single thought but what is respectful and kind in my mind concerning her

The fact is, I sometimes think she covets my wife and baby, and is hard towards me for keeping them here; and with her love for those I love, how can I quarrel?

She really must forgive me and restore me to her love again, and then perhaps, I shall tell her a secret I am sure she would like to know.

And now I must close. Jeanie sends her sweetest love to you all and we both desire our loving remembrances to our other father and mother, and to every member of the family tribe, whom may God bless.

I am,

Your affectionate son,

John Alexander Dowie.

(Replies to a minister who writes protesting against the circulation of tracts in his parish —May 22, 1879.)

Dear Sir

In reply to your rude note of yesterday, I have to say,—

1. I do not recognize your right to request any information from me concerning any of my actions, or as to what instructions I give to those who are kind enough to cooperate with me in Christian service.

2. At the same time, I may say that your existence, much less your Sabbath School, has never been mentioned by me for I should say, over a year, and that, whilst I leave my people entirely to their own discretion as to where and to whom they distribute my weekly tract, I gave them no instructions to distribute them in P— and was entirely ignorant that they were distributed there until I received your note.

3. Had I any respect for your judgment of anything I might say, or do, or write, I would feel that your assertion that my tract of last Sabbath "was calculated very seriously to unsettle the minds of the young and injure their moral tone", to be a statement demanding instant explanation; but, as I consider your judgment to be as feeble and incapable as your ministry, I do not reckon it to be of the slightest value, and it would be foolish to be angry or vexed about it, much less to be "filled with indignation", as you say you were with my "obnoxious paper".

4. It may interest you to know that no fewer than 14,000 of these very "obnoxious papers" have been circulated, and that the liquor dealers and modern Pharisees generally agree with you in your opinion, but that there are many thousands of persons who hold a different opinion and have actually said they did good, which is of course quite a mistake in your profound judgment Also that 100,000 similar tracts written by me have recently been circulated in Sydney.

5. I wish I knew who distributed these "obnoxious tracts" among your flock, I would certainly commend his choice of a field, and will certainly do nothing to hinder "perpetuating so gross an impertinence", notwithstanding your awful (ridiculously so) threat to "take very vigorous steps to put a stop to it".

With profound pity for you, I am,

Truly yours,

John Alexander Dowie.

(Written to his father, Sept. 26, 1879)

.. There is no true "honour" but that which "cometh from above", nor any "nobility" but the aristocracy of grace   How few men seem really to believe this, and whilst they profess to despise mere worldly applause who name Christ's name and say they glory in the Cross and its attendant shame, yet even of these there are few who are not seekers of human honours and worldly applause

I want my boy to obtain "a good degree" in heaven, and if he does that I care not if he never gets a degree of any kind of honour on earth.

Though I am poor, I never more cordially despised all who make gods of riches, and not for all the gold of Australia and all it could purchase, would I bow down and worship the golden calf which is the leading Divinity of the day   Empty honours and soulless gold go hand in hand with every form of hypocrisy and uncleanness to demoralize our fair Australian land, and every day supplies abundant proof.

> "Ill fares the land, to hastening ills a prey,
> Where wealth accumulates but men decay."

And Sydney, sometimes, seems to me to be literally "rotting" as to its people, for in body and in mind the decay, through iniquity and vanity of every kind of the people is evident to all who have eyes to see and ears to hear. I had rather my boy would die this day than live to be the corrupt beast that thousands of men are in this city, and only the hope that he will be a blessing in his time could make me wish him to live at all. If I thought he would be a "wretch con-centered all in self" in days to come, my misery would be greater than I could bear and live. But I pray and toil on in the hope and earnest desire that I shall in him give to the Lord and for His service a man who shall "destroy the works of the devil" wherever he finds them, set free the captives, bind up the broken hearts and homes around him, and extend the Kingdom of Righteousness and Joy and Peace on the earth, and then go to be forever with the Lord

.   You will see that page five of this letter bears date September 26, or more than a month from its beginning   Interruptions, cares, toils, difficulties, dangers, temptations, weariness, sadnesses, victories, conflicts, watchings, studies, deaths, births, burials, baptisms, marriages, writing, speaking, and employments of all kinds have intervened within that month enough, if written, to fill a volume. I know you would like to know and I to tell, more than time and pen and ink will enable me to express. How gladly would I spend an hour with you every day if you were near and tell you of the way the Lord has led me, of how good and merciful He has been, how He has sustained me when ready to faint and delivered me from despairs and doubts, doing great things for me "whereof we are glad" He has given me victory over devils invisible, and very visible too ; and "in perils amongst false brethren" He has brought me through. This day I stand amid many dangers, but my feet are on the Rock, and my head is above the waters, nor can I dare to despair. for the Lord will bring me through. "What shall we say then to these things? If GOD be for us, WHO can be against us?" He that spared not His own Son, but delivered Him up for us all, how shall He not also with Him FREELY GIVE US ALL THINGS?" With such assurances, to doubt is to dishonour God, and with such provision as ALL THINGS needful for life and work I am ashamed to reflect upon my weariness and discouragement Who can be against me, since God is for me?

What is the chaff, when the breath of God's Spirit can in a moment drive it away?

There is not a shadow of doubt in my mind that

my way would have been a thousand fold brighter and more successful had I feared none and nothing but had trusted constantly and fully in the Lord So that though I have to record triumphs, yet it is my disgrace that, with such promises and such unemployed powers, I should have done so little, where there was so much to be done.

You would see from the tracts which I have sent to you from week to week that I have preached every Lord's Day in the Victoria Theatre, Pitt Street, since the second Sunday in this year. Our audiences in the morning have been small from many evident causes; but I am sure that in the evening I have had the largest regular congregation of men to be found in any building for Christian worship in this city, not excepting Pitt Street Congregational Church and its "found-wanting" minister. He has not dared to attempt a word of reply to my lectures on "The Drama, the Press and the Pulpit," and to other severe criticisms of his foolish speaking on the Roman Catholic and Educational questions. The press and he form "a mutual admiration society," and flatter each other in fine style; but the people are beginning to get free from being press-ridden as well as priest-ridden, from the tyranny of the "scribe" as well as the "Pharisees." I often launch out against our corrupt press, but though there are reporters there every evening, they dare not print what I say nor dare they attack it; for like other scribes long ago, they are saying, "we fear the people: for all hold John as a prophet"

I dare say you will laugh, as I do, whilst I write, and doubtless the quotation does not exactly fit, though it is not without force, since friends are pretty well agreed that the people generally have a general respect for me, of which I have many evidences—not the least being that thousands of them hear me gladly, and that for months past I have been asked to become a candidate for their representation in Sydney at the next general election, a fact which seems to be widely known, and which I am sure very largely accounts for the comparative silence of the press against me just now. But enough about the press, which is one of my abominations—as at present conducted: for its deity is Mammon.

Our audiences have often filled the theatre to its utmost capacity with even the standing room occupied, and I think that for the last thirty Sundays our average has been fully 1000 We have written 20 tracts and printed and distributed 200,750 copies—thousands of which have been sent to all parts of the Colony, to other Colonies of Australia and to many lands.

The results of this preaching God alone knows and only eternity will disclose, but we have been privileged constantly to see results to some little extent, and I do not know of a single fruitless service in the theatre, or a tract from which some good has not come Were I to go into details it would be too much for my time and perhaps your patience. Drunkards reclaimed, infidels converted, sensualists purified, homes made happy, and sinners in various conditions reconciled to God in Christ.

We have also fought a good fight against the foes of the Lord who rule in this city and land—especially against the Liquorocracy and Snobocracy of Sydney who are such a curse to the people generally. In political and social life these are serious hindrances to real progress in spiritual life. They who despise the Lord are the honoured of the land, and false and foul and devilish principles are the laws of their lives. There are few who do not worship the golden calf, and there can be no more debasing idolatry—none more cruel or heartless Vice is under high patronage, and money covers a multitude of sins. There are hundreds of dens of iniquity in this city where awful deeds are done, such as lands sunk in barbarism and ignorance could not exceed in horror, brutality and shame. Diseases of the foulest kind are literally corrupting the bodies and cursing unborn generations with a heritage of pain, crime and misery awful to contemplate. But to all this the Church of Christ seems deaf and blind, and most certainly it is for the most part dumb. I see clearly that unless I can carry my principles into practical effect in our legislation, I shall only be beating the air for the most part, as so many are doing, and I believe that my ministry in this city must carry me into the legislature ere I can fulfill it.

There are many hundreds who desire it, and they say there are thousands who will hail my candidature for East or West Sydney with delight, and send me into the House with a large majority. I do not know if this be so to the extent my friends imagine. I know the enemy is numerous and strong, also. But at the same time necessity imposes upon me the duty, as from the Lord, of my offering myself for this work, because I do not see who is likely to do it if I decline.

Of course, my preaching and church work will go on. I do not see why it should cease. Paul could be a tent maker and an apostle, I can surely be a law maker and a minister. I do not covet it for position, it can give me none higher than I have; but since I am determined to do all the good I can while I live, I do desire now to be in the position to do it in the place where it will be most far reaching and effective in its influence. It seems to me that a reform of our social life is impossible without a reform in the laws which now license vice and promote crime.

Politicians are not in earnest in their professions, and a new class of men must come to the front in Australia if good work is to be done. We are now on the eve of great changes. Old political parties are dying out, and a few years more must see the end of political tricksters, to whom legislation has been a form of gambling for the most part. Our care must be to take advantage of the present position to do our part

8

to promote righteousness in our Government and laws, for triumphant iniquity everywhere opposes the spread of the Gospel and sows future harvests of awful sin and sorrow. Our young men are decaying fast, and a kind of dull despair of all change for the better is seizing upon many who see things as they are, whilst the great majority walk about as in an opium eater's dream, so far as acute perception of present dangers is concerned Nothing but God's own Spirit can revive them I look for a revival in politics, family life, social intercourse, business pursuits, etc., where God's truth shall purify and bless the people so that they toil not in vain This revival will not proceed from the churches as they are now constituted. They will need to be purged ere they can bless others. . . .

The work is the Lord's and wondrous in my eyes. But I know it might be better done. Indeed, were we free from money care, I am sure it would be. Would that the Lord's time were come to favor us in that way! It would take long to tell you all about these matters, and only worry you needlessly; for I am sure if you were rich in earthly treasures you would be forward to aid us I feel sure of that, and I therefore do not care to bother you about these matters.

Some day, I am certain, the Lord will remove this trial and meanwhile I go on, not doubting His promise. I would rather be poor and in need, than rich and heartless

Whatever will some Christians say when they see the Lord and give an account of their meanness towards His work? They spend thousands on houses, lands and luxuries, and grudge shillings to extend the Kingdom of Him to whom they owe all. If I were engaged in establishing a business, I might get a thousand pounds to help me, far more readily than I would now get a thousand pence to save immortal souls from death and ruin.

But do not let us forget that the Christian Church

never owed its origin to the rich on earth, but to the poor, even to Him "who for our sakes became poor," and the Apostolic Missionary Society had probably no balance at its credit anywhere on earth—and yet what Society since, has done such work for the Lord? "God hath chosen the weak things of the earth."

Among those present at our services there are frequently several ministers—indeed, there are always one or more present. They are, of course, principally ministers from other Colonies or from another country. My sermons are, I know, constantly discussed and are evidently not without interest to the sermon-makers who visit the city. In my afternoon addresses, I have seen city ministers of various denominations present. I tell you these things that you may know that my work is an object of at least curiosity to the churches, and, I am afraid, of distrust to many who dislike its nonsectarian character, and, what is more felt, find that there are sheep from all their folds who are getting too much attached to us for their liking.

Of course, humanly speaking, the task has always been too great for me, and I gladly acknowledge that only God's own power could have sustained me and made me thus useful to many; and to God, therefore, I very sincerely give the glory. But it is a satisfaction full of cheer that should the work cease tomorrow, it will not be that my work has been unsuccessful in every sense as a preacher, but because it has not been financially supported as it ought to have been. Yet that reproach would fall upon others, not on me. My hope is, though, that it is being wiped away, and that God will carry the work through, and not let such reproach fall upon any. Now, even one year and eight months have proved my part of it, and I look back and say gratefully that it has covered the ablest and most fruitful period of my ministry. God has "sealed" it in an unmistakable way, and if we can only overcome present difficulties, there lies before us a glorious future, if spared to labour in this city. Yet, I am not anxious about the matter, assured that it is God's own hand that leadeth me There must always be work for me so long as the world is before me for my parish, and a field for labour whenever there is a man who knows not the Lord I want to go on here, if it be God's will, and I think it is; but most of all, I want to do right and to go or stay as the Lord may decide. "A good soldier" must be ready to fight any enemy, at any time, and anywhere. I want to be such a soldier Therefore, 'tis for me to obey, and for my Leader to direct. I bless God I have come to that. I am sure it is right I shall work as if I were to stay all my life in Sydney; but I shall hold myself ready at any time to go to London or anywhere. To do that "will" is my increasing delight, and that I only care that I bear to those around may do it in every relation that I bear to those around me, and to those whom God has given. And my keenest sorrow is to err from the way that "will" so lovingly appoints.

But I daresay you will be wanting to know about our great International Exhibition There is no doubt it is a grand display of manufactures from Europe, America and even Asia (for Japan and the Straits' Settlement and Ceylon are well represented.) There is a good display, too, from the other Colonies, but I am sorry to say that South Australia is about the poorest and shabbiest court in the building. I am sure you could have done better had you tried New Zealand appears well and so does Victoria. But in my opinion, Queensland has about the most interesting display of its natural products, arranged with great taste and skill, of any.

The building is very finely decorated within and occupies the finest position in Sydney. The view from the towers is indescribably beautiful, even to us who have it before us so constantly, in part; for it is most comprehensive—the city, the suburbs on every side, the harbor, the hills, etc., around make up a living picture of great grandeur

In front of the great building—The Garden Palace is its official name—there is a great pyramid, colored like gold, showing that no less than 274,000,000 pounds worth have been raised since the discovery of gold in Australia.

But that is only enough at the most to pay for England's drink bill for two years, and at the rate we are now drinking that sum is drunk in about ten or twelve years in Australia. Our portion of the gold raised is valued at about 35,000,000 pounds—but we drink that sum in seven years. The pyramid is very suggestive looked at thus; and I fear it is but too poorly regarded

It is very late and I am very tired. You are all ever in our prayers and in our hearts. We meet you every night at our Father's blessed mercy seat   We desire you to accept our warmest love, and our keen regret we cannot better manifest it   I would like to have you all here, had I as much room in my house as you occupy in my heart, I could entertain you grandly, but I cannot. Remember us with all affection, for we love you all. I am sorry there is a cloud anywhere; but I shall do nothing to increase it. Life is too short for needless strife. I need all my strength for the Lord's battles. I do trust this will find you well, dear father and mother   May the Lord bless you. I bless you in my heart for all your goodness to me, and I pray the Lord to give you every needed grace, and everlasting love and joy and peace.

Your affectionate son,

John Alexander Dowie.

. . . . God has been very gracious to me in the midst of many conflicts and trials; for He has sustained me and my dear ones in life and peace, He has rewarded my "little faith" with great blessings, such as make men to wonder and ponder; He has defeated my foes and disappointed their evil desires and predictions; He has encouraged the drooping hearts of some whose faith had well nigh failed; He has filled with alarm and fear the souls of evil men and evil spirits, who would fain have destroyed me long ago; He has opened up before me such far reaching harvest fields of labour, and filled me with such desires, and supplied me with such powers to do good, that I am sometimes lost in wonder, love and praise, as I see all His mercies, which form so glorious a crown to His goodness. How can I praise Him,—my tongue cannot find words to express my imperfect conceptions of His great grace to me in all my past, in all my present, and in all I hope, by His grace, to be and do!

Sometimes my inexpressible thoughts of God's goodness and care for one so unworthy as I am fill me with awe, and a deep sense of responsibility, lest I should prove unable or unstable, and so bring reproach upon the glorious name I bear as the redeemed and regenerated object of Jesus' love and power.

For I am utterly weak in myself—neither body, nor mind, nor spirit are strong enough to bear or do His will, unless He strengthened me at every point, in every moment of my life. I lean, then, and I desire now and ever to do so, upon Him "Who not in vain experienced every human pain," and there I find it true that His strength is made perfect in my weakness, and His grace is sufficient for me.

The future is solemn, the present is full of perils, and of golden opportunities too; but I need prayer from praying hearts on earth who love me well—and who can tell how much I owe, under God, to the faithful prayers of humanly obscure but divinely powerful souls, who have unceasingly prayed for me since I came into this city, alone in a human sense, to do battle for the Lord?

(Written to his father and mother, in March, 1879, Sidney, N. S. Wales.)

. . How the world turns at the very words "He's rich!" But it need not try its blandishments— rich or poor, I am against all that is wrong in the world. I will still be the foe of its vices, the friend of all whom it oppresses I value my probable power in a money sense most of all for the good it will now enable me to do, and the evils I may now resist, check, and so far as I can, destroy. I look forward to my church, my house, my control of a newspaper, my seat in the Legislature, my increased and strengthened influence upon the public mind, as so many possible talents to be employed for my Lord I hear Him say —"Occupy till I come"—and in His name I shall make these means for extending His dominion amongst men and seizing, so far as I can, upon the fair provinces which Satan now rules over in social, ecclesiastical, and political affairs. I want to "occupy" these provinces with permanent garrisons—"armies of occupation" in fact—for the Lord Jesus Christ, and glad will I be, if life is spared, to hand over my sword to my son, and noble men yet to arise, that they may carry on yet more fully what I have begun. But who can tell what may happen? Life is very uncertain. Tomorrow's sun may never shine on earth for me. I may never see the desire of my heart. There is often but a step betwixt one and death

This was the case last Wednesday night. I fell, when crossing the railway line alone on a dark night, about five miles from town, as I was running to the station in time for an approaching train, the rumble of which I could hear in the distance I came down with a terrific thud upon my face right on the rail, over which the coming train must pass, and for a few seconds lost consciousness, or nearly so; but remembering my peril, I managed to roll off in some way,

and got to my feet In less than a minute or so the
train dashed up to the station, to which I was close,
and just reached as the train did. Then I found that
I was bleeding profusely from a rather deep cut on
my left eyebrow I bound up my head with my
handkerchief, jumped into the train, and when I got
to Sydney drove home in a cab, feeling very faint.
But, by God's mercy, I got over it quickly, and the
wound is now nearly quite healed up

Was this not a providential escape? I was quite
alone, the night was very dark, it was past ten o'clock,
I had been conducting a marriage near P— and afterwards spent a few hours in the house of Mr. S—, one
of my old Newtown deacons, about a mile and a
half from the station Had I remained unconscious
for two minutes, I would have been without doubt
cut to pieces, for no eye of man saw me fall, so far as
I am aware. But God saw me, and He in His mercy
rescued me from so sudden and terrible a form of
death.

I have a good hope, though, that to die for me is
gain; yet it may be for the sake of others, and my
Lord's work, best for me to live awhile yet on earth.
Indeed it must be, since He delivered me, for I am
sure He did This nearness to death has made me
realize more deeply how serious it is to live. . . .

Your most welcome letter of various dates reached
me on March 1st. We experienced a very great
pleasure in reading it, and I thank you for your kind
words, which are in such marked contrast to those we
have received from South Australia, but of which I
do not intend taking any notice whatever—I would
scorn to defend myself against charges which would
fain place me on a level with a liar, a thief, a hypocrite,
and a fool. My only observation to you concerning
these wicked and foolish Kenttown letters is, that
they are as untrue as they are unkind and unchristian.

If they had been true, then I could not have done better than followed Judas Iscariot's example, who "went and hanged himself," for I should have been unfit to live, so intolerable an existence as must have been mine.

I do not envy the polluted mind from whence such evil thoughts and words could flow, nor the sublime compound of impudence, ignorance, and peerless egotism which shines in every sentence of these productions, in which there does not throb one feeling of love to God or man, nor one single word which recognizes the dignity and glory of self-denying service for Christ's sake.

They breathe the meanness of a soul which never rises above the pecuniary estimate of life, which would have called Christ a fool for not making friends with the Pharisees, or a spendthrift because He was homeless and moneyless, or a lunatic because He preferred death and a Cross to life on earth and a Crown. Does such a man dare to call himself a follower of Jesus, or dare to say his highest glory is in treading in His footsteps? I tell you that there are charges in these letters, and sentiments too, which even the Devil himself would more than hesitate to utter concerning me —for, even in Sydney, my enemies would call him a fool for his pains. But I will say no more. Lies are not immortal, and sooner or late they return to their parents, and driven out of the world with scorn they return to the heart from whence they came out, no longer plausible and fresh looking, they are vile, loathsome, stinking, slimy reptiles with poison fangs, which coil themselves around the soul which produced them God have mercy upon the liar, for he burns in the unquenchable fire which falsehood kindles and which only eternal love can supplant!

But not to me belongs vengeance—'tis to God that belongs, with Whom also is power and mercy, and, as for such power of forgiveness as I possess, it was exercised long ago. My one regret is that I am under temporary monetary obligations to one who has acted in such a way, and my consolation therein is that I never incurred such obligation by my own action, but that it all sprang from his own first origination, as I can easily prove. Meanwhile, my hope and faith are strong that ere long the Lord will deliver me out of the hands of this Philistine, who is, also, so closely related to me I cannot doubt that the Lord Jesus is a stronger friend to me, than this man can prove a foe I know them both, and God knows whom I trust. He has delivered from all my fears, and it sometimes makes me smile to see how weak and powerless men are to hurt me, so safely and tenderly does the Chief Shepherd keep and care for me.

However, this is the first reference which I have made to this matter in my correspondence with you, and I have done it, not to vindicate myself—for "God is my judge"—not to condemn others—for to their own Master they stand or fall—not to give anyone pain needlessly—for that would be sinful—and not to invoke comment upon the matter from you—for that would lead to endless letter writing without good result. I have only written what I have because I am your son, who does not wish that any shadow should rest upon your thoughts of me, and because I am sure you will believe me without further proof, when I solemnly declare to you, that the charges which have been made against me are utterly baseless in fact, so far as they reflect upon my character and uprightness in conduct.

There is, at the same time, another object which may be obtained by this reference and it is this, that you may use your discretion in communicating the position which I take in this matter, respecting further intercourse I may say that, after long meditation and prayer, I came to the conclusion that I would not write another line nor hold any further correspondence, for if I had answered, or were not to answer his last letter, as it must be dealt with if I replied at all, I would, in his present state of mind and heart, fail to do good, so far as I now see. Therefore, I shall hold no intercourse with him whatever, and neither wish to see him nor hear from him any more, unless he is prepared to recall the shameful insults he has heaped upon me. He has vexed my heart, and hindered my work more than all my difficulties put together, and if men generally had dealt with me in anything like the same spirit, I must have failed long ago There is not one kind word of encouragement, or of hope, in all his writing Had I been living the life of an abandoned prodigal, he could not have employed harsher terms of reproach. He classes me with those who "have denied the faith and are worse than infidels;" he tells me that I have incurred God's curse by bringing to Him robbery for a burnt offering; he declares to me "your" (that is, my) "conduct has been simply disgraceful," he says I have shown "an ungovernable temper," he tells me that "it now appears that your work in Sydney is a failure," he calls me "a fool" in half a dozen places, ignores all I have written, misrepresents facts which were set before him with the utmost clearness, and abuses me from beginning to end, without exception, through a letter of eight pages The only pause in this raging is when he pauses to contemplate, by way of contrast, his own spotless virtue, and his exalted position as a prosperous man To give you an instance, take the following words, which succeed the epithet "pauper" as applied to me, which word doubtless suggested the remarkable sentence. "I firmly believe" (this then is his true creed), "that the secret of my prosperity in Adelaide is the fact that I leaned upon no one whatever for help in money matters; but trusted entirely in my own energies and good management" Is not this a most astounding creed for a professional Christian man? Has God no part in that which this man possesses? Then, though I am no prophet, I may prophesy that, unless he repents quickly, God will write speedily his epitaph, as He did on the tomb of the rich man in Christ's parable, in two emphatic words—"Thou Fool." I say to him, he should read these words,—"Who maketh thee to differ from another? and what hast thou that thou didst not receive? Now, if thou didst receive it, why dost thou glory, as if thou didst not receive it?"

Let him take care lest the angel of the Lord smite him as he did king Herod, "because he gave not God the glory." That proud fool was eaten up with worms, and I fear me the loathsome worms have begun their work on thy proud heart that sayest, "my prosperity is my own doing; I leaned on no one, I trusted entirely in my own strength and my own wisdom!" Didst thou never read, "Trust in the Lord with all thine heart, and lean not to thine own understanding," or, "He that trusteth in his riches is a fool," or, "He that trusteth in his own heart is a fool?" These words are Divine, and will last long after thou hast, in body, mingled with the dust; long after thy ledgers have vanished into the smoke of the last fire, should they last so long; and these words will appear awful to thee at the judgment seat of Christ, unless thou dost repent, O miserable boaster. "Lo, thou trustest in the staff of this broken reed, in Egypt (the world), whereon if a man lean, it will go into his hand, and pierce it." Yea, and it will go deeper still, it will "pierce thy heart through with many sorrows," and then fling thee overboard to "drown in sin and perdition," unless thou hast a care for thy soul's true welfare

'Tis in these words that I would reply to such blasphemous boasting and pride

As to the charges, of which I have quoted a few in this boaster's own language, I am under no necessity to reply; they bear their reputation on their face, as lies generally do, and I can dare proof of one of them with a calm conscience. God has justified me, and is justifying me; and He will give such an answer yet as will put this man to shame, who dares to make out that I am rather a son of Belial, than a son and servant of God. Indeed, ever since I received that letter, now more than a month ago, I seem to hear a voice Divine saying, "The Lord shall fight for you and ye shall hold your peace," and I have obeyed the word. What has been the result? This: the work has been blessed in an unprecedented degree, and now appears to be entering upon a period of most hopeful character, and I do from my inmost soul give all the glory to God, from whom alone I receive power and blessing. The marvelous success I now enjoy is God's answer to the declaration of my traducer that I had failed.

I will not go further back, at present, than the beginning of this year, on the first Sunday of which I preached my first sermon in the Masonic Hall, where for seven months I had preached, under circumstances I venture to say of such keen trial as few men are called upon to pass through. God alone knows my temptations and distress during that time. It was one unbroken period of faith endurance—there were few sunny days, and there were protracted drouths, as it were, mingled with dark nights of tempest, when we must have gone under had not Christ been in the vessel. The place was a most unsuitable one, and that alone greatly damaged the work. But I dare not just now attempt a history of that time—which I now see was most blessed to my own soul, and which most thoroughly sifted my people. I do not complain of one single grief or sorrow the Lord permitted me, in His unerring love and wisdom to me; for they have all been blessings in disguise, or have been overruled for my good, without a single exception.

They were painful, but now I sing already "the conquerer's song," for the Lord has delivered me, or is delivering me, out of them all

"Why should I complain of want or distress,
Temptation or pain? He told me no less
The heirs of salvation I know from His Word,
Through much tribulation must follow their Lord."

I dare say, when Gideon's host melted away from 32,000 men to 300, he was not without temptation to fear that he would be crushed by the Midianitish foe. But the Lord took "the fearful and afraid" away, ay and thousands beside, "lest Israel vaunt themselves against me, saying, Mine own hand hath saved me"

He did that, too, with me. He emptied my exchequer often; He reduced my congregations to a very small number often, He diminished my helpers, and took away all my trust in man until I leaned on Himself alone; He pointed the way to bolder enterprises in the face of an utter want of apparent resources, and then when I obeyed, He proved His faithfulness by giving me the most glorious victories I have ever won, in this battle which is the Lord's

Tomorrow will be the tenth Sunday of preaching in the Victoria Theatre, and I can say that every Sunday has shown a steady and large increase in the attendance, an increase in spiritual results, and an increase in material resources As to the last of these, I will only mention this fact, that last Tuesday evening in the Temperance Hall a meeting of my people was held at which the sum of 15 pounds per week, for all expenses, was guaranteed for the next three months certain, and a committee was formed to relieve me entirely of all perosnal responsibilities.

The expenses of Theatre, handbills, advertising, etc, come to 7 pounds per week, which will leave me 8 pounds for my personal income, and if our prosperity increases, then I shall see my way to more.

Of course, I shall need to have to pay up what I am behind now, but, if the Lord spare my life and give me health and success, it will not be long ere I shall "owe no man anything" but to love them, as God requires, and as I do—I feel I owe love to all men, when I remember God's love to me

Does it look like failure, or does it look like something very different, even from a temporal point of view? Of course, I do not expect that it will please my traducer, even though it is the Lord's doings; for I fear that he imagines God's way of dealing with me could be greatly improved upon, if application for advice were only made to him But I believe in "the Lord's doing" infinitely better for me, than if I "lean on no one," or "trust entirely in my own energies and good management." In fact, I have such confidence in the Lord, **even** "in money matters," O mine enemy, that I am determined He shall be my Banker and my sole Executor should I die tonight, or should I live for forty years, and for this reason, He has never failed those who have "**put their trust in Him**," which can be said of no other.

I would reckon it to be a shameful insult to God were I to say I could trust Him with my eternal spirit, and yet would hesitate to entrust Him with the care of my body, and I know of nothing which can be meaner or more detestable than such a course would be.

I am afraid that many men are treating Christ as if He were a kind of spiritual Assurance Agent who takes the risk of insuring their souls for a small premium of money or lip service, so that, in case of accidents, heaven may in this way be bound to make things all right Oh, what a terrible awakening awaits those who make a "house of merchandise" of God's Temple, and who reckoned their "prosperity" and that of others to depend on pounds, shillings and pence, and that God had no part in even that!

I have had very keen trials in money matters; but I and Jeanie have no personal extravagance with which we can reproach ourselves 'Tis the work which has demanded of us heavy sacrifices All the way through I have believed that it would be blessed And God has rewarded the faith which His Spirit has sustained in my heart

The work which I am now doing I think is quite unique in its character, so far as I know, in any of the Australian Colonies Connected with none of the denominations, aided by none, hindered by many, and looked askance at by all, I have gathered one of the largest congregations of men to be found in this city —and largely of such men as never enter a Christian church edifice. Nine-tenths fully of those attending are men from twenty to fifty years of age with some older and younger—there are also not a few gray heads. This kind of congregation is rare here, and most of the churches are three-fourths female in their congregations.

But most striking of all, I have won the respect and confidence of Free Thinkers in no small numbers, and I never preach at night without seeing among my audience numbers of men who have been connected with the Free Thought and Spiritualistic Societies of this city. I have the joy of knowing that some of them are free thinkers now of the right stamp, made free by Christ, the Truth

But I could fill pages with the stories of strange people we have drawn up in our deep sea fishing net. Perhaps one of the strangest just now is a giant looking gray headed old Mormon—I believe he was an Elder or something of the sort—who has been in this city for many years—generally known as "Mormon Joe." He is a most singular man, and, I cannot say that he would pass muster anywhere as an orthodox Christian, but he is an acute thinker, a fluent, earnest

240

talker, and a stern lover of Truth and Righteousness, according to his light. Then, as a different specimen, there is a Scotchman, whose case is most remarkable, and the details would fill pages. Drink had been his ruin and nearly his death. It had got him into bad company, and into prison for various offenses in Victoria, and here, during the last five or six years. He was three years in Pentridge Gaol, Melbourne, for horse-stealing when on a drunken spree; then, after various adventures, he came to this colony, and at New Castle was more successful in his business, but spent it all in drink shops. Eventually he came to Sydney. However, being utterly godless and passionately fond of drink he again got into trouble, and was sent for several days to prison because he could not pay a fine imposed upon him at the Central Police Court. After this he drank harder than ever, and at last, feeling very ill, he wandered away out into the country, until he reached the foot of the Blue Mountains, then a fearful time followed, for he was in the awful grip of delirium tremens. Wandering into the mountains he got lost in the bush, extraordinary fancies possessing him in the intervals of his increasing bodily torture. One of his fancies was that he fought with bushrangers and was severely wounded by their swords.

Poor fellow, his wounds were self-inflicted. He had cut his throat with a razor which he carried, and nearly five days after he left he was found on the railway line through the mountains by some plate-layers in a horrible condition, covered with blood, unable to speak, and apparantly dying. He was removed to the Sydney infirmary where eventually he recovered. He was then tried at Quarter Sessions for attempted suicide, and in consideration of his great sufferings he was discharged. He wandered about the streets in great misery, constantly tempted to spend for drink the few pence which he had, and, finding that he could get no

241

employment, he became very despondent He had
had very little food, and had only four pence left and
was utterly without hope As he wandered through
the streets one of our young men accosted him and
gave him one of our handbills and got him to promise
to come to the service. But, when he came to the door
his heart failed him, and he was shrinking back, when
he heard my voice, and some words fell on his ear,
and into his heart, which caused him to go in at once.
Everything seemed intended for him. Old memories
of a Christian home in Glasgow were awakened, and
new thoughts, too, in his despairing heart, and ere the
sermon had closed, he had given his heart to God.
Deeply moved, he went out with the crowd As he
approached the door he saw the collection plate, and
was regretting his poverty, when suddenly he remembered that he had four pence left. He put the four
pennies in the plate, and passed out into the night,
knowing that he would need to sleep in the streets or
in the park But he scarcely slept at all, he prayed
a good deal, and asked as a token of mercy that he
might get work the next day. The morning came
He got work early that day, and since then—more
than a month—he has procured decent clothes, I have
had long conversations with him, and dressed so
respectably, with a pleasant countenance, and calm
manner, it is difficult to imagine him as he has been,
until you hear him speak of his past, when the tremor
of his speech and the emotion which fills his eyes with
tears, shows you how he has sinned and suffered.

But it would not be right for me to leave you to
think that our congregation solely consists of such
classes as are represented by the two I have named
There are many in it who have been connected for
many years with every denomination in the city, I
think. There are others, besides, who come irregu-
larly, and whose prejudices are passing away Nor
must I forget to name the noble band from my late

church at Newtown, who have stood by me with a splendid courage and self-sacrifice which is beyond praise, coming in three miles, fair or stormy weather alike,—nearly all of whom are the fruits of my ministry there, and all of them coming without a word of solicitation on my part; for except the outcast and careless, I have never solicited a single human being to attend my ministry

In the front of that noble band, who are the very heart center of my people, there stand two men— Frank Allum and Thomas S Hutchinson—and, under God, it is to these two men we owe very much of our success In point of honour they stand equal in my love and confidence, and in the respect they receive from every one who comes into contact with them. They are both the fruits of my ministry at Newtown. Such men as they are rarely found amongst men on earth, and for real goodness of heart, cheerfulness of manners, coupled with simplicity of faith, and perfect consistency of life, they have never been surpassed in my experience These two men are representatives of not a few who are attending my ministry. Surely there never was a more singular company banded together to sustain a Christian minister

We are, by God's mercy, building up a church which shall yet do great work for the Lord in this city and land. I do not fear either the dangers or difficulties which stand like "lions in the way," if God give me only bodily and mental health, added to "the grace sufficient" which He has never withheld when I have gone forward with the rod of faith, which is mightier even than Moses' and Aaron's rods.

But there is need for every virtue and every grace; and were I not sure that I am where the Lord would have me be, the great burden of this work would be too much for me Yet as it is, loads which seem as mountains to many outside are feathers light as air to me, since God puts in me the strength of His own

Spirit to bear them. I do humbly hope, that I am now at the end of the difficulties as to the finances of the work, and that we are about to enter upon a period where the only concern will be how best to do it

My rather bold use of the printing press has been fully justified by the results, and I am now speaking weekly, through my weekly tracts, to many thousands of homes in this city. People send them to their friends in the country districts, in the other Colonies, and in England; and you will find them here and there pasted up on the walls of offices, in the cabins of sailors, etc. On the Sundays, I observe many persons reading them in the parks and on the streets, and many persons stop our distributors now and ask for one. The Theatre is situated in the very center of all the traffic in the city, and many passers by to whom they are given under the gas lights of the front entrance, stand and read them, and often afterward turn and go in. I shall keep on, therefore, writing a new one every week

My successor at Newtown has been telling his audience that "amusements," so-called, ought to be indulged in, and that he would as soon die playing a game of billiards as in a prayer meeting, etc. Not to be outdone by his neighbors, Mr. J— followed suit, and made a great panegyric upon the Theatre and its noble capabilities.

I can stand it no longer, so I have now entered the field, and shall lecture, if God will, on Sunday evening next on "The Drama, the Press, and the Pulpit." I am especially provoked by the gross ignorance, and daring untruth of his representations concerning the ancient Greek drama. He says,—"The tragedies of Aeschylas and Sophocles contain high moral and religious teaching. They represent men as they ought to be, not as they were. But the theatrical assemblies of the ancient Greeks were no more satisfied than theatrical audiences of modern Englishmen with ideal pictures of a noble life."

Now when I tell you that the three tragedies are so disgustingly filthy in their plots, full of incests, parricides, fratricides and horrible fornications that it would be impossible even among men to read them aloud without shame, and that some of them set forth the disgusting lasciviousness of the gods and their bestial natures without any sense of shame, I ask you, wherein lies their "high moral and religious teaching" in this nineteenth century? What have these heathen poets of five centuries before Christ to tell us of "high morals," when the most shameless immoralities were ascribed by their worshippers even to the gods, and what kind of "religious teaching" is that which peoples the heavens with monsters, who hated and fought with each other, and wreaked their diabolic passions in leading men to commit the foulest of deeds? The "Agamemnon" and "Libation Pourers," two of "Aeschylus'" tragedies and the "Oedippas Tyrannus" and the "Oedippas Coloneus," two of Sophocles', are so horrible that one shudders even to recall their plots, and so filthy that they would not be tolerated for a moment on the boards of even the vilest theatre. In the first two named, a wife of a great king dishonours herself and, aided by her paramour, murders her husband, both of whom are in turn murdered by a son of that husband, whilst, as episodes, Agamemnon, leader of the Greeks at the siege of Troy—sacrifices to the gods his own daughter, and returns home with a concubine from Troy, named Cassandra. In the other two, a child is exposed on a mountain to die by order of his father and mother, who are king and queen of Theks. but is preserved, and afterwards, when grown up, in ignorance of his birth, murders his father and marries, horrible to relate, his own mother, Jocata, by whom he has four children, all which ends in the suicide of the wife-mother, and in his two sons murdering each other in battle fighting for their father-brother's throne. Then, remember too, that the gods are at the bottom of all this abominable crime, and now here Mr J.— says that these tragedies are "ideals of a noble life". These are strange words from a Christian preacher, or one who professes to be such, and I, for one, think that an ignorance so extreme must be dealt with in plain language. If the modern drama is capable of purification, certainly the filth of Sophocles and Aeschylus are poor purifiers. I had rather the worst of modern dramas than that. And, if Christian ministers are to aid in that talk, they must have clearer ideas of "morals," "religious teaching," and "ideals" of noble living than this man, who talks of writers of whom it is charity to suppose he is wholly ignorant I shall do my best to deal fairly and plainly with the whole subject, and in such a way as shall show that I have no sympathy with dramatic performances as a rule, nor can I see in what way the drama is to be made a beneficent and progressive power, which it never at any time has been, so far as I can find, and let those who say the opposite prove the contrary. . . .

Your offer to send me a black suit as a present touched me, and seemed most kind, but I feel almost ashamed to accept so costly a gift My present frock coat is rather old and shabby, and I have only got through the summer by getting trousers and vest and wearing my dress coat, which you made in 1867, under a yellow silk dust coat I need, it is true, a frock coat immediately, for the present one is more thoroughly worn out than any of its predecessors Therefore, I will accept, upon condition that you will accept in return a few books it is in my mind to send you, and a little money when I can I assure you money has been very tight, indeed, often with me, and I have, with Jeanie, been most parsimonious in personal expenses—it is the establishing of our work which has taken the money. I often regret my inability to provide help for mother, who should rest more than she does, I fear, and I hope I may yet, for the future looks brighter.

My measures, taken just easily, without straining the tape, are, chest 40 inches—waist 39 inches. You may be surprised at my corpulence. I do not understand it myself. for I am a moderate eater and a hard worker. But I sleep well, and live regularly as to meals, etc I weighed, two or three weeks ago, no less than eleven stone and six pounds, and yet I do not look the weight for I flatter myself I am not disproportionate in figure—although I do not see myself as others see me.

To all our friends remember us with kind wishes.

Pray for us daily yet more and more—it strengthens me to know you and many more do—and remember that you are always in our hearts and in our prayers that you may be supplied "in all your need" out of the fullness of God's infinite love in the Lord.

I am,

Your affectionate son,

John Alexander Dowie.

(*Answers anonymous writer who criticises work—Jan. 8, 1880.*)

My Dear Mr. Editor:

When I read today in your issue of January 2, the spiteful misrepresentations of some correspondent signing himself "Spectator," I was reminded of a story told of one of my "brither Scotts." He was for some reason, or more probably for the want of reason, a subject of many unpleasant gossiping tongues, and at last in cynical defiance he wrote over his gate, "Men say; what say they? Who cares what they say?" Now, although no cynic, and by no means regardless of the opinion of my fellow men, I always treat anonymous attacks as I do anonymous letters, with both of which I have for years been largely favoured, with the utmost contempt; and seldom do I now bestow a second thought upon them. During more than six years' residence and public life in this city, and for the last three years bitterly opposed by all sections of the Philistine Press which curses this city and defends the grossest iniquities of our social and political life, I have only once appeared in print in self-defense. Frequently, I have been attacked by all four newspapers in one day. The "Herald" would sneer loftily in its ignorant, purse-power, important way at my "fanaticism" concerning the Liquor Traffic and Intemperance; its evening "Echo" would virulently stab at me through its "Funny Man" in its "Zigzag Papers" column, where roundabout lies abound on every subject, the vile sheet called the "Evening News" would follow suit, a paper which feeds on garbage and exists to glorify vice and liquordom generally, and then the new paper, "The Daily Telegraph", must needs have its little fling, to please its pro-liquor editor and proprietors. And now, my friend, you must see it would never do to begin attempting to fight these valiant "we" people on their own midden heaps: for there would be nothing gained worth the effort, nor would I be wiser in pursuing these critical flesh flies into their malodoring dens. In this city I leave my daily life and work to answer these cowardly anonymous persons, but it is a different matter when they cross to your city, where my work is less known, and endeavour to needlessly blacken me to a people among whom I lived without reproach for nearly one fourth of my life, and where slanders against me are but cruel wounds to the hearts of my nearest kindred who have lived in your city for twenty years. For their sakes, principally, I feel it my painful duty to make an example of "Spectator". and since I shall need to speak of myself and my affairs in doing so, let me ask you and your readers to do me the justice to keep in mind two facts, first, that I do not willingly write concerning myself, but of necessity imposed upon by my traducer, and, second, that the facts which I shall mention I am so little in the habit of boasting about, that they have never been made public through the press before, even in Sydney, although I have had abundant opportunity of so publishing them.

Now let me proceed to my unpleasant task of unmasking this nameless slanderer, and disproving his false assertions.

"Spectator" denies the accuracy of a paragraph concerning me in your issue of December 12th, and boldly asserts, "Mr Dowie's work in Sydney has virtually collapsed."

As to the paragraph referred to, it is for you, Mr. Editor, to defend its accuracy in its first instance, by calling upon those who supplied the substance of it to you

You know that I did not, either directly or indirectly, and I have not any knowledge of who did.

During my short stay of five days in Adelaide, I did not see you or any one connected with the paper, and neither sought nor inspired the paragraph, and first saw it after my return to Sydney.

The principal portion of your paragraph concerning my work here was quoted from another paper, and was written entirely without my previous knowledge by its able and well known editor who resides in Sydney, who has attended the services in Victoria Theatre when he could scarcely find a vacant seat in that large building, who has many independent means of judging the value of the work he has written of so kindly, and is probably as well fitted as any man in the Australian Colonies to write concerning its spiritual results.

He is quite impartial, for though I think sympathizing generally with the work, he is not one of its direct supporters or co-operators

He is a "Spectator" whose unsolicited testimony and statement of facts is entirely opposed to your anonymous correspondent and I venture to say that fact entirely condemns the slanderer. And as to the other portions of the paragraph, I do not know who wrote or inspired them, but at the time they were written, they were literally true in every particular. I challenge "Spectator" to prove a word in the paragraph to be either false or exaggerated, and I further demand that he will not sneak behind the coward's cloak of anonymity, but write boldly under his real name

Not content with disputing the truth of the paragraph he propounds his first false assertion that my work has collapsed, when my work is going on, and in the opinion of some qualified to judge, is more likely to be firmly established than ever. Perhaps the fact that the Sunday previous to the late election for East Sydney and for the Sunday after, I did not preach as usual, made this ignorant traducer to say the Mission had virtually collapsed. But let me tell this "Spectator" that the Mission was all the while in full working order, and had regular weekly business meetings during my brief absence, and actually arranged for a twelve months' lease of a new hall—the International—in a central situation in Pitt Street. I preached there, on the day appointed when I left Sydney for resuming work, viz· December 28th, and the place was comfortably filled on that first Sabbath evening, although the weather was unpropitious, the Hall almost unknown, for it has not been finished a month, and it was only advertised the previous day.

Last Sunday I preached there to a large audience, and had what I fear "Spectator" cannot appreciate, the joy of being followed to my home by enquirers, who are asking with tears, "What must I do to be saved"? So far as man can judge, many received the blessing they acknowledged to have desired I was delighted to find God thus signally blessing my offer of Christ's glorious salvation as a New Year's gift, and I take it as a loving token of His continued approval on the work of which I and the faithful band of Christian men and women associated with me have been engaged for nearly two years   Week evening services are held in the same hall by me, work among the young is begun with good promise, and it is quite possible that my committee may secure the Hall during the whole week for my various operations, and indeed I may say that pending that possibility, the lease for which they have agreed has not been signed.   Many are of the opinion that for our evening services the Hall is too small, but it is a most convenient building, and more liked by my people than the Victoria Theatre

These are the simple facts.   Does not their mere statement completely demolish the slander of "Spectator" that "Mr. Dowie's work in Sydney has virtually collapsed"?   Surely the wish was father to the lie At any rate, the probabilities are, you will see, "Spectator's" statement is in a state of actual collapse.

But I proceed to examine another statement of "Spectator's" which is of a retrospective character. He says, "that while **some** good has been effected, it has been an utter failure pecuniarily".

I will deal at once with the first portion of that remark that seems to contain half a sneer, as to "some good" being done by our evangelistic services   It will lead me to give you a brief outline of the origin and progress of the Mission, which may interest your readers, and be of some service to my friends and foes alike.

In the first week of February, 1878, I retired, entirely of my own free will, from the pastorate of the Newtown Congregational Church, which I had held for exactly three years, and from all formal connection with the Congregational and all other denominations This I did for reasons which then and now seem to be sufficient, reasons entirely of an impersonal character, not the least powerful of which was, as it seemed to me, the absolute necessity of reaching the utterly

Godless majority of this city by means of an entirely free Christian organization, where no Talmud of tradition nor fetters of unbelievable creed, would stand between the preacher and his expression of what he believed to be the truth of the Word of God. I believe that it was the will of God that I should take that position, and that confidence was the result of more than a year's direct prayer and thought upon the matter. Therefore, I came into the city, took the Theatre Royal; I did not then, and never have at any time, asked any one to join me, and at once set to work. The Lord gathered around me devoted friends and larger congregations than any I had ever preached to before for over four years in Sydney.

The work has gone on ever since without the intermission of a single Sabbath service, excepting the month's rest which it was agreed I should take in December, and during that period my fellow workers met together every week, and kept up their contributions. And what has been the good done? Who can tell or dare to estimate? I cannot, and dare not.

Eternity alone will declare the results of these two years of unremitting and delightful work. But of what has been apparent, I may be allowed to speak, and tell, to the glory of God alone, from Whom the power and blessing came, some of the work done and its results

Severe trials, disappointments, and temptations I have had and do experience; but these are what I expect True, they have been severe, and sometimes of a kind unexpected, but I have not murmured, nor will I murmur at that I humbly hope I have learned that God's will is always best; and my confidence that His love has never permitted aught but what was for my highest good, and that of those whose welfare I sought, has been my constant strength and joy.

During 1878 the services were conducted in the Theatre I have mentioned, and in two of the largest

Halls of this city; and I do not think a week has ever passed without evidence of God's Spirit working in the services, amongst people of all ages and classes.

But during 1879 the work was carried on entirely in the Victoria Theatre, except on week evenings, and for many months every available seat was occupied before the service began, and on more than one occasion many unable to get seats went away, and many stood throughout the service.

During nine months of last year I wrote twenty imperial octavo tracts, and had them stereotyped. These were printed, with an invitation to each Sunday's services on the other side, and a weekly average of nearly 6,000 copies were distributed gratis on the Saturdays and Sundays. A total number of 210,750 were printed and given away—of these 89,500 were direct appeals to the heart and conscience to accept God's gift of pardon, peace and life in Christ under various titles, 79,250 were connected with the evils of intemperance and kindred social evils, and 42,000 were addressed to Roman Catholics especially and set before them the errors and evil designs of Rome, with particular reference to the pastorals of the Archbishop and Bishops of the Church of Rome.

Two pamphlets of 2,000 each edition were written and printed, and that entitled "The Drama, the Press and the Pulpit" has been widely read, and a very large number of a reply to Dr. Vaughan, entitled "Rome's Polluted Springs" have been read by persons who were connected with the Church of Rome when they first read them and are now Protestant Christians. Lectures and addresses on many subjects were delivered during the week in various Halls, and I have repeatedly been chosen spokesman to successive Premiers with a view to induce Governments to introduce a reform of the Liquor licensing laws and Sunday closing of public houses—not without good result. I know of many cases of conversion through the

tracts, some of whom joined churches of various denominations, and it has been my joy to hear many
say, "I yield myself to Christ and trust Him as my
Saviour," or, "I will drink no more," or, "I doubt no
more," or, "I have done with the Church of Rome."
In my Committee I could find some of each class
named, and, whilst I would not wish, through inadvert-
ence, to overstate in so solemn a matter as the conversion of souls, yet I think I should be within the mark
if I said that about 200 persons have given
themselves to the Lord under my ministry during
these two years Nearly one half of these are with us,
and the remainder in the country, or divided among
the churches—some are now in other lands, and a few
are safe over in the better land above. Very heartily
do I recognize the noble help and prayerful sympathy
of my devoted fellow servants of the Lord in this work
as the secret spring of many a soul being won from
sin in my ministry, and I do wish again to most
humbly acknowledge all the blessing is from the Lord

Will you permit me, then, to give this, necessarily,
most imperfect outline of the "some good" to which
"Spectator" so sneeringly alludes as having been done
in the work, which I am afraid he will be disappointed
to see has not collapsed. It is a duty I owe to my
gracious Lord and Master to record thus gratefully
my testimony as to His faithfulness, in blessing so
richly the mission which I entered upon alone, believing that I was simply obeying His will, and I believe
now still more firmly that this work is of God, and
that it will not cease until His objects in it are accomplished

And now what of "Spectator's" statement, "It has
been an utter failure pecuniarily." Suppose it true—
what then? Who claimed that it had been a pecuniary
success? Certainly I never did, for it has been a very
great pecuniary loss to me. But Paul could say the
same, and much more , and I am afraid that "Spec-

tator" would have been compelled to pronounce the Redeemer's own earthly ministry "an utter failure pecuniarily," as did His treasurer, Judas Iscariot, who could only make money out of it by selling his Master for silver. That was the only pecuniary success I read of in that Mission Yet who would dare to even mention the fact of its impecuniosity as a charge against the Lord? Is it not indeed one of Christ's glories that "for our sakes He became poor that we through His poverty might be made rich"? And, if I am poorer through my ministry, I am no more disposed to write "failure" upon it, and abandon it on that account, than I am to brand Paul, John Bunyan, or John Wesley as "failures" because they cared more for the souls of Christ's sheep than for their golden fleeces But it would be a shame to me were I to allow the Mission to be branded "an utter failure pecuniarily". More money has been raised and spent upon it during the two years than was raised and spent in actual work, apart from ministerial salary, in any church of which I know in Sydney—for the actual sum paid to defray the Mission expenses, apart from anything to me, has averaged nearly 10 pounds per week That work is not an utter failure pecuniarily which has done that The burden and anxiety concerning means has fallen entirely upon myself, and I do not doubt that the Lord will take care that I do not lose in His work. He is "good pay", even although He keeps His servants waiting long, as it seems to them. We have made no appeals for aid outside the circle of our immediate friends, and beyond the money given by our own hearers, the outside help has been a trifle, comparatively. I have a shrewd suspicion that "Spectator" knows nothing about the matter, except from idle gossip, for which I am a fair target, and I think it very probable that, notwithstanding even he admits we have done "some good", he has been "no good" pecuniarily

or otherwise to our Mission. But let me tell him this
is an old story of his, and has been often repeated by
him and others, doubtless in the hope that the fact
might be so This is a fair specimen of much of the
pretended Christian charity with which my work is
regarded by many denominationalists, whose churches are doubtless pecuniary successes, but at the same
time huge spiritual failures, offensive in their pride,
laziness and worldliness, both to God and man.
"Spectator" may yet be found to be one of the "greedy
shepherds who feed themselves", with whom I am no
favorite, you may be sure.

And now in a word, I desire to say this: that come
pecuniary failure or success, this Mission will go on,
whilst God preserves my strength and gives me souls
for my hire. This work does not depend upon money,
but upon God's grace; and I have learned that "power
belongeth unto God" alone. I say, I will tarry at
Sydney for the same reason that Paul once said he
would at Ephesus,—"for a great door and effectual is
opened unto me, and there are many adversaries".
One of the clearest signs that I ought to continue here
lies in the very fact that people like "Spectator" abound
here, and are very bitterly opposed to me. That is a
clear proof that the great Adversary does not like me,
and therein I rejoice; for as the song of the Salvation
Army has it, so also say I:

> "The Devil and I, we can't agree,
> "I hate him and he hates me "

Perhaps "Spectator" may turn out to be a partaker
of or a trader in those poisons which the state has
established by law as a traffic to destroy, and which
have been called by Robert Hall "liquid fire and distilled
damnation," which is an apt description Now all men
know where I stand upon that question, and that I
have contracted with the Lord to spend my life in

doing what I can to crush that modern Moloch, the Liquor Traffic, which is perhaps a "pecuniary success" after "Spectator's" own heart.

I shall hope yet to convert even my traducer to my way of thinking about that trade in human misery and despair.

Now let me refer to another statement of "Spectator's". He says, "There is no likelihood whatever of a building being erected in which to carry on the services."

Now, even whilst you were printing his letter, we had just entered upon a building erected for the purpose, although not by us. Two newly built Halls were offered to us, and if they had not offered, let me tell "Spectator" that in all likelihood we would have leased a central block of land, and built a large, temporary building thereon at once. But when the Lord had built us a central and fairly suitable place, we did not need to face the larger undertaking until we were stronger. By God's bessing, we shall ere long erect our Free Christian Tabernacle, which faith has long planned, and I do not despair of seeing this poor despiser a wondering "Spectator" in that House of God which we shall yet preach in, if spared to continue this blessed work for the Lord Jesus.

Here, my dear friend, I leave "Spectator" for the present. With my very earnest good wishes and prayers for you and "The Christian Colonist," I am,

Yours in the Lord Jesus,

John Alexander Dowie.

(Addressed to his friend, Holding, Sept. 3, 1880, Darlinghurst, Sidney.)

My Dear Q:

Although it is only three days since I sent to you my last letter, yet as an opportunity offers by the "Chimborazo" which leaves Melbourne on the 7th I write you again, knowing you would like to hear from us as often as possible.

9

I am glad to say that two days ago I received your letter from Auckland dated August 17th, and was delighted to get it and all the dear, loving words contained in it   It was like "cold water to a thirsty soul": for it was truly good news from a far country. I had almost given up all hope of getting it, and so it was the more welcome. I have read it over and over again, and carry it about with me in my breast pocket to re-read when I am quietly sitting somewhere outside. Surely our love has been Divinely given · for it is beyond all ordinary love of men, my best beloved.   I thank you for the nice letter—no eye but mine has read it, as you desired; but I have read from it to Jeanie, and when G— comes tomorrow I will read part of it to her   You may be sure that every letter you write to me will be appreciated   Write freely all that is in your heart, so far as that is possible, and I will guarantee that your letters will but strengthen the ties which bind us to each other—ties which neither earth, nor time, nor distance, nor every evil power can weaken—for our love is from God, I believe, and that kind of love never faileth.

You will now be getting near San Francisco, and are I trust well, my beloved. My prayers are unceasingly for you, and I have a sure belief that they are being graciously answered   You are safely encompassed by God's hosts, and no evil can hurt you. "The angel of the Lord encampeth round about them that fear him and delivereth them". And who is that angel, but Jesus, who says, "Lo, I am with you alway." May you rest secure in His loving promise.

The meeting of the electors of South Sydney who were favorable to my candidature was held on Tuesday night. For a first meeting it was large and very enthusiastic. My supporters are growing more and more numerous and confident daily. They anticipate that I certainly will get in as one of the four to be elected for that constituency and that I may even head the poll I am neither too hopeful nor too fearful I shall do my best to win, and I shall not be disgraced even if I am defeated The elections do not come off until next month and perhaps not until November, so that it will not be necessary for me to speak much upon politics for a month As you know, I do not seek to enter Parliament either for its honours or rewards I simply desire to initiate legislative reforms on social matters such as the liquor traffic, the whoredom traffic, and the official corrupt trafficking I want to put legal hindrances in the way of immoral and destructive pursuits I want to do something to elevate the tone of public life, and to get the rising generation, especially, to see that "politics" are not synonomous with lying, trickery, and successful Parliamentary corruption I want the people to know that "politics" rightly understood mean patriotism, self sacrifice, high moral, intelligent action, and purity of speech and life. "Salus populi suprema est lex" was the noble old Latin motto—that is—"The safety or welfare of the people is the supreme law " And so every Christian man must hold The people, Christ lived for, 'twas the people whom He taught, for them He suffered; for them He died; for them He ever liveth to make intercession, for them He bids His followers live, suffer, and if needs be, die, and for the people, therefore, in this spirit I desire to labour Hence "politics" is an essential part of my ministry, and on that point I am glad you and I agree, as indeed I believe we do on all matters, for I do not remember anything on which we seriously differ.

I have taken for myself a room in Stephen Court—in 99 Elizabeth Street, where I will place my library and study fittings, and a sofa bed I will stay at "Coolabah", as much as possible of the week, and get the good air and rest of the Blue Mountains to prepare me for the Hill Difficulty, which lies before me in the shape of "politics", which when climbed will, I doubt not, lead to the House that is called "Beautiful", as well as to the House of Legislature.

I am not very well, my best beloved, and friends are beginning to say that lately I have looked worn and weary—and they must be right, for I feel weary. I have had a very distressing cough day and night for weeks past, and a pain in my chest and languor very unusual to me. But during the last two days I am feeling a good deal easier, and I hope, if it be God's will, I shall continue to improve. The contemplated change gives me hope, and I thank God it has come at this time.

Stephen Court, where I intend having my room, is next to Temple Court, only that it enters from Elizabeth Street, round the corner from King Street. It is most convenient and central in situation.

Rent is 12s. 6 d. per week—2 s. 6 d. for cleaning, etc extra—and I can get my meals at the Coffee Palace and even sleep there, if I please. I think I have done right. To have boarded with anyone would have been expensive and inconvenient. I avoid both evils and get cheap and good quarters.

You will, I know, forgive all that is amiss in this letter No doubt it will be chargeable with faults of omission if not of commission, but you will know one thing, surely, that every word of it is written by the hand of one whose heart is full of true, deep, and strong love for you. Look upon every word in that light, and then you will see, that which I see in your letter, love shining like the sun with its radiant beauty in every line; for love is the light of life, and nothing that is unclean or false can be concealed in its presence, whilst every thought and word and deed and memory is clothed with beauty and filled with sweetness and gladness by its presence Love never faileth, it ever groweth, it cannot die.

How comforting to know that come what will, love cannot fail.

"They err who tell us love can die!
With life all other passions fly,
All others are but vanity;
But love is indestructible."

I feel the words are true of you and I: for our love is given by God, and, therefore, cannot be destroyed. That conviction keeps our hearts at rest, though seas and lands divide us: for love unites us.

How I wonder, as I sit here quite alone in the silence of the night, where you are; how you are; what you are doing; what has happened to you, what will happen, before this reaches you? What condition you will be in at the time you read these words, etc. etc. But all that is in vain. I can only pray, be patient, and wait By and by we shall tell each other all. . . .

Interruptions, indeed! Why, I have been a prophet beyond my wishes very, very much: for it has been nothing but interruptions, and about the busiest week I have had for years On Tuesday night I was up all night engaged in writing a letter to the Attorney General, pleading for a young man who had got into great trouble with his Department, through a series of blunders, if not crimes, which led to his suspension and threatened to lead to his imprisonment. He is a young man of great ability, of hitherto unblemished character, and most respectably connected in London I had and have the highest respect for him: for I am quite sure that he committed himself while suffering from mental abberation, and that he did not intend to commit a crime or wrong the Government of a penny.

This view of the case I have induced the Minister for Public Works to take, who is the head of the young man's Department, and I think my letter, which dealt at great length and most exhaustively with the whole subject, will induce the Hon. R. Wisdom to take the same view. In fact, he did so unofficially through my conversations with him in his office. The members of the Government treat me with much personal respect, and from what I have heard, I have reasons to believe that Sir Henry Parkes desires to have my support very much, or that at least I shall not go against his Government at the approaching General Election The case of which I have been speaking has caused me much toil and anxiety, and hindered me from the pleasanter task of writing to you, my dearest boy

But you will, I know, not complain because of my doing this good work—for if I save a soul from death, and I have every reason to believe that by God's grace I will, and save aged and pious parents from going down to the grave with broken hearts, I am engaged in work wherein I know you are heart and soul with me, work which it will be our joy to do much of together in days yet to come.   .

My dear ones are, I hear, getting on well at Coolabah in the Mountains. I hope to see them all on Monday night and to see them getting fat and rosy cheeked   They like, Jeanie says, the place well, only they miss me very much and want me there—flattery, you know.

But to keep me humble here is an antidote in the unflattering impudence of a "poem" from the comic organ of the Spiritualists, from whom, by the way, I have received several new abusive letters since you left

The "Bulletin" also has been at it again

I will cut out a few of their would be funny paragraphs, and send to you.

But wait. We shall have our turn some day in the press, and meanwhile, it does not hurt me. I laugh and pass on, and as people tell me, I am growing fat upon it—hard work, no sleep sometimes, and all. . . .

I am wondering today whether you are in New York. Dear brother,I do feel for you in your visit there; as you stand beside your dear one's grave I seem to be with you in spirit. "Be of good cheer", there is much to live for. Let your dear ones all live so that when they end this life those they have left behind may bless the world through ages yet to come. I shall, with you, one day see them: for

> "Bye and bye we shall be standing,
> "Bye and bye, bye and bye,
> "At heaven's shining landing,
> "Bye and bye;
> "And our friends will round us gather,
> "Saying, 'Welcome,' for the Father,
> "Loves to have His children nigh "

Blessed thought—so shall we be forever with the Lord, and with all these dwell with Him in the many mansions above. . . . Beloved, I must close or I will miss the mail Forgive me for being so hurried. But you know how you are ever in my heart, in my prayers, and in all my plans. . . . .

After posting my letter to you last night, I returned home to write my tract. I was interrupted by a visitor, and did not get to it until late

However, I stuck to it, and finished it about three this morning It is entitled "Seducing Spirits and Doctrines of Devils," and is the second against Spiritualism. I think it will be good: for it goes straight to the proof of most serious charges against this abominable superstition. The Freethinkers and Spiritualists are getting very angry, but that is a good sign. I hear from many of good being done to many who were on the brink of the abyss of Atheism, and only yesterday I received a letter from a workingman cheering me on, and saying that I was on the right track as to his class

I have had a good long sleep, and am now fresh again, in a quiet house, with time for at least two hours' writing—and for that time purpose to have a quiet talk, as it were, with you, although it won't be nearly so pleasant as were our long night conversations in the room above me.

Every minute I expect to hear the bell ring and the telegraph boy appear with a message from you telling of your safe arrival in Adelaide   Day and night I have besought the Lord to take you safely   there and to strengthen you in body and soul   I expect a gracious answer: for I am sure that the Lord has preserved you for His own gracious purposes, and these will, it seems to me, be best fulfilled by your life being spared. "The fields are white unto the harvest," and ere your day declines and the sun of this life be set, you may labor with me to bring in and fill with Purity and Peace and Joy those who are weary amidst the world's mad, mock-ing mirth, and groaning amidst the unrest, the unclean-ness, and the sorrows of sin in the city and throughout the otherwise beautiful land   I want to have you with me to say to the wanderer "Come in!" and then to seat them at the Banquet of Love   I want to see your hands spread the first communion table in our new Tabernacle, which the eyes of faith often see.   Last night, or rather this morning, I dreamed that I was passing, a stranger in the city, through the streets, when I came to a large, well lighted, comfortable, even cheerful looking building   The brilliant light from the street lit up the whole front, and above the wide door-way on a white marble slab, I saw, carved in large letters which shone like gold, the words "Have Faith in God".   I entered the door, thrilled to my heart by these words, and saw a sight which stirred my soul with deep emotion.   The building was full—tier upon tier the seats rose upon every side, from the platform down to the farthest end of the building.   Every eye was turned toward and every ear was listening to the speaker, who was saying, "O my beloved, believe me, God is Love!"   And above the speaker's head, on a wide, beautiful scroll on the arched recess behind the platform, there were these words in shining letters: "Christ is All." And, whilst I looked, behold, I found the speaker was myself, and in front of me, and all around me, I saw the faces of all my dear ones—wife, children, brother, parents, friends from far and near, and a multitude of eager, softened eyes of waiting souls were looking upon me from every side, as I awoke repeating, "Yes, He is, He is Love" But it was no dream, after all It was only my waking thoughts in our "Free Christian Tabernacle "

But enough of dreams, however beautiful. Thankful am I for such thoughts, let them but nerve us for realizing them! "To the work! to the work! we are servants of God, let us follow the path that our Master hath trod." . . . . .

(*Feb. 12, 1880—gives account of campaign for a seat in Parliament—his defeat—its resultant effects—gets deeper into mire of debt—resolves to close the mission in Sidney—sudden change in material affairs is wrought which is ascribed entirely to Divine intervention—plans for speedy organization of church.*)

My Dear Father and Mother·

Your most welcome letter of 5th has just reached me and I thank you from my heart for all the kind words and wishes you have written therein

You might very reasonable have complained of my silence; but you do not, and thus find excuse for me. I cannot so easily excuse myself; for I feel it would have been far better to have written at once after the East Sydney defeat, since neither after reflection nor knowledge of facts have in the slightest degree altered my convictions concerning that event. On the contrary, everything has confirmed my statement that Dr P—achieved a disgraceful victory by employing the vilest means, and that events would cause the electors yet to be ashamed of their choice—and they are so now, so far at least as the Temperance and Educational

(Protestant) votes are concerned, as I shall show you. But I was too sad and disappointed to write to you. God's goodness to me was very great, and I was wonderfully supported amid the conflict. But the strain of rapid traveling to and from Adelaide and the toil of brain and voice and body from my arrival here the 11th, until the following Wednesday, told upon me very heavily, and indeed, I have not yet recovered from the effects. Then it is so difficult, almost impossible, indeed, for one to write or even speak in such a way as clearly to put before you at a distance the whole facts concerning so intricate and deceitful a batch of lies as for the most part an election here is. However, I will try to give you some idea of the facts in this letter, or else I fear I will never be able to give you my version of the affair. Every one in Sydney who knows anything about this election knows that I was not defeated. I was sacrificed, in a panic, through greed and fear, which is not an uncommom thing, and shows us yet more clearly than ever before that money and alcohol are the slaves and yet the tyrants of men who are the destroyers of the people and dishonorers of God.

Mammon and Bacchus are the supreme rulers in the political arena here, and unless God prevents they will enchain and drag down fair Australia into the depths of an awful political hell. Approved by the press, applauded by society, smiled upon by the churches, and placed in the most influential positions by a deluded people, the high priests of Bacchus and Mammon are the rulers, and "they love to have it so." Nothing can be clearer than that awful fact.

God help Australia! God awaken a slumbering Church to see the serpents and adders which are being nourished in its bosom! God help the bruised and bleeding and dying multitudes who are wailing in their despair and struggling amid the seething, blood-dyed waters of the abyss of Intemperance, whose cries are being drowned by the drum beat of vicious pleasure which Mammon and Bacchus keep ever sounding to stifle the sounds of the perishing crowd of souls whom they are pushing below these dark waves, having destroyed for them all human hope!

God help the faithful few, who are found amid a faithless world and a hypocritical Church, and who will not bow the knee to Baal! God help me, too, I cry this day; for I am sorely tried and diabolically tempted to fight no more! O, Thou blessed Lord, who did say to one, when he in vain self-confidence boasted that he would not fail Thee, "I have prayed for thee that **thy faith fail not**;" pray Thou, too, for me, and deliver me from Satan who desires to have me that he might destroy me and destroy my power to serve Thee! O blessed Saviour, I would have a part in the restoration of the world for which Thou hast died! If I may but see Thy love in my trials, Thy strength in my weakness, Thy light in my darkness, Thy good purposes in my crushing disappointment, I will be able to bear the load and say "Thy will be done."

How hard to say, when all is dark above my head, when dreary is the path I tread; how hard to say, amid the triumphs of the Evil One; but though I die I yet say, "In me, my God, Thy will be done!"

I am very full of prayer tonight: for I do want to know and do the right, and I am surrounded by many dangers.

But I must tell you about the election, and then about our work, for the one is connected with the other, and you will understand our present position better if I tell you how we were affected by the political contest The contest lay between myself and Renwick. Knowing the claims I had upon the Temperance and Protestant voters, with the support of the working classes, I went into the contest with every hope of winning, although I knew that my opponents had spent a great deal of money in carousing for weeks.

267

My first meeting was a great success and gave me a unanimous vote on the evening of the day I arrived at Adelaide   The next evening I had a splendid hearing at my principal address in the Temperance Hall and a unanimous vote.

That night I sat up and finished my address to the electors, which was published in the paper of the next day and in the "Herald" and "Telegraph" of Monday and Tuesday   Ten thousand copies of it were printed   It did me a lot of good, and every one seemed to have a good word to say for it   The meetings on Saturday were splendid—I had three—and had unanimous votes.   When the week closed I had addressed about six thousand persons.   The Renwick party were in a dreadful scare   But Saturday night brought them their opportunity, and the unprincipled rogues began their game on the husting.

A very influential deputation from Renwick's Committee sought an interview with me   Dibbs, an influential merchant, was spokesman   He began by praising my address, and said, "We know you are the ablest and best man of the two.   But why not split the votes?   You are too late in the field.   Retire in favor of Dr. R—now, and we will pay your expenses and help you all we can the next General Election."   I said, "Gentlemen, you have brought your answer"   They asked me what I meant   I replied, "If you tell the truth, I am in your opinion the best man   Then why ask me to retire?   Gentlemen, the best man, whoever he may be, should go into the House: go and ask the next best to retire, and like honest men give your votes.   But whatever you do, say no more to me about paying my expenses: that means dishonour, it means bribery to my mind."   I had them fairly in a corner, but of course they were not to be moved by logic.   I knew they were insincere and unreliable.   They tried then to bribe my Committee to get me to retire.   Two did fall into their hands, if not more

Allum, the Treasurer, and Hutchins, the Chairman of the Committee, were offered 100 pounds each, they said, to get me to give up; and on the Tuesday evening four members of my Committee were told that if I would retire—the very evening before the election— a check for 500 pounds would be forth-coming This was looked upon as trickery, or bribery, and rejected, of course, by them.

But it shows how they feared me. Do you imagine that I had "no chance at the beginning" when this was their conduct on the very eve of the election? What I tell you are indisputable facts But they played their cards well that evening and gained an important point at a meeting of the Orange Institution, whose great lodge, it appears now, had pledged them- · selves to Renwick before my return; and false friends stood up and said that though they had the highest opinion of me, and under other circumstances would have supported me, they advised Temperance men and Protestants not to vote for me but for Renwick, saying that Renwick was right in his views with both those parties. The paid officials of the Temperance Orders,who had also in my absence pledged themselves to secure the Temperance vote for Renwick, without even consulting the members of these orders, aided to get a mass meeting of Temperance men at the Tuesday evening to declare against me.

They failed: for though my friends had only a few hours' notice, they rallied and outvoted the traitors, who abruptly closed the meeting, amidst great confusion. But the "Herald" falsely declared the next morning that the vote had been against me. The said "mass meeting", too, was a contemptible failure as to numbers; for even with my hurriedly summoned Temperance friends, it did not number three hundred. An address which I delivered to a large meeting, exposing the treachery of Holdsworth, Davies and others, at the Bathurst Column, not far from the Temperance

Hall, an hour before their "mass meeting," effectually prevented a declaration on behalf of Dr. Renwick by the Temperance men. But still the poison told, and with a Protestant Hall meeting of which I have written above, it fairly frightened my supporters Then the next morning the papers came out with strong, leading articles for Renwick, of course, and whilst they, for policy's sake, refrained from attacking me to any great extent, yet they warned the electors that there was a danger of Tooth going in if they voted for me. Lying rumors of my retirement were then circulated, bills were printed and posted about, which stated the fact that I had withdrawn, and paid touts hung around the polling booths and repeated that and similar lies. They did this with a thoroughness and success which surprised themselves, and left me far away out of the running They spent money like water, and beer flowed freely at Hodges' Hotel, their Central Committee rooms, while scores and scores of vehicles drove about the voters, and the unclean political vultures who swarm about on every side at such times doing all kinds of dirty work.

Of course we did nothing of the kind, and every vote cast for me was in my eyes worth a score of Renwick's, who was, I knew, deceiving the people and especially the Temperance and Educational Reform Parties—if indeed there exist such Parties where so many are rogues or fools. Thus was the disgraceful victory won.

Had the Temperance men voted on principle, they would have voted for me.

I was a lifelong abstainer—Renwick was a "moderate drinker"

I had led in many movements against the Licensing system, had advocated every plank in the Temperance Platform, had preached constantly against it, delivered over forty special sermons and lectures against Intemperance, and written, printed and circulated from

80,000 to 100,000 tracts upon the subject within two years, had been chosen as spokesman to Government after Government at the head of large deputations, and never had I once flinched or failed to do my duty in the matter, in private or public life.

Renwick had done absolutely nothing, was relying for support upon the publican ex-mayor, Roberts, who was his first advertised chairman, and though the false Temperance men **said** he had adopted the Temperance Political Platform, I did not believe it, for he cunningly avoided saying so himself, and his notorious actions in the House since he took his seat have fully proved before the whole country that I was right

Had the Protestant Party voted on principle, especially the League, they would have voted for me.

Three years ago I fought that battle in my reply to Dr Vaughan, ("Rome's Polluted Springs") and in my preface I warned the country that "the true friends of National Education should arouse and look to the guardianship of the National Treasury upon which Papalist leaders have dangerously affectionate designs, at present artfully veiled under liberal phrases" On pages 82—4 of my pamphlet I announced the views I hold today, and exposed the fallacy of the cunning scheme which Dr Vaughan had advocated in his "Hidden Springs", under another name I had delivered six lectures in Sydney, Newtown and Newcastle at that time, and had printed 2,000 pamphlets at a cost of time and strength and money such as Dr. Renwick never has dreamed of giving to such matters Then I delivered a series of six lectures upon the Roman Catholic Pastorals in the Victoria Theater to crowded audiences from July 13th to August 24th last year, and one on September 14th on the Roman Educational Agreement which I denounced and exposed; besides which I wrote, printed and circulated over 42,000 tracts in connection with these lectures I also delivered the series in the Temperance Hall on week evenings.

Where was Dr Renwick then? His voice was never heard, he never uttered any protest, he never exposed the Papal plots, he never sought to enlighten the people, he was busily making money and doing well to himself in worldly things, and no one ever heard his new born zeal in those days when my pen and brain and voice were found in the forefront of the stern conflict. No, he reaped what I and others sowed, and he reaped it by fraud, deceiving the people into the belief that he was their champion, when he was only making them tools for his ambition. In his written address he expressed no opinion on the Education question and it was only at the last moment that he adopted the role of Protestant champion, and hoodwinked the League into a pretended belief of their platform, as he has shown by his votes upon the Bill now under discussion in the House Assembly.

But in the panic and whirlwind of lies which swept over the city within two days, like one of our dust storms, my services were forgotten and hundreds admitted that they voted for Renwick only to keep Tooth out, whereas had they voted for me who believed in me and in my principles, neither Tooth nor Renwick would have gone in, I verily believe, but I should have won the seat.

This is now admitted by many who intensely regretted their votes when they saw how they had been tricked, and who regret them still more when they see how he votes in the House.

Briefly I will tell you how he has already voted and acted.

His first public act after he took his seat was to introduce a deputation of wine and spirit importers and of brewers and distillers to the Colonial Treasurer, Mr Watson, whose object it was to protest against the proposals of the Government to increase the duties upon imported intoxicants and to impose an excise duty of 3d per gallon upon all beers manufactured in the colony—and the first speaker he called upon to address the Treasurer was Mr Mitchell, who I am informed, is Mr Tooth's partner in the Liquor Trade (!!!) Was not this a consistent beginning for a Temperance reformer? Does it not prove that he knew he was indebted to the liquor dealers for some support, or at all events that he meant to support them?

Why, Mr. Tooth could not have done more He would scarce have been important enough to do as much as introduce his own partner as first speaker

Then his next act of gratitude to the Temperance Party was to vote against increasing the duties on spirits, and his reasoning (!) upon the question shows clearly that he would approve of reducing present duties: for that would reduce the danger of smuggling which he says he fears, and cheapen the drink to the consumers, thereby increasing the quantity consumed, and so promote temperance (!). Beautiful Temperance Reform this, ye Temperance traitors! But the Government carried these proposals—no thanks to the chosen representative of the Temperance Orders.

Then his next stroke in Temperance Reform (downwards) was to miss the first chance which has ever presented itself in the history of legislation in this Colony to tax the manufacture of beer, and to bring the breweries under inspection

He voted against the 3d per gallon excise duty, the voting, had he gone on the Government side, would have been just equal, and the Speaker, it is believed, would have voted with the Government, so that Renwick's single vote was sufficient to turn the scales and squeeze a 100,000 pounds this year out of beer, which at least was the estimated revenue expected from the tax by the Treasurer. Glorious achievement for Holdsworth, "The Social Reformer", the Temperance "Orders," etc. etc.! It has put back Temperance legislation for years. If the present "strong Government", as it is called, cannot with its large majority carry taxation upon beer, you may depend upon it their successors will be chary ere they attempt such proposals in days to come   Had I represented East Sydney then, we should have carried the tax, and driven in the thin edge of the wedge of further restriction, if not of prohibition.

This, however, would not have been the new Temperance principles, I suppose.

And now the fourth and latest act is on the Education question   It was proposed to amend the Bill now before the House by introducing one of the principles of the League, which did so much to put Renwick in, and of which both he and I are members—the principle that there should be no fees, that education should be like police protection, free to all, since it was to be provided by the state from the taxation of all   Dr Renwick voted against that proposal, and voted for 3 d per week being paid by every State School scholar, arguing that the Treasurer could not afford to lose the 35,000 pounds which that fee would bring   Here again you see the traitor's footprints.   Of course the Treasurer could afford to lose 100,000 pounds duty from beer, but scarcely a third of that sum from Education   Heigh for the New Reformer, set this bright boy up in the corner, he'll muddle the brains and rivet the chains of children and father and mother!

Having reformed the liquor traffic by restricted taxation, he reforms Education by imposing taxation "Hurrah for stunting the mind and muddling the brain!" should be the rallying cry of these new reformers

Now do you not think my epithet upon the hustings was most just, and that Renwick won "a disgraceful victory"? He could not give clearer proof of its truth than is supplied by these indisputable facts. But do you think our Mammonized Press notice these facts or would insert this summary of them? Nay, "the tabernacles of robbers" prosper by their aid, and woe to him who would root out the nest of social and political pirates who prey upon the people in a thousand forms. Our Press is their shield, for it is in their pay, and those who write therein must obey—or— away they must go.

And now, having given you this long account of Renwick and how I was defeated for East Sydney, I return to tell you how that defeat has affected the work in which I am engaged for Christ, or rather its influence upon my fellow workers and upon my personal affairs. The "work" cannot be affected for permanent injury by anything except sin, and I do not believe I sinned in standing for East Sydney. However, the effect upon the workers is another matter, and this has been a time of the severest testing. How far they have stood the test will appear from what follows.

You will remember that I told you when I left Adelaide that it was the telegram from my people here which decided me to accept the nomination for East Sydney, in the firm belief that they would not have impressed it upon me without good reason and a pretty sure prospect of success.

Knowing that Mr. H—, my Secretary, a man of nearly sixty years of age, was an old stoger politically, having been Secretary of Sir Henry Parke's Committee for East Sydney, I relied largely upon his judgment. Then the letter from the Political Reform Union and the subsequent adhesion of their President and a large number of their Council to my Committee was of importance.

I am bound to say, though, that my friends were not sufficiently cautious.

They failed to make certain inquiries which would have shown them that there would be a strong opposition to me amongst the rulers of the "Orders" or Secret Societies, and relied more upon my general popularity with the body of the people, and my personal

275

influence through my speeches during the contest than upon pledges of support by prominent persons This would have been all very well had it not been for two facts, the first of which they should have suspected and ferreted out, and the other was plain enough for those on the spot to see These were, the fact that the leaders of the Secret Societies were pledged to vote for Renwick before I appeared on the field, and also this fact, that he had made most extraordinary progress with his canvass, and through dint of a plentiful use of money in paying canvassers he had compiled a list of promised votes which included large numbers of my friends ere ever I left South Australia. Under these circumstances, it was not important to bring me over, where there was so much to be risked. I certainly would not have come had I known the real state of affairs, and I am sure that it would have been, so far as man can see, better for myself and my affairs, had I done what I purposed to do when I left Sydney for a month. But as it is, I fear it has proved disastrous to me in a financial sense, and that it is by no means the remote cause of that which will no doubt greatly surprise you, my determination to close the Mission in Sydney, for the present at least, on Sunday week next.

And now I must explain how this comes about and how it is connected with this East Sydney affair, though of course there are other contributing causes towards this result, which I shall not fail to lay before you, yet chief, or rather to speak more correctly the most important, is the political one

You will remember that I told you the understanding with which I left my people, as to what was to be considered by them and accomplished during my absence if I was to go on with the Mission when I returned. It was decided at a large meeting of my friends held the evening before I left that whilst I was away they were to consider and decide upon a distinct guarantee of at least 7 pounds per week to me as a salary besides the expenses of the Mission, and I most firmly told them that unless that guarantee was of the most reliable and businesslike description, I could not go on at all It was also decided, that arrangements were to be made to secure for a short time a suitable place, other than a Theatre, if possible, and that we should as speedily as possible face the building of a large, temporary edifice, in which to found our permanent organization When I returned, they were to be in a position to show me the result of their month's work on these matters, and meanwhile they agreed to keep up their weekly contributions, and to meet frequently and to work with their might. The meeting was without exception the largest and most enthusiastic and businesslike I ever had, and we all parted in the confidence that when I returned everything would go on better than before.

Their first meeting was to be held in two days, on the Wednesday evening.

But the very next day, Tuesday, the day I left, the announcement was made in the evening papers of Mr Alexander Stewart's resignation, and therefore, that East Sydney was vacant. The idea of my candidature immediately seized a number of the men on my Mission Committee who, finding that a good many outside were thinking the same way, seemed to me to have been suddenly seized with the idea that my election for East Sydney would be a short cut to success for our Mission, and save the trouble of organizing in my absence. Indeed, both Allum and Hutchinson said as much to me, when I returned. Consequently my Committee and friends threw themselves into the election contest, to the utter disregard of our arrangements. Indeed it could scarce be otherwise if they were to work for my election—and that I do not blame. What I feel about the matter is that their desire to get success by a short cut blinded them to two things, first, the danger to the Mission if I failed; and, second, the difficulties which really existed to my being successful, and which I particularly mentioned to you. Having failed, you will see at glance the blow it was to the Mission. True, I began again on the very date arranged, but it was without the guarantees I had required, and would have had, I believe, had my people been working for the Mission, instead of toiling for a week at the election with such discouraging results. True, we secured a place for our services, the International Hall, but it has proved too small for our evening audiences, is badly ventilated, and has proved unsuitable in many ways; nor can we secure it for the year, if we would, the party who lets it to us having misled us, as we find he has no power to sublet for any term, besides he uses it on other nights for a dancing saloon. But the **prestige** of the work has suffered by my defeat. Many butterfly, fair-weather friends have forsaken me, and some of my apparently firmest friends have lost much of their courage and faith, the sure result of rashness and over-confidence. It took us a good many weeks to see this at all clearly for we resumed work in the holidays and have had a good many wet or threatening Sundays and so could not be sure of things. Public interest in our work is not, I think, at all diminished; but our building being so small and unsuitable, we cannot possibly get our Theatre audiences. But the fact is indisputable enough, we are much weaker.

I have not changed, there have been no differences of opinion nor reason why any of our regular subscribers should fall away, so far as the work is concerned.

But they have fallen away, and in considerable numbers within the last few weeks, and consequently our small income has been smaller still, and quite insufficient for our support. I, therefore, called our people together to consider the state of affairs, and made the condition of my going on, to depend upon their giving me a sum of at least 6 pounds per week, independent of all expenses, which are at present, say, 3 pounds per week; and that a number of persons, not more than 15 or 20 in number, should become responsible for the regular payment of that sum to me weekly. Many faithful ones were willing to do this if it were possible, and four or five meetings were held without the result being attained.

At last, on Wednesday evening, a final meeting was held to see if it could be done; for I was getting deeper and deeper into the mire of debt, and it was imperative upon me either that the Mission should be self supporting, or that it should cease forthwith, at least for a time   The meeting was held, I attended it before it closed by arrangement, and it was found that the average collections in addition to subscriptions, there were only about 6 pounds available, and even with that, there was no absolute guarantee. There was, therefore, no alternative but to give up the Mission. for it did not leave me enough to live upon, and I consequently said so   Of course, there was general sorrow and regret. Those present had for the most part done what they could, but the defection was too strong. for many had quietly dropped off, and amongst them our secretary, Mr H——, who had been loud in my praises up to the very day of my defeat, who had really wrought hard in the election and through the whole of the Mission had done finely, though   by no means active as an organizer, and irregular and impulsive; yet he was a most faithful friend in my private difficulties, and indeed it is to him that I am at this moment chiefly indebted, which makes his defection now the more serious and painful to me. That is one of my severest trials. I have had and lost troops of what are called "friends", and who have really for a time been friends, but who have gone back and walked with me no more.

Often do I search my heart and conduct to see whether the cause be not in myself; but, though it would be of course, untrue and absurd in me to say that I am wholly without blame in my work or methods, I do find myself compelled to conclude that it generally arises from some prejudice against some unwelcome truth, or from mere love of change and inconstancy of mind, or from the lies and slanders of my numerous enemies in the Church and the world .

What an entire change has passed over the whole state of my affairs as described in the previous part of this letter! Ten days have passed since I wrote the above words which show you how desperate seemed the very existence of the Mission, and my personal affairs looked equally black   Truly, God is good

Everything is changed. The Mission is to go on. A reliable guarantee is given   Very substantial help has been given me in my private affairs.

There are difficulties, but we do not shrink from and will overcome them, there are dangers, but we do not fear them: for we see more clearly that God is indeed for us, and we cannot but be victorious   If we wanted a motto for our work, we might find an appropriate one in Exodus 3·2—"And the bush burned with fire, yet the bush was not consumed." Our fiery trials prove to me more than any other test could, that the Lord is with us, and our Mission stands therefore on holy ground. My faith may have sometimes varied in its strength, but it has never from the first failed concerning my call to do this work being from God, and that He would see me through. I believe now more than ever, that this is indeed the fact. And we have reason to bless the Lord for the trials we have passed through—and they have been indeed severe—for it is quite apparent to us all that they have brought us every one nearer to the Lord, and developed a more prayerful spirit of dependence upon Him alone.

The change is so great, and so unexpected, it is so sudden and so complete, and yet so thoroughly and apparently reliable, that I shall find it hard to tell you how it has been brought about. Indeed no circumstances will account for it, no mere human action could have produced it; we ascribe it entirely to Divine intervention

But I will tell you briefly the course of events.

You will please remember that I am writing this on Tuesday, February 24th, and that the facts recorded were written on Saturday, February 14th.

On the following day, Sunday 15th—the second anniversary of our work—I announced that I would preach, in all human probability, the last sermon in connection with the Mission on that night week But ere the evening service closed, at which there was a large attendance, although the night was very wet, I was asked to request the friends to remain at the close They did so in considerable numbers, several short, pithy, heartfelt speeches were made, and it was determined to hold yet another meeting on the following Tuesday evening, to make one more attempt to keep me, and continue the Mission I agreed to their doing so, and the meeting seemed delighted to think there was yet hope A kind spirit of loving appreciation was shown towards me, and it was determined that I should receive some tangible token of their esteem, should I leave

But the larger part seemed determined to put the idea of my leaving away from them.

Well, the meeting was held, and was successful in getting a reliable minimum guarantee of 8 pounds per week, with every hope of increase, for which a certain number are responsible in the fullest sense for its due payment. This leaves me 5 pounds weekly for my home and pastoral expenses—which is just enough— but it is a guarantee of such a nature as makes me feel sure of a speedy increase. I accepted it, and from that moment our winter has turned into a glorious spring.

Instead of the intended final sermons last Sunday— of which however no public press notice was given— I preached two of a totally different kind—and in the evening we had an after meeting for prayer and enquirers, which was most encouraging We had in the afternoon about 40 children to begin our new Sunday School, and Jeanie and I are forming Bible classes for young men and women, which are likely to be well attended. There is such a fine spirit among the people.

We hope to form our church, and establish the ordinance of the Lord's Supper, in about six weeks. An evangelistic choir in the city has offered us a service of song to aid our funds. We think of having a social gathering soon again to celebrate the entry of the third year of our work, and its formation into an organized church I intend to lay aside entirely for the next three months all dealing with political or social affairs in my sermons so far as possible, and concentrate my whole efforts upon the comforting and edifying of the church, and direct evangelistic effort to rescue the perishing souls around

Our friends are rallying. Mr. H— is, I am glad to say, as fully with us as ever, and last Sunday evening he was much affected by the after meeting. He and Mr A— and a Mr. McI—have stood by me most nobly in money matters during this last week; and for their kindness I feel no words could express my gratitude.

No men could have behaved better or more generously. They knew well how I had wrought and incurred these liabilities, and they have nobly aided me. Will you join with me in praising God for these friends, and in praying that the Lord may prosper them in their families and affairs, and in their spiritual health?

We have had sent to us a young man who is a very good organist, and who will throw himself heartily into the work or reorganizing our choir Good singing is in every sense a great help, and I hope soon to see our choir stronger and more efficient than ever. We have quite a number of good voices in our congregation. We aim at congregational praise in singing. It is, however, as needful that the choir be prepared in heart and voice to lead the voices of the people, as it is for me to be prepared to lead the prayers and thoughts of the people.

I attach, therefore, great importance to the organization of this choir, and pray that we may get the right people in it Satan often makes discord, among those who should most of all be in accord, both in spirit and voice. I pray it may not be so with our choir—nor have any reason to think otherwise

We will go on for the present in the International Hall and take God's time for a better place. The idea is gaining strength that a building of our own is needed, and that the success of our church will be largely affected by delay in getting it. Had we a roomy, plain, well arranged hall in theatrical form, with class rooms, and built in an unpretentious style in a central position, we could get two thousand persons to hear, as readily as we can now a few hundreds On several occasions lately our Hall has been far too small for those in it, the heat has been very distressing, and hundreds more might have been present had it been larger This is a very deplorable fact. But I will not worry about it. The matter is in the Lord's hands He will provide. I will do my utmost to raise "The Free Christian Tabernacle" whenever the Lord sets it before me, and raised it will be, I believe.

But "Except the Lord build the house, they labor in vain that build it." I know that we must wait until He has first found "the people", and then He will give us a house where we can worship Him and into which we can welcome the rich and poor, diseased and dying souls, who are spiritually starving in the streets and the lanes of this city for whose salvation I hourly long.

Will you pray especially for me in this matter? We want the Lord to send us some of His silver and gold. He can do it quickly, and I am sure He will, if we are faithful in seeking it from Him alone, if we desire to use it only for His glory, and if the time has come for Him to entrust us with it for this purpose. Surely we have now come to the place where we should say, "Let us build a house for the Lord" Surely we shall have grace to be faithful and unselfish. I really do think we are ready, or nearly so, to "go forward", exercising faith, in this matter From this day, I intend to spend half an hour daily in prayer for the Tabernacle for the Lord, until He grant me the desire of my heart, or make me clearly to see that it is not in accordance with His will

If you will join me in this, I believe we shall not pray long ere the first money will be sent for this purpose, and all the rest in due time. Let us especially keep before us in this matter the Lord's own promise—"Again I say unto you, that if two of you shall agree on earth as touching anything that they shall ask it shall be done for them of my Father which is in heaven" When we get the building, we will carve upon a stone above its central doorway this inscription "Have faith in God." Now do join me in this matter, and tell me how you are impressed concerning it. Remember, it is to give a half an hour each day to this matter alone We shall not ask without receiving.

And now I must draw this letter to a close. for I do not wish to be any longer silent Write me very soon, if you please, in reply and it will help me to write the quicker in return I desire to write oftener, but how to perform I know not I need reforming in the matter of letter writing. It would be better, doubtless, if I wrote shorter and more frequently. But I always dread to write what may be misunderstood, and brevity has that danger

284

I can imagine that my letter will give you mingled pain and pleasure as you read it; but you will doubtless feel as you read to the end, that I have reason to rejoice in God's deliverance and to praise Him for His present grace. If you read Psalms 124 and 126 they will express exactly what I now feel. But I must not close this matter without a few sentences concerning personal and family matters And first I must say concerning the five pounds you were good enough to lend me to pay my passage, that I deeply regret that I cannot at present send it to you. I advanced to my Election Committee all the money I had in hand, and **never got a penny of it back again**, although I hope I yet will. Then the unexpected cost of the overland passage, and the many extra expenses and heavy losses I have lately had, has made me to be not only short of money, but in plain language, embarrassed, for want of it. I hope, however, to be able to send it to you ere long, and much do I wish that I were able to send you a great deal of money, if that would be good for you, for at all events I am sure it would be well for you to have a little more than you have at present. If ever the day comes when I can, you may be very sure I gladly will help you thus But I am engaged in a work where the earthly rewards are but small at the best.

Our new house will be healthier, it has a bathroom and other conveniences that this house lacks. It is situated on one of the highest points of the city, and overlooks a considerable part of the harbor and city. There are many reasons which caused us to change, but if there had been no other, the fact that this house is very old and cockroachy and above all that the neighborhood is becoming more unhealthy and overcrowded every month would have been reason enough. This house lies in the valley near Woolloomooloo Bay. Our new home is about a hundred feet higher, I should say, and perfectly drained We move there, God willing, on Monday next.

Jeanie primus is in good average health, and is still my good, patient, industrious, and prudent wife. She is increasingly useful to me and much liked in the work She has quite thrown her heart into the school and will doubtless become a very efficient teacher I wish she had less domestic care, but she bears up well and will get through splendidly. She has a treasure of a servant, Annie Macy, who never counts anything she does for us a trouble.

Jeanie secundus, that is, Jeanie Macfarlane, is just the sweetest little pet you ever saw. She is always a picture of content and beauty She is always ready to smile with her eyes But I wish she were stronger. She does not seem to suffer, and never gives any trouble, sleeping all night through and never rejecting her food. Yet she does not seem to keep herself up, her head seems almost too large for her dear little neck—they say it is like mine, and mine is heavy enough, sometimes, I can tell you. However, we have no cause for any alarm, only that she will need care, and we are hoping that the fresh breezes on the Darlinghurst Heights will give a little more color to her pale sweet face and strength to her little body.

As for Gladdy, he is perpetual motion embodied. He is growing every way and says and does the most astonishing things. He never does, and never will do, things by halves. If he is naughty, he is naughty, and it needs "father" to put down the rebellion. When he is good, he is good, and no infant Jesus artist painted ever had a sweeter expression than he

His imitation of me is said to be very exact. Occasionally he delivers a sermon to goats and naughty boys whom he sees from our back window. This is an exact report of one the other day, and you will perceive the theology is quite original, even if it be scarcely orthodox, according to Dwight "Goats!

286

you are nasty. But, goats, you should be good. Be good goats, and perhaps God will make you little lambs of Jesus "

On another occasion, he startled his mother by climbing on a chair, then he opened a little book and gravely addressed an imaginary audience as follows: "Now, all you little children who have books, turn to the fifth hymn." And then he went on, "Take the name of Jesus with you," etc The other day when she sent him for something, he must have found a blind stick loose and pulled it out. When he appeared in the presence of his mother with it, the inquiry was immediately made as to where he got it. With great earnestness he said, "God gave it to me, mother." That assertion being at once contradicted, he fell back on another, "Grandfather sent it to me, mother"—which was too much for our gravity, although we did not fail to bring him to a full confession and due repentance concerning his having become unlawfully possessed of the said blind stick.

He adores "dear little Jeanie Macfarlane" or "dear little sister." He firmly believes she never gets naughty, and that "no goat" or "naughty spirit" has ever "got into sister's heart," although he will freely confess that is not the case with himself. .

(Dated from North Terrace, Adelaide, Feb, 9, 1881, whence, after breaking up his home and leaving his work in Sidney, he had gone, en route to England to meet a scoundrel by the name of Holding, who under the guise of religion and friendship had gained his complete confidence and who had promised him a large sum of money with which to build a church. The story is told in the succeeding group of letters, the last one, dated six years later than the present date, being published in The Christian Colonist)

My Darling Wife:

I today received your sweet letter of 1st with our dear little son's letter to me enclosed full of "thick love," and indeed they both cheered me very much

287

I now sit down to write the first of the long letters which I promised yesterday in my telegram; and I sincerely hope that I may be able to tell you of money on the way even before you read these lines

When I wrote to you my last letter, I was with our dear friends the McD—'s at Birnam Wood, and I am sure that I very narrowly escaped a severe illness by going there: for I never remember to have felt more brain weary and pained in all my life than I did when I went there. And yet I could not sleep until after dawn for a long time and found myself quite unequal to any long sustained mental or physical exertion, and after the services which I wrote to you about at Crystal Brook were finished I suffered a relapse from having overtaxed my head However, I was by God's goodness amongst the very kindest of friends, and Mrs McD—especially deserves every good thing you could think or say of her: for she counted no trouble or labour too much to give me ease or comfort. Had I been in a palace I could not have had more willing servants or more tender care, and I must get you one day to tell our friends in your own sweet way how deeply you value their kindness

It is indeed a mercy for which I cannot be too grateful to God that I am spared to you and to my dear ones, if indeed my poor, weak life is after all of much use to anybody, for sometimes I get to questioning very much if it is, and wonder whether after all I would be much loss if I were removed from earth—even for your own dear sake I have sometimes been tempted to ask whether it would not be best. But that feeling does not last long when I think of you and your true heart's love for me and of my dear little son and daughter—to whom I never can be replaced: for even though it might not be difficult for you, dearest, to get a better husband,—and I say it with sincere humility, yet they could never get another father. And I do love these children very dearly, and wish it were in

my power to be at their side this very moment. They
and you are worth living for, and I sometimes feel
as if I could wish to live more for you than I have
done I am tempted to ask sometimes if I have not
lived too much for others, and verily if I were to decide
that question by men's gratitude, for the most part,
or even the approval of the church generally, I should
answer, Yes, I have lived too much for others But
when I remember that all the noblest and most fruitful lives which have ever been lived on earth have
been for others, and when I remember the Grandest
Life, that of the Sinless Man, was lived without even
a thought of self and entirely from first to last for
others,—then I am ashamed to think of my poor, puny
self-denials and trials when compared with His—our
Pattern.

"Wearied and faint" in my mind as I often become, when I find my noblest deeds unheeded or misrepresented by those who should joyfully recognize
them, I find I can only be comforted by turning to Him
who has trodden every foot of this path, and in considering Him who endured such contradiction of
sinners against Himself, I alone find peace and rest.
He forgives my sins, carries my sorrows, comforts my
soul, strengthens my faith, brightens my hopes, and
crowns me with His love Oh, how kind and how
good He is to me, and but for Him I should indeed
despair. for I am weak, and lonely, and prone to
wander even though I love Him. But He is patient,
and without upbraiding receives me to His heart
again.

I have learned, though, one lesson very thoroughly
since I have left you, and that is that we ought not
to be apart for long, since Satan can make use of our
separation to create a temptation and hindrance, to
me at least, which I fully determine shall not exist one
day longer than I can help I am glad now, therefore,
for my detention here, so far as that is concerned, be-

10

cause it has resulted in my determination that whether I go to England after Q—comes or not, you and my dear ones shall go with me or stay with me, wherever it may be I now feel that it would have been wrong for me, and not good for you, for us to have been on other sides of the world Circumstances have made us to be very dependent upon each other for sympathy in an unusual degree, and I feel that we must never leave each other for so long again if it be possible to avoid it

But this is beginning at the wrong end of my letter, and telling you first what properly comes last as to arrangement, though indeed it is first in point of importance ˙You will want to know, however, what has happened to me since my last letter of nearly a fortnight—indeed to my amazement I see it is sixteen days—ago, when I wrote to you from Birnam Wood

Well, don't be alarmed if I tell you that much of it seems like a horrid dream which I only dimly remember, and would find it impossible to write—for my head was more queer than any one knew and had my bodily strength not kept pretty fairly up, I would have gone down never to rise on earth again. But I never entirely lost faith and courage and consciousness, and kept my deepest troubles to myself for the most part My severest trials arose one-half, and now arise, from the extraordinary attitude which my father has taken up toward me in this whole matter; and the utter shattering at one blow of the confidence of a life time in his integrity, and fearless courage, and superiority to all low views of self-seeking And I know that it will be impossible for me, even if I were willing, to put into any letter of mine words to describe what he has said and done against me in Mr H—'s matters, or the strange position in which we stand towards each other now by that conduct.

I came down from Birnam Wood late on Wednesday last, and hoped to find my father in a frame of mind ready to pursue a more straightforward and kindly course towards me, but it was entirely the reverse. He had received another of those extraordinary letters from Mr H—reflecting upon me, and seemed rather to glory in the fact, although the matters upon which he remarked were entire misunderstandings on his part, which a few minutes could set right with an honest man any day when face to face

He asked me to tell him my plans and to hear and take his advice. I said I would only tell him my thoughts and intentions if he would promise not to tell A—one word of what I said. He refused to give the promise, and became very angry and abusive. But I refused to say any more or to hear or take his advise, telling him a few plain truths as to his position towards me He was in a most extraordinary condition of mind, but I had recovered my strength to some extent—though this scene threw me back for a little—and was strong enough to keep from getting very indignant with him, because, painful as it is to say it, he seemed deliberately to provoke me with a view to getting me to commit myself to the use of expressions of which he might hereafter make some use against me with Mr H—as he has now threatened to do. This was on Thursday

I left him as quickly as possible, and had no more conversation of any kind with him until Monday—waiting to see what news the English mail which was delivered on Saturday night would bring Meanwhile, I was very little in the house, and on Sunday evening I went to Hindmarsh and preached for my old friend John McE—, coming back to the city with him after service On Monday morning my father came into the room with a letter in his hand which he flung down before on the table,—"Read that!"

It was a letter from Mr. H—and was certainly a very strange production, and a fitting climax to those which had gone before. It seems someone had written from Australia (father volunteered the information that it was not him and was sure it was not A—; and if the one is as sure as the other, then neither assurance is reliable)—this "someone" had written last November saying that I had stated to many persons that he (Mr. H—) was quite unfit to do anything for himself and that I would require to go home and do everything for him, etc —all which you know is quite as true as the other fact which someone sent him, namely, that I had gone to Melbourne to plead for the life of the bush ranger, Ned Kelley. But, believing at once this malicious invention of someone, and apparently forgetting everything he ought to have remembered just at that moment of numberless lies which he knew to have been invented concerning me, he writes in a most angry and I must say foolish fashion, concerning me He says he will still give me the 21,000 pounds and even pray God to bless me, but he does not trust me, I am a bad business man and not discreet, and not like father, and wishes I was, nor like A—in whom and in father he expresses full confidence, and winds up by saying that he has been obliged to show all my letters to his trustees, who have requested him not to write to me, to which he has agreed, and that he is coming out to Australia by the "Cotopaxi" which leaves England (or has left now) on February 5th.

This is a fair summary of his letter and is the strongest proof (if he is, as I will still hope and believe, an honest man) that he has been for a long time continuously subjected to a stream of evil influences. The only other conclusion is that he is a rogue and a fool, which I will refuse to believe unless it is proved beyond a doubt.

But will your ears, or eyes, credit what I am now going to tell you? When father saw I had finished the letter I looked on his face, and there was a smile of quiet satisfaction.

"Well?" he said, waiting for me to speak.

"Well," I said, "I see this pleases you, but it will be a short lived pleasure; for an hour with him face to face will be quite enough to put all these lies for ever to flight, if, as I believe, H— is a true man at heart. That letter does not alter my plans in the least" At the last words he started and seemed agitated a little.

"Then you still intend to stay and meet him," he said, "and your mother tells me that you are even thinking of bringing Jeanie and the children over here, too."

I replied, "Yes, I will stay, and perhaps,—indeed very likely,—I will bring Jeanie over, but not to this house, depend upon it. for I see more than ever clearly that you are against me, and want to see the will altered to serve your own purposes, many of which I now see through."

He put a strong restraint upon himself and began in a coaxing tone—"Now, I would just advise you to accept the position this letter places you in, your home is in Sydney and your friends back there; you will never alter Mr. H—nor get more than the 21,000 pounds; and if you stay you will only make a mess of it all." I waited with as much patience as I could to hear this precious piece of advice to its close.

"Well," I said, "whoever would have thought that you could have been so wicked and yet so foolish as to show me your hand. You certainly are my enemy in this matter. You advise me to accept the position in which that letter places me, and yet dare to call yourself my friend. You know that letter is entirely based upon false reports, and advise me to let them remain in his mind as true. You know how A—, whose tool and helper you are, is false and wicked, and want me to let my friend think him true and good, **you** know you are crooked in this matter, and are afraid of my staying here, you try to frighten me for the loss of all, but I don't care for that compared to the loss of my character; and you say Mr. H—will never change, but that is the worst of all: for that would be to write rogue on his face, since if I have been misrepresented and am unchanged then there is no need for him to change if he is good—and your bad thought that he will never change towards me is fathered by a bad wish in your heart" So spoke I, and I was angry, but spoke coolly and slowly, letting him feel the force of every word

"What wish do you mean," he said, boiling over with rage

I said, "The wish to get as much of the money as you can for yourself. I see that has been your aim for a long time; and long ago you conspired with A—that he should give H—money, and that you would make it pay him and you well.

"What," he roared, "I conspire with A—to get money out of H—? Take care what you say, sir; it is false "

"Oh, no," I said, "the money was to be got out of me, and what I say is true "

"How out of you?" he said, looking very uneasy.

"This way," I replied, "you were heard by one whom I can trust to say to A—when Mr. H—needed money in Adelaide just after making the will in my favor leaving me nearly all, or about 200,000 pounds, I say you were heard to say—'Yes, give him the money, give him all he needs, he has made a will in John's favor and if he dies, as he thinks he will, I will make John drop 20,000 pounds."

"How dare you say that, you mean, contemptible fellow?" he asked when he got voice

I answered, "'Tis not I who am mean and contemptible, but the man who could use such words; and you cannot deny saying them · for I can produce the man who heard them."

"I do deny saying them," he said.

"Oh, your answer is a mere quibble," I said, "but you used words conveying the same meaning, I am sure, and I tell you more: you hope he will live now, and that you and A—can do better without me; A— knows he has nothing to hope for now if the money should ever come to me, and you fear you won't get so much from me, if it does, as you might, and therein you are quite right. Hence you are anxious to get me out of the way. But I should not wonder if you were terribly disappointed yet: for see him I will, if I live, when he arrives, and unless he is another man than my old friend and brother, he will not allow base-less lies to alter his affection and purposes. But he can do what he pleases. He is a free agent, and I never did aught to bind him, and never will And but for the good it might do in my hands I could curse the money, and wish none of it might ever come to Australia, and perhaps that will be the end of it for God sees what a curse it has already been to you and A—even in anticipation, and what a heart break it is to me "

With these words, or similar,—I have tried faith-fully to preserve and record this conversation—I left him. That was on Monday forenoon. I am now writ-ing these words on Wednesday night But we have never uttered even one word to each other since, al-though living in the same house We, by mutual con-sent I suppose, avoid each other; never eat together; and in short keep entirely apart. My dear mother is most kind and very wise She sees the trouble is too deep for her to meddle, and so she just quietly goes about her work, and is very good to me but says nothing. Of course this state of affairs is most un-natural, and cannot long continue. But I leave it with the Lord. He only can put things straight.

This only I can say, I did not make them crooked for you know my father has been all my life until now the very embodiment of integrity and courage to me, and that I relied upon him absolutely

Judge, then, how deep my sorrow, my misery, to find my idol to melt away when tried, like a snow man when the sun shines on it—ay and that man my father, whom I had ever honored, and, as far as he had right, obeyed

My whole nature seems to be torn asunder in this trial, and every nerve of body and soul seems to have been separately tortured by it —and these words but faintly express what I feel and have felt.

And the worst is, I see no remedy for this in the future. Only God and time can heal this sore heart. But I am sure your sympathy and love and presence here would help me tonight But, alas, a thousand miles divide us Yet in spirit I am with you always, and bending over you now I say "God bless you, and good night;" and God bless our three little loves for ever and ever. . . .

Dearest. after a rather restless night I feel very weary, but still am decidedly improving. No one to look at me, would think there was much the matter; but it is not the body, but the mind, from which I suffer so much. However, I feel I am getting stronger daily, and I doubt not that God will restore me to you again. I find it so very, very hard to write, and it takes me so long: for I have to rest every few lines. It seemed to me as if I could not write until I began this letter, and God only knows how painful it has been for me to write what I have done

It has taken me a very long time indeed, and yet I have not told you all my sorrow, no, nor the half.

Had it not been for my awful troubles, I might have been further forward in money matters, but I have been almost afraid to move about much, too soon: for my head has been "shaky" and dizzy with strong rushes of blood to my heart and brain, causing me to be very careful.

I have not quite got over my fainting fit in the Baths at Glenelsy; but I have no doubt I will

Of course the worry of thinking about you and the children—rent—store—and other accounts—was very great; but you will remember that I was nearly 200 miles from town and ill, and I am sure you won't think I could be wilfully careless for one moment. It will be a pleasant minute when I send you money I have had one consolation, that my noble friends, A—and S—, would stand by you and do their best to get you time and save you worry and help you all they could And then G—'s kind sympathy and love were with you, and the joy and comfort of our dear little ones, and many kind hearts were sympathizing, and many more of our good people were praying, and then I was every hour thinking of you, and praying God to bless, sustain and comfort you—so I felt often comforted in prayer amidst my inexpressible loneliness and weariness of heart.

I close at last in haste not to miss post. Kisses and love to the dear children.

Your ever affectionate husband,

John Alexander Dowie

My Darling Jeanie:

It is now more than a week since I wrote to you, but you must not blame me, dearest, for I have been very unwell, and indeed it is only since Saturday night that I have known any ease from the pain in my head, or had any really refreshing sleep

But by God's goodness I now feel so well and free from pain, that I can scarcely credit the change I dared not even try to write to you before: for my attempt to do so was most distressing in its effects upon my head.

Our dear friends have been most kind and atten-

297

tive to me, and their love and esteem is evidently greater than ever. The harvest has been very poor owing to red rust, and as they have been adding to their farms by large purchases last year, they find it rather hard to pull through this year I have told them well nigh all about our affairs, and they will help me all they can, I am sure I expect in two days to know what that is, and will then return to town and remit to you all I can

I am grateful that my reason and life are yet spared, for your dear sakes very largely

I love you all very, very dearly, and it is an increasing trial to part from you for my still contemplated journey to England But God will help us to bear it and to do His blessed will.

Kindly remember me to S—and A—. I am sure they will do their best to help you until I can send. Once or twice I feared you would never hear from me any more on earth; but God has been good in sparing me. . . . .

Last night I preached for an old friend at Crystal Brook to a crowded chapel—subject, "Peace." Crystal Brook is about seven miles from this farm to which I have been asked to give a name, and have accordingly baptized it "Birnam Wood," from the beautiful scrub belt around it, and the romantic name is very much appreciated

But my head is at it again a little, and I must stop Love, love, love to all Kisses to my dear little son and daughter.

My darling, for you every prayer and wish is for your good, sweet love of my heart, and I shall count it long till I embrace you and tell you all I never can write The Lord bless you and all our dear ones always.

Your affectionate husband,
John Alexander Dowie.

My Dear Mrs M—.

I return herewith that arch-liar and hypocrite H—'s letter to you of June 9, and thank you for your kindness in permitting me to copy it.

The amazing daring of this scoundrel in writing such a letter within ten days of his complete exposure by your relatives in London, and his confession to the detectives, astound me beyond measure

However, as he has in his later letter of June 30, announced his intention of departing this life, it is quite possible that your next letter will be one from some of his confederates in this little game, giving you a touching account of his pious death It will be interesting to observe the handwriting of that epistle should it arrive I have a perfect recollection of the style of writing in the two forged letters of Holding's which he placed in my hands—one from New York and the other from Washington Both must have been the work of criminal confederates, as must also have been the letter forged in your name which he showed to Mr S—.

Probably he is one of a gang of thieves and forgers.

You will remember that two or three days were e-nough to enable him to get the letter forged in your name, so that his accomplices could not be far away.

I confess that the conduct of his relatives appear strange to me, and I cannot think they are without blame For instance, his uncle knew where to address a telegram to him concerning his sister-in-law's death, and, probably, his father and brother also knew where he was staying—at a rich gentleman's house—and yet, though they knew he was a penniless adventurer and thief of a widow's savings in their own neighbor-hood, they never say anything until it is too late. This does not look well on the face of it. But there may be some explanation possible which can free

299

them from blame or guilt. I sincerely hope so Still, the matter looks suspicious until that is given.

The effect of H—'s heartless deception will be felt by you for many a day, and my own suffering and loss through him, makes me to feel all the more sympathetically for you and your sons.

To them it is not merely a temporal loss but a spiritual danger for the hypocrisy of the villain was one of the most powerful helpers in his nefarious, diabolical schemes But I earnestly trust that they will look at this matter in its right light, and see in it, not a reason for keeping their hearts from God, but an awful reason for fleeing from sin and Satan which, this wretched man proves, can tie a soul hand and foot, and cast him into a living hell, even on earth.

I have long believed in demoniacal possession of those who give themselves willingly to the service of Satan, and I see in H—a striking confirmation of what I see round me every day. "The spirits of devils," you will read in Revelation, 16th chapter and 14th verse are "to go forth;" and I am sure they have come, and are possessing the hearts of those who are sleeping in Zion, and careless about having on their souls the spotless robes of Christ's righteousness.

"Blessed is he that watcheth, and keepeth his garments, lest he walk naked, and they see his shame."

And to do the opposite is to be cursed, and deceived by "the spirits of devils." Now, if there is a man on God's earth today who has lost his garment, who is walking a naked liar in all his vileness, and whose shame is seen, it is H—, held and led as he is in chains of sin by the Devil at his will It is an awful warning God have mercy upon that damned soul, and though he has made his "bed in hell" may the "right hand" of an Omnipotent God of Love draw him up out of "the horrible pit," into which his sins have cast him I recall most vividly this afternoon the awful terror which used to possess H—whenever

Spiritualism, against which I was lecturing in July, '80, was mentioned. It was remarked at the time, and set down to his sensitiveness and weakness. Little did I think he was a devil-possessed soul then, and that he shrank at his demons' bidding, from contact with the subject. I observe the same shrinking from it, in others whom I know are not right with the Lord. O that the Holy Spirit of God might work mightily upon the sin and Satan possessed hearts of men! It is a fearful thing to fall into the hands of living devils; and I do pray that from henceforth we may have discerning spirits, so as to know more quickly a man of evil spirits when he comes to us in any guise. "Beloved," (says the Spirit of God in the first epistle of John, chapter 4 and verse 1) "believe not every spirit, but try the spirits whether they are of God; because many false prophets are gone out into the world." This is a most important command. Let us ask from God the Spirit of Christ to obey it; no other power can give us the victory. I realize that, more and more every day I live.

How foolish we are to forget what our "weapon" as Christians is. Look at the epistle to the Ephesians (6th chapter and 10th to 12th verses, revised version) and you will see to what I refer: "Finally, be strong in the Lord, and in the strength of his might. Put on the whole armour of God, that we may be able to stand against the wiles of the devil. For our wrestling is not against flesh and blood, but against principalities, against powers, against the world-rulers of this darkness, against the spiritual hosts of wickedness in the heavenly places"—or "in the upper air," as some translate the words.

But I fear I am wearying you with too long a letter. Its importance is my only apology. May it lead you, my dear lady, to rest your whole heart entirely upon Him who is "mighty to save" from every foe in earth or hell.

301

May you all be guided and blessed by God—**His** blessing "maketh rich and addeth no sorrow with it," and that cannot be said of any other kind of blessing: for every rose has a thorn except the Rose of Sharon. every crown is a burden except the Crown of Life, and every death has a sting except where God gives the victory

---

My Dear Madam:

It has been in my heart for some weeks that I should write to you concerning the work of the Lord in this city, with a view specially to enlist your sympathy, prayers and help in the efforts now being put forth by the Salvation Army. But I have been deterred by several causes, one of which was my own indecision as to my official relations to it, and the difficulty, nay, the impossibility, of writing all I would wish to say, and of answering the numerous enquiries which would very properly arise in your mind concerning its operations

Therefore, I have determined to write and ask you if it is convenient and agreeable to you for me to visit you on Monday next. If so, it will give me pleasure to come and plead the cause of this great work, and its claims upon the Lord's stewards, of whom you are one.

I have given between three and four months diligent study to the history and organization of this marvelous association, and to an active co-operation with it in Adelaide. Last night was held the anniversary of the formation of the First Adelaide Corps and the opening of the second building, "The Salvation Army Academy," now occupied by the Army here.

Eleven souls professed to find peace with God through Jesus at the prayer meeting, which makes about twenty saved in the last three days God is working mightily amongst us; and I realize His Spirit's guidance in my long and wearied detention in Adelaide through business, and the entire break up of all my plans of work consequent upon the discovery that my supposed great benefactor and friend —W. G. Q. H—is only a great swindler and hypocrite. You were good enough to express the desire to know the sequel to what I told you about him in May last, and if I have the pleasure of seeing you, I promise you a story which is fit to rank in clever audacity with the most romantic of swindles, his career in England being a most extraordinary series of adventures and impostures.

It has been a most painful and trying experience.

It is a melancholy satisfaction, however, to know that he deceived clever business men of high standing in England for months as to his alleged, but really mythical, wealth: for it can no longer be said, if it ever has been, that he practiced upon most immoderate credulity in my case, seeing that for many months he lived with persons such as I have referred to without detection or suspicion. It has been a most mysterious affliction, and productive of much anxiety to me, and to many. . . .

Dear Brother In Christ:

Enclosed I hand you three clippings from our local papers, which are fairly correct reports of the case which is of some interest to many of your readers; and I shall be glad if you will find room for them in your next issue of the **Christian Colonist**, which I always read with much interest.

You can imagine my surprise to find H—, dressed in full Salvation Army uniform, selling all sorts of things, with radiant smiles and coaxing words, to admiring customers, at the Trade Tent of the Salvation Army at their Annual Demonstration on the South Melbourne Cricket Ground. I had just been conversing with Commissioner Howard, and after a few words with him again, my long lost, and, according to a funeral card now in my possession—once deceased, deceiver, was confronted with me.

What a change! Smiles vanished, and fear and guilt and shame chased each other over his ash-colored face A few minutes served to make his real character so clear that he was at once removed from the Trade Tent, and dismissed from the ground I advised him to get away, by sea, as quickly as possible, failing which he would certainly be arrested, and I spoke earnestly to him in urging him to abandon his miserable course of deceit, and seek God's mercy And so we parted on Friday—New Year's Day.

But on the following Monday he came to my house, looking most unhappy, and said, "I can't go away—I want to make a full confession to you, and give myself up to the police, or do whatever you tell me." After consideration, and in the presence of witnesses, I took down, with many cross questionings, a most extraordinary story of crimes beginning in 1877, with minute details of a band of about thirteen clever associates, amongst whom are two solicitors, a doctor, and men of various professions

These swindlers had offices in New York and other parts of America, in Paris and Mentone in France, and in Leicester, Bath, and London in England. By their aid, fraudulent correspondence and forged legal documents, with all sorts of skilful plans for swindling, were employed; and H—appears to have only been in the outer circle of this long firm of swindlers—as they are called by the detectives, who say that it is very rarely that they extend their operations to these colonies. Long before he came to Australia he had helped in some of their villainous schemes, and he gives minute details of a funeral in Derbyshire, at which he was chief mourner, where the whole thing was a sham—stones and packing taking the place of the supposed corpse. From that and other circumstances, it is evident that they were engaged, amongst other things, in Assurance frauds.

They frequently had a good deal of ready money, which they used freely, sometimes renting for a period large mansions and estates the owners of which were abroad, and from one of these the bogus funeral in Derbyshire took place. There are many strange things in this story, also, to which I can make no allusions: for it is now in progress of investigation by the police, and the names of wealthy merchants, manufacturers, and even bankers who were deceived would require to be given—a proceeding which could only cause pain, and defeat the ends of justice. Several times ere it happened, he was nearly found out, and when the discovery did come he was on the most familiar terms of friendship with a large circle of persons of wealth and social position in various parts of England, upon whom he was most skilfully imposing. One of these. a member of a firm, whose name is widely known in these colonies, was about to lend him 1500 pounds, and I found that he had been making use of the friendly letters of that gentleman, in which he somewhat pressed the little loan, and regretted he could not make it larger just then. These letters were in his pocket when he was ignominiously expelled from the house of Sir J. S—with whom he had been living for nearly six months, with brief intervals. I made him give me these letters, and they are now in the hands of the detective police.

On Wednesday, H—came to my house again, by appointment, and gave himself up to Detective Sergeant Walsh there, and the same evening he was lodged in prison. Two days after, as the appended reports show, he confessed his guilt upon a formal charge which I had made, and was remanded for sentence.

But a difficulty arose—and it is a practical comment upon the need of Federation—, it was found that the Courts here had no jurisdiction, since the offense had been committed on the other side of the River Murray; and, although he had pleaded guilty, and all the parties were here, the police magistrate was compelled to discharge him, unless I would incur the cost, time and trouble of going to Sydney to lay an information, get a warrant for his apprehension, wait for a writ of extradition, and then remain to go on with the prosecution before the police court, there, with a probable prospect of having to return to Sydney in a month or two to give evidence at this trial before the court there I, therefore, viewing these facts, and above all having the conviction that he was really penitent before God for his wickedness declined to give any promise that I would go to New South Wales and initiate the proceedings afresh there It was the most perplexing position in which to be placed, and I believe that I was rightly guided in my decision

Will you, then, kindly publish this letter in the "Colonist," so that the many sufferers through H—'s deceptions in your colony may know the facts connected with this matter; and, probably, this will be reprinted from your columns into some of the papers here, and in the colonies of New South Wales, Queensland, Tasmania and New Zealand, for the poor, wretched fellow has committed acts of fraud in all of the Australian colonies, except Western Australia. It is due to my many Christian friends in these lands that I should make these explanations; and it may possibly put an end to the further circulation of one of the numerous falsehoods of my enemies, namely, that I received a large sum of money from this adventurer with which to build a tabernacle in Sydney.

Strange to say, a Christian brother from Ballarat, Mr. Elias Hoskins, was visiting me on the day when H—came to make his confession, and at my request, he with two others witnessed every word he spoke.

Afterward Mr. Hoskins told me that only a few days before a prominent Christian worker in Ballarat had taken him aside, and with shrugs and whispered confidence had warned him against me, **because I had never accounted for the 21,000 pounds which I had once received by deed of gift to build a church.**

Excuse the length of this letter, and let me add that, with the exception of a few words in the Introduction to my pamphlet on **Spiritualism Unmasked,** published here in 1882, I have made no public explanations concerning this matter which nearly six years ago caused me to break up my home, and leave my dear people and work in Sydney, en route for England to meet this adventurer, whose letters detained me at Adelaide for many months until authentic news reached me of his imposture. What I, and mine, have suffered and lost through that, God only knows; but since His love and mercy have sustained me amidst all, I rejoice to have had an opportunity of showing mercy to my enemy, and with that act closing this page of my life's history.

I am,

Ever yours in Jesus,

John Alexander Dowie.

(Dated from the Victoria Coffee House, March 29, 1882—almost despairs—suffers for food—ready to die or live—true to the service of his Lord.)

Beloved Wife:

It is hard and bitter for me to have to write to you today; but it would have been impossible for me to write to you two days ago.

Once more, I have to write the discouraging word "failed."

But I live, and God lives, and it cannot be that the night will long endure, and that one who strives to do His will shall always fail.

I will try again in another direction—indeed, I am already at it, and will hope on: for there is still a guiding Star which shines on through the darkness, although for one long night I almost doubted that. But, when I "saw the star" again, I "rejoiced," as did the wise men of old, as did the true sons of God in every age, and I am sure it is the "Morning Star" Only for this comfort I would die, and I have seemed to be near dying many times. It is and has been hard to bear; and "my feet were almost gone" into ways of doubt, and fear, and sin, and death for that is the way of the backslider and forsaker of his Lord But He kept me

Last Friday evening the Executive Committee met and decided to make no appointment for the present

This was done after Mr M—, the Secretary, had employed every measure to delay a decision, and to thwart Dr. S—'s action He failed to find any means of prejudicing the Executive against me directly, but he succeeded indirectly at a small meeting, in which he got a majority to support him His point was that Dr. S—was thrusting me upon them, and that it was taking all power out of their hands, to make his offer to raise 100 pounds dependent upon my appointment. This was wrought with success upon a majority who were attached to him for various reasons.

But it was a farce: for they had in their letter expressed their "deep regret" that they could not comply with my "esteemed proposal;" and we were informed that the only difficulty was the want of means

Dr. S—removed that, by guaranteeing the first quarter of my salary for a year at 400 pounds; and this then brought out Mr. M—in his true colors He feared loss of prestige and of position, and determined to resist the proposal. He tried to weary me out and disgust me by delaying a meeting and, when that failed, he excited the unworthy and unfounded prejudice against Dr. S——, to which I have referred. It may work his own undoing yet; but at present it has prevented **my appointment.**

It is a miserable story and another instance of the fact that in Australia the Temperance cause is hindered by ignorant, mean, incompetent men, who cannot lead themselves, but are strong enough to hinder others; so, apart from all personal considerations, a most deplorable position and, in consequence, the liquor traffic is becoming daily stronger, the laws which have been passed to restrain it, such as the Sunday Closing Act, are openly defied, and vice, crime, disease and pauperism are increasing in most alarming proportions. This traffic stands in the way of all progress, and yet the churches are almost entirely inactive, and the Temperance workers are a miserable, disunited rabble, envious of each other, and not true to the cause, so far as organized effort against the drink traffic is concerned. Oh, the sad, heart-rending scenes of misery which I have seen! They would wring your heart and horrify your soul Yet the scenes are but the story of ten thousand homes.

Oh, it has been a weary time for me, since last I saw your face Alone in this great, cold city, I have spent some of the most sorrowful hours of my life. Anxiety concerning you and my dear ones, who are so near my heart; fears for the future of this uncertain life; doubts as to the past; questionings as to why God was permitting these fiery trials; strugglings with the dire realities of the present, with its poverty, weakness, my growing shabbiness, and ofttimes positive hunger—all these, and more, have been my companions day and night for months Do you remember the date when I told you I had 6d left to face the week with? It was more than a fortnight ago, I think.

Well, when it was spent, I did not have a penny until yesterday. I made up my mind that I would die, rather than ask Mr. D—or any one for money help again, and I just lived upon what I ate at the house of Dr T—when he invited me there, and at that of Mr. C—, a Christian bookseller with whom I am well acquainted. I did not average one meal per day up to yesterday, and sometimes I have gone forty-eight hours without breaking my fast—on one occasion, I had only one meal, tea, for seventy-two hours. But I did not cease to pray for deliverance, and watch for an opportunity of doing something to earn money I was asked to write something for printing, which I did, and yesterday I received 5 pounds from the gentleman to whom I read the MS and it is to be printed at his expense very soon I am to get, by and by, a little more money from it This money was God's direct gift: for I did not tell this gentleman my necessity, although I intended doing so at the last extremity But I did not need to do so He gave it to me without a single word from me, in the nicest way It seemed a little fortune to me, after my distress, and I praised and "thanked God and took courage." I had to pay away at once a large portion of it on account of what I owe the manager of this place for my lodging; which should have been paid in advance, which is the rule.

So that I saved very little of the money; but I shall be very careful with it and watch for ways of getting more I am a good deal thinner, a little paler, and there are a few more gray hairs in my head, but this is no doubt due to my fasting, added to my sad thoughts and disappointments But I do not think any permanent injury has resulted

Do not let this trouble you, I beseech you. The Lord will not suffer me to be tempted beyond my strength.

Oh, for the end of all this sense of pain and sin in this false and cruel world which Satan rules! ..

The Church of today is as unlike Christ's example as it was eighteen hundred years ago when it crucified Him. Perhaps we may be nearer "the midnight" than we have hitherto believed; and it may be we shall soon hear the cry at midnight, "Behold, the bridegroom cometh: go ye out to meet Him!" Let us be ready. Let us keep our light burning, our lives shining for the Lord and filled with all the fullness of God's Spirit.

Do not let us be found slumbering and sleeping, when the "Cry" comes, with "lamps gone out," as also seems to be the case with many whom we love; who have a name to live and are dead, and who mock me in their folly, because I love and serve the Lord.

Oh, what an awakening it will be for them should Jesus come now, and find their hearts empty of love to Him, and their lives dark and cold, like burnt out lamps. I feel as if I wanted to warn and entreat them all to awaken out of their sleep lest they should awaken only to find it "too late," and they shut outside the gate. I do pray for them all, from my heart: but I feel I should do more. Oh, it is terrible to think of the long night, the darkness, the sighing and gnashing of teeth, the company of the damned who have sat down not having on the wedding garment, and to think that many of our friends will be bound hand and foot and cast out there. I know God's mercy never dies, and that He will receive at the end all unto Himself. But oh, what long and weary ways amidst the torments and fears of an existence where they continue to deceive and enslave their souls in the service of Satan as they did on earth. My heart is sad and sorrowful when I think of it; and I only hope that they may really be converted ere it is "too late:" for the night cometh, and the last storm may soon rage around us which will prove if our souls are built upon the Rock and our names written in the Book of Life. . . . . .

God knows me, and he knows (despite many shortcomings, mistakes and sins which He has pardoned) that I am true to the service of my Lord and Saviour, and true in my love to every soul of man, for every one of which He tasted death.

. . . And now—"Be of good cheer:" it is the Lord who calls me on; and I will follow Him wherever He doth lead. If it be for His glory and your good, may He spare me yet awhile.

I do not fear either for you. dear ones, or myself, should the Lord call me hence by His sweet messenger, Death, who but opens, like a porter, the gate of the City of God: for He who in His wisdom takes me, will care for you, better than if I lived.

"Be of good cheer:" for the morning is coming of the endless day. I do not fear to live: for life can have no bitterer cups in store, or if there are, then His love will sweeten them, since I can trust Him now more fully than ever, and can say: "I am persuaded that neither death, nor life, nor angels, nor principalities, nor powers, nor things present nor things to come, nor height, nor depth, nor any other creature, **shall be able to separate me** from the love of God: which is in Christ Jesus our Lord."

"Be of good cheer." I am not ill, or apprehensive of any immediate danger to my life. But I am wanting to be more than ever "ready" either to die or live.

I have sent by this post two beautiful cards, which I got from my friend Mr. C— this morning.

One is for all the children. It is an Easter card.

I have addressed it to Gladdy; but he is to give it to you to keep. You will tell him about the Resurrection to which it refers—first to Christ, and then to us through Him, the Ressurrection and the Life. The other, with all the cupids, is for you.

All these sweet angels are but emblems of the sweet thoughts of love for you in my heart. Gladdy may look at it, but must not soil it, for I want mother to **keep it.**

Tell the dear little fellow to keep on praying to God to send the money to father to bring you here, and to ask until He does.

Give him many kisses, and say I will write him another letter soon. Say father wrote him to be very obedient and to grow up a good little son, and please God, and be like Jesus, as far as he can. Tell him father prays very often every day for him, and wants him to be always happy and good. He is much in my thoughts and prayers.

I have answered Mr. McD—. I did not like your comments concerning his letter. But I say no more. Send any letters you receive to me without any comment. I bear these burdens. They are quite heavy enough. Do not add to them by inconsiderate words. I am sorry to the heart about the matter; but they know as much as you do as to how things have gone, and did before I left Adelaide. I am doing in all things the best I can—an angel cannot do more. God is my judge, not any man or woman. I have learned this lesson, at great cost; but it is worth all the price: "Wisdom is justified of all her children."

Kiss my sweet little "angel," and tell her all kinds of sweet things from father. I dreamt about her this morning just before waking. She was smiling at me, and holding out her arms for me to take her, and I did so with gladness, and awoke laughing. I am grateful to your mother for taking her to Dr. Henry. I am sure it is general weakness, from that first loss of blood soon after her birth; and it will only be time and care that can restore her, if indeed she is to stay with us: for she is ever to me "my angel" Jeanie.

Kiss the darling "Queen" for father. The sweet little "mystery" is very dear to me; and I long to have you all around me in a home, if it be God's will, once more.

313

Still, I say from my heart, "Thy will, not mine, be done."

And now I close. The night is far spent, and I am getting tired Pray for me, with increasing faith.

"Faint not at my tribulation." God will show you yet it is "your glory." The Lord ever bless and keep you. .

———

(Story of how he came to preach Divine healing—later published in tract form—although it was not until six years later—1884—that he entered fully upon that ministry)

.... I sat in my study in the parsonage of the Congregational Church, at Newtown, a suburb of the beautiful city of Sydney, Australia My heart was very heavy, for I had been visiting the sick and dying beds of more than thirty of my flock, and I had cast the dust to its kindred dust into more than forty graves within a few weeks. Where, oh where was He who used to heal His suffering children? No prayer for healing seemed to reach His ear, and yet I knew His hand had not been shortened. Still it did not save from death even those for whom there was so much in life to live for God and others. Strong men, fathers, good citizens, and more than all, true faithful Christians sickened with a putrid fever, suffered nameless agonies, passed into delirium, sometimes with convulsions, and then died And oh, what aching voids were left in many a widowed orphaned heart Then there were many homes where, one by one, the little children, the youths and the maidens were stricken, and after hard struggling with the foul disease, they too, lay cold and dead. It seemed sometimes as if I could almost hear the triumphant mockery of fiends ringing in my ear whilst I spoke to the bereaved ones the words of Christian hope and consolation. Disease, the foul offspring of its father, Satan, and its mother, Sin, was defiling and destroying the earthly temples of

314

God's children, and there was no deliverer

And there I sat with sorrow-bowed head for my afflicted people, until the bitter tears came to relieve my burning heart Then I prayed for some message, and oh, how I longed to hear some words from Him who wept and sorrowed for the suffering long ago, the Man of Sorrows and of Sympathies. And then the words of the Holy Ghost inspired in Acts 10: 38 stood before me all radiant with light, revealing Satan as the Defiler and Christ as the Healer. My tears were wiped away, my heart was strong, I saw the way of healing, and the door thereto was opened wide, and so I said, "God help me now to preach that word to all the dying round, and tell them how 'tis Satan still defiles, and Jesus still delivers, for 'He is just the same to-day.'"

A loud ring and several loud raps at the outer door, a rush of feet, and then at my door two panting messengers who said, "Oh, come at once, Mary is dying; come and pray." With just such a feeling as a shepherd has who hears that his sheep are being torn from the fold by a cruel wolf, I rushed from my house, ran hatless down the street, and entered the room of the dying maiden. There she lay groaning, grinding her clenched teeth in the agony of the conflict with the destroyer, the white froth, mingled with her blood, oozing from her pain-distorted mouth. I looked at her and then my anger burned. "Oh," I thought, "for some sharp sword of heavenly temper keen to slay this cruel foe who is strangling that lovely maiden like an invisible serpent, tightening his deadly coils for a final victory."

In a strange way it came to pass, I found the sword I needed was in my hands, and in my hand I hold it still, and never will I lay it down The doctor, a good Christian man, was quietly walking up and down the room, sharing the mother's pain and grief. Presently he stood at my side and said, "Sir, are not God's ways mysterious?" Instantly the sword was flashing in my hand,—the Spirit's Sword, the Word of God. "God's way!" I said, pointing to the scene of conflict, "how dare you, Dr. K—, call that God's way of bringing His children home from earth to Heaven? No, sir, that is the devil's work, and it is time we called on Him who came to "destroy the work of the devil," to slay that deadly foul destroyer, and to save the child. Can you pray, Doctor, can you pray the prayer of faith that saves the sick?" At once, offended at my words, my friend was changed, and saying, "You are too much excited, sir, 'tis best to say 'God's will be done,'" he left the room. Excited! The word was quite inadequate for I was almost frenzied with Divinely imparted anger and hatred of that foul destroyer Disease, which was doing Satan's will. "It is not so," I exclaimed, "no will of God sends such cruelty, and I shall never say 'God's will be done' to Satan's works, which God's own Son came to destroy, and this is one of them." Oh, how the Word of God was burning in my heart "Jesus of Nazareth went about doing good, and healing all that were oppressed of the devil; for God was with him" And was not God with me? and was not Jesus there and all His promises true? I felt that it was even so, and turning to the mother I inquired,, "Why did you send for me?" To which she answered, "Do pray, oh pray for her that God may raise up." And so we prayed What did I say? It may be that I cannot now recall the words without mistake, but words are in themselves of small importance. The prayer of faith may be a voiceless prayer, a simple heartfelt look of confidence into the face of Christ. At such a moment words are few, but they mean much, for God is looking at the heart Still, I can remember much of that prayer unto this day, and asking God to aid I will endeavor to recall it I cried:

"Our Father, help! and Holy Spirit, teach me how to pray. Plead Thou for us, oh, Jesus, Saviour, Healer, Friend, our Advocate with God the Father. Hear and heal, Eternal one! From all disease and death deliver this sweet child of Thine. I rest upon the Word. We claim the promise now. The word is true, 'I am the Lord that healeth thee.' Then heal her now. The word is true, 'I am the Lord, I change not.' Unchanging God, then prove Thyself the Healer now. The word is true, 'These signs shall follow them that believe in My Name, they shall lay hands on the sick, and they shall recover.' And I believe, and I lay hands in Jesus' name on her, and claim this promise now. Thy word is true, 'the prayer of faith shall save the sick.' Trusting in Thee alone, I cry, oh, save her now, for Jesus' sake, Amen!"

And, lo, the maid lay still in sleep, so deep and sweet that the mother said in a low whisper, "Is she dead?" "No," I answered in a whisper lower still, "Mary will live, the fever has gone. She is perfectly well and sleeping as an infant sleeps." Smoothing the long dark hair from her now peaceful brow, and feeling the steady pulsation of her heart and cool, moist hands, I saw that Christ had heard and that once more, as long ago in Peter's house, "He touched her and the fever left her." Turning to the nurse I said, "Get me at once, please, a cup of cocoa and several slices of bread and butter." Beside the sleeping maid we sat quietly and almost silently until the nurse returned, and then I bent over her and snapping my fingers said, "Mary!" Instantly she woke, smiled and said, "Oh, sir, when did you come? I have slept so long;" then stretching out her arms to meet her mother's embrace, she said, "Mother, I feel so well." "And hungry, too?" I said, pouring some of the cocoa in a saucer and offering it to her when cooled by my breath. "Yes, hungry too," she answered with a little laugh, and drank and ate again, and yet again, until all was gone. In a few minutes she fell asleep, breathing easily and softly. Quietly thanking God we left her bed and went to the next room where her brother and sister also lay sick of the same fever. With these two we also prayed, and they were healed. The following day all three were well and in a week or so they brought to me a little letter and a little gift of gold, two sleeve links with my monogram, which I wore for many years As I went away from the home where Christ as the Healer had been victorious,I could not but have somewhat in my heart of the triumphant song that rang through Heaven, and yet I was not a little amazed at my own strange doings, and still more at my discovery that HE IS JUST THE SAME TO-DAY.

And this is the story of how I came to preach the Gospel of Healing through Faith in Jesus

---

(Written Nov. 9, 1885—tells of the death of his little daughter, Jeanie.)

Beloved Friend

Again I have stood over the open grave, and laid aside the earthly garments of my little "Angel," whose spirit quietly stole away just as the day was dawning on Lord's Day morning last I can scarcely realize it yet. for it was so sudden and unexpected; but I bow, with my dear wife, in resignation, though in grief, and say "It is the Lord, let Him do what seemeth Him good."

When we returned this day week from Sydney, we found Gladdy almost entirely recovered, and our two little daughters apparently well—our little Jeanie—the "Angel"—being especially delighted to see us, clasping us around the neck and kissing us again and again. The following day, Friday, she was toddling about the house, stronger, as we thought, than ever we had seen her, and our hearts were glad to look upon her sweet, pure face and happy smile That evening, however, we noticed one or two little spots which looked like measles on her face, and the following day, Satur-

318

day, she slept a good deal—it was a very hot day.

In the evening she seemed very bright, and when I came in to tea I found her sitting on our maid's lap being fed. I lit the gas in the dining room, as it was getting dark, and when I did so she laughed and clapped her little hands together.

I said, "You dear little Angel, father is so glad to see you bright and happy;" upon which she looked up into Ettie's face and smiled. We then sat down to tea and had scarcely commenced, when Mrs. Dowie, who was sitting near her, said, "Come here, John, and look at Jeanie's eyes." I immediately went over, and saw she was insensible and in a fit. I took her up at once, and besought the Lord for her; but she was by that time in strong convulsions. I then carried her into her own room, and kneeling down with her alone, besought the Lord again for her that the fit might cease; and it seemed almost as if a voice replied, "Yes, the fit will cease; but the Lord will take her now."

I then called Mrs. Dowie, and told her of the answer, and shortly after the fit did cease, and our little pet lay utterly exhausted. To avoid an inquest, I sent for a neighboring doctor, who took the same view as myself, namely, that there was an effusion on the brain, and no hope of her recovery. From that hour she slept, opening her eyes at intervals in response to our loving words, and at times breathing heavily, but entirely without pain. About four o'clock on Lord's Day morning, the end came, and, opening her eyes wide, she looked, oh, so beautifully, upon the faces of the unseen angels, and, without a sigh, her sweet spirit went away with them to dwell forever with the Lord. The daylight saw only a beautiful, white, marble-like form lying with closed eyes, and hands gently folded on her breast, and a look of holy peace upon her little face, which looked so calm, with the dark hair parted from her placid, broad brow. Ere the Sabbath songs of earth swelled from shore to shore, she was singing above in the presence of the King, where there is no night, but one endless day

Earth has one angel less, but heaven one more, since last Lord's Day. Our home has lost its purest, holiest child—our hearts are torn and bleeding—light has gone, in some degree, from everything around— but heaven is nearer, Christ is nearer, and our darling has gone where we shall one day go—often I care not how soon—and we shall meet her there, with all our loved ones gone before, and never, never part again We know where to find her, and, although we weep, we rejoice for it is well with the child.

Although I had not slept, I went through all the work of the Lord's Day, preaching in the morning from 2 Samuel, 12:23—"But now she is dead, wherefore should I fast? Can I bring her back again? I shall go to her; but she shall not return to me " How I preached I cannot tell, except that it was often with tears streaming from my eyes; but I did, and God blessed the word. In the evening I went out into the open air with our workers; and afterwards preached to a large audience

Many remained to the after meeting, and I am sure we shall see good fruits. But the evening "Herald," an organ of the liquor dealers, attacks me every issue since for my utterances, and gives utterly false reports of what I said Two leading articles and many paragraphs have appeared in its columns this week. It first invents a lie and then proceeds to comment upon it as an accepted fact. Its object, of course, is to render me ridiculous and unpopular; but it does not succeed in really injuring me permanently, although it gives many who never saw me false impressions

But all this draws me nearer to Him who "was despised and rejected" when He taught and wrought the will of God on earth—and I rejoice to be counted worthy to suffer for Him and with Him. This city is in an awful condition of open and secret depravity; and there are few bold or faithful enough to speak out in God's name.

The anger and hatred of the patrons of the Cup against me for calling it "The Cup of Death" is very great, so much so that I am sure my life is often in real danger from the infuriated, maddened men who are Satan's tools in this city.

But "none of these things move me;" for doing God's will is more than life to me. Last night there were violent knocks and then stones thrown at our front door, and when I went to the door the persons who had done it stood a little distance off, and shouted forth a volley of oaths and threats and obscene curses and then ran away as I moved towards them. It was late, then; but my duty took me out a half an hour later, and I went unhesitatingly and without fear. Do not be surprised if you should hear some morning, that like Faithful in "Vanity Fair" the Lord has honoured me by permitting me to seal my testimony with my blood, and be taken up, as Bunyan took "the nearest way to the Celestial Gate." But there is much good work to do here; and if it be God's will, I want to stay and do what I can to spread the Gospel of saving, healing, and sanctifying power and love, through faith in Jesus Christ, our Lord.

The books arrived quite safely, and are now in the cases in the room where I am now writing. They are like the faces of long absent friends, and although I have not been able to open them and let them pour out their treasures of wisdom and knowledge to any extent yet, still they have been useful already, and are likely to be still more so in days to come. There are a few missing which have possibly got mixed with yours, and one especially, a little black book of about four inches by three bound in leather,

11

entitled "Vetus Testamentum Cum Apoc. Graece"— i. e. The Old Testament, with the Apocrypha, in Greek. It is a little volume which, for many reasons, I much value—I purchased it in Adelaide thirteen years ago. Our late visit has drawn out our hearts very much to our Sydney friends, and there are times when we could wish it was our earthly home again. But God appoints our habitation and our work, and where the Spirit leads we desire only to follow.

> "So with my God to guide my way
>
> 'Tis equal joy to go or stay."

And now, beloved friend, on the eve of the Lord's Day I close this letter. Let God comfort thee; for the Holy Spirit is the Comforter. "As thy days, so shall thy strength be. . . The Eternal God is thy refuge, and underneath are the everlasting arms." I and my dear wife can, and do, sympathize with you more than ever,—we have both new treasures in heaven: Let us go forward and upward—we'll soon all meet again in the happy home above. . . .

(Memo made by himself regarding the case Cameron v. Dowie— tried in Fitzroy Police Court, April 20, 1885, for violation of bye-law prohibiting street preaching, and of which he was found guilty, fined, and suffered imprisonment for thirty-four days—receiving unconditional release by governor.)

Before the case was tried, Mr. Marsden, one of the oldest local magistrates, stated that he was conscientiously convinced that I was right in conducting religious processions in the streets, and that the Bye-law I was charged with breaking was ultra vires, and contrary to the fundamental British principles of civil and religious liberty. He offered, therefore, to the solicitor for the plaintiff (Mr. Lewis) that he would retire, if he wished. Mr. Lewis said that he thought Mr. Marsden's position was akin to that of a juryman who had a bias in, or had already prejudged, a case. Thereupon, Mr. Marsden said he would not take any part in it, and sat aside.

The case was tried before four magistrates, Messrs. Robb, (chairman) Cowie, Rowe, and Best.

The Town Clerk and Mayor having given formal evidence as to Bye-laws, and no permission having been asked or obtained, I, in cross examination, elicited from both the fact that I had on Tuesday evening, March 3, attended a meeting of the Council at which I had shown cause why the Bye-law should not be confirmed, and had declared that, as I conscientiously believed it to be ultra vires, and a direct infringment of my civil rights, and an attack upon my religious liberty and conviction of duty, it would, in the event of its passing, become my duty, and that of many others, to meet it "with the most determined passive resistance" within our power.

The plaintiff (a constable named Cameron) then proved the alleged offence, and admitted that the procession was orderly and caused no obstruction to traffic, nor had he ever seen or heard of any of our processions being otherwise.

Mr. Lewis (plaintiff's solicitor) then said that was his case; and resting upon the decisions in the cases of Rider V. Phillips, and Bannon V. Barker, (Law Reports for 1884) he claimed that the magistrates must uphold the violation of the Bye-law, and fine me accordingly.

I then called Mr. Robt. Smith, as a witness, simply to prove that the procession was orderly, and productive of no obstruction, or disorder.

I then endeavored to address the Bench for the defense, and had scarcely begun when a Mr. Lyons, solicitor, rose, and in a most insulting manner interrupted me, and addressed the Bench, and asked them whether I was to be allowed to preach there, etc. Mr. Lewis (plaintiff's solicitor) protested against the interruption, and demanded that I should be heard.

Somewhat ungraciously, the Bench concurred, and

I proceeded to show (1) that I was exercising what I believed to be my rights to the use of the common highways; (2) that I did that in an admittedly orderly way; (3) that I did so not for any private gain, nor from any wilful desire to come into collision with the municipal authorities, but to do good to my fellow men, in obedience to distinct commands of Scripture (See Luke 14:21, Mark 16 etc); (4) that I had done so in this city for more than two years previously without interference or complaint, and that, for more than thirty years, I had taken part in similar work, in many parts of Great Britain and the Australian colonies; (5) that the Bye-law, therefore, had created a crime, of that which had never been attempted to be shown to be a crime, and (6) that for reasons which I would then give, I held the Bye-law to be **ultra vires**.

Here I was again interrupted by Mr Lyons; and I again claimed the protection of the Bench, who were most evidently not in sympathy with me.

The chairman here said that it was not within their power to hold the Bye-law to be **ultra vires**, in the face of the decision quoted by the plaintiff's solicitor.

1 contended it was within their power to do so, if I was fortunate enough to convince them by the arguments that I was about to adduce—and I went on to say that Lord Chief Justice Coleridge had decided upon appeal from the magistrates of Hastings, England, that a similar Bye-law was ultra **vires**; that the Hon. W. B. Dalley, Attorney General of New So Wales, had last year given a similar opinion, in consequence of which religious street processions are, at the present moment, protected in Sydney, Newcastle etc, and that recently, the Court of Appeal, in Adelaide, South Australia, had upon appeal from the magistrates of Kapunda and Strathalbyn decided that similar Bye-laws in these municipalities were **ultra vires**.

Mr. Best here blurted out, in a most angry manner, that I had broken the law, and must be punished, or words to that effect, and the other members of the Court, who seemed to take no notice of what I was saying, but were excitedly conversing, seemed to be ready to concur with their colleague.

I endeavoured in vain to proceed with my argument, which was making no impression upon, and receiving no attention from, the rude and angry persons on the Bench; and, therefore, I said that if they had made up their minds to inflict a fine, I would ask them to fix it at a sum sufficiently large (plaintiff's solicitor had only asked for a small penalty) to enable me to appeal to the Supreme Court of this colony, from which, if unsuccessful, I would endeavour to carry it to the Supreme Court of Appeal in Great Britain.

The Chairman immediately said they were unanimous in upholding the Bye-law, and in finding me guilty of having broken it, and would fine me L5:5:—

Mr. Lewis applied for L3:3:—costs, which sum was granted.

I said—"That is an additional wrong. I give notice that I will appeal."

———

(Sept. 2, 1885—tells of attempt to wreck Tabernacle—narrowly escapes death—has premonition of danger.)

Dear Brother in Christ:

Your usual weekly note duly received this morning, just as I was about to go out for our day's work in the Healing Room. I praise God for His goodness to the brother restored in the Home and for the grace given to you all who are promoting the Gospel of Healing and Holiness, through Jesus only, in Ballarat. Kindly greet them all in love from Mrs. Dowie and myself.

When we reached the Tabernacle this morning we found that, by God's mercy, I had narrowly escaped being seriously injured, or killed, by a dynamite explosion which happened shortly after I left last night.

The explosion was heard by many living around, about 10:30, and many came out of their houses, amongst them the Fire Brigade people near; but seeing no fire or smoke they could not tell where it had happened   When our caretaker opened the place for the meetings today she found my room a wreck

The flooring boards beneath had been broken and had smashed in the drawer of my writing table, my chair had been thrown up to the roof and was lying with the other chairs in a confused heap; and had I been sitting there, it is very likely I would have been in heaven ere this   The side walls were partly blown out, some of the planks being broken into small fragments, and generally the room is damaged throughout, the window sill being partly torn out.   It was my intention to have remained in my room until past 11 with candidates for fellowship; but about quarter to ten, I asked four who were waiting if it would be equally convenient to see me this evening, and as they said "yes," I went home, for I felt weary—an unprecedented thing for me to do

All day, however, I had felt the shadow of death around me, and I had actually filled up, for the first time in my life, a proposal for Life Assurance, telling Mrs. Dowie that I felt well but had a feeling that I would at some time, perhaps soon, be called away suddenly

So you see the Devil is busy, and wants to kill us outright by violence, failing his being able to cover us with disease. "But none of these things move me, neither count I my life dear unto myself, so that I might finish my course with joy, and ministry, which I have received of the Lord Jesus, to testify the Gospel of the grace of God."

He has cast us into prison, and now he would kill us, but we cannot fear: for to us "to live is Christ, and to die is gain."   But for my dear ones' sake, for my dear people, and for the work's sake, I am glad the Lord delivered me on this occasion.

The police and detectives, under Inspector Brown, have been working at the case all day, they have found remnants of dynamite cartridges and they have some clues as to the perpetrators of the outrage.

Of course this broke up our Healing meetings today: for which I was sorry, as I understand many came from long distances; but doubtless I shall see them again, or rather, if the Lord be willing, I shall.

Ask all the friends to pray for us. We shall, the Lord willing, go to Sydney for two or three weeks about 21st inst., and we hope to proclaim the Lord as Healer there. . . .

(Sept. 6, 1886—protests against linking the doctrine of Divine healing with Spiritualism, Mind cures, etc.)

Dear Brother in Christ:

I very much deplore the article in your issue of 27th ult., entitled "Mind Healing," based on Dr. Buckley's article in the Century for June last: and I am sure the day is not far distant when its writer, whoever he may be, will deeply deplore the evil which it will work.

Dr. Buckley errs "not knowing the Scriptures nor the power of God," as I will, God helping me, endeavour to make plain in a pamphlet which I intend to write during this month, before starting upon a tour of Divine Healing Missions in New South Wales, New Zealand, and Tasmania.

I therefore write simply to enter my public protest against linking the Christian doctrine of healing by the Holy Spirit, through faith in Jesus, with the diabolical performances of evil men and evil spirits, who today, as in apostolic times, worked miracles and deceived mankind.

The design of Satan has ever been to destroy belief in the reality and Divine nature of Christ's work,

327

by producing diabolical counterfeits, and that Mother of Harlots, the Roman Church, has manifested its Satanic character by joining hands with its sister impostor, Modern Spiritualism, in showing mysterious power, and signs, and lying wonders. It ill become Protestants and evangelical Christians to confound the permanent "gifts of healing in the one Spirit" which our Lord promised to give His true Church with the magnetic, mesmeric, and psychopathic mockeries of ancient and modern heathenism, by whatever name that heathenism may be disguised. I do not write, like Dr. Buckley, who boasts of his skill in making people fools, and seriously injuring them, by the way, in the process, as his article abundantly proves. He is a confessed practical mesmerizer: and I have the greatest horror and detestation of such practices, knowing that they are injurious to all concerned, and are always the primary methods adopted by "seducing spirits" in leading many to "fall away from the faith," giving to Paul's prophecy a very practical fulfillment.

But I write as one whom the Lord has used for four years in the Ministry of Healing, and for nearly twenty years in the Ministry of Salvation through faith in Jesus I know in Whom I have believed, and that all who have been healed, and they number many hundreds to my certain knowledge, like all who have been saved, and I believe these number thousands in Great Britain and Australia, were healed and saved by grace through faith in Him of whom it is written, "The chastisement of our peace was upon Him, and with His stripes we are healed."

This testimony of practical experience, added to the published public testimony of large numbers of persons, such as those you published in your issue of February 26, of this year, ought to go for something as against the mere assertions of Dr. Buckley's article, and the "Mind Healing" echo of it in your columns. Besides, the whole world is full of living, rejoicing witnesses to the power and willingness of Jesus as an unchangeable Healer of "them who believe" for healing. It will take something more than sneers to convince these that they are suffering from "imaginations," or, as he also puts it, from "abberations of the imagination." People don't imagine cancers and blindness, and we can supply many very tangible facts of instantaneous, perfect, and permanent healings which no one has ever disputed in this city. But alas for truth, men like Dr. Buckley are ready to admit every explanation for phenomena, except that of Divine intervention, and no facts or reasonings from my standpoint are ever likely to affect them, until they bow to the supremacy of the Holy Spirit in their warped and blinded intellects, where a false conceit reigns to the exclusion of all else.

I promise him and all who attack God's truth, and want to link me by a scientific chain, as he does, with Mormons, Spiritualists, Mind-curers, Roman Catholics, and Magnetizers, that I will do my best to repudiate and disprove the alliance, which would be as repugnant to my vows of loyality to Christ, as the practices of these enemies of God are to my experience.

One thing I imagine even my bitterest critics will admit is, that his charge that belief in what he calls "faith-healing" produces an "effeminate type of character which shrinks from any pain and concentrates attention upon self and its sensations" is not true in the case of myself or my people; for, by the grace of God, we have been able to make the opposite tolerably plain to all who know us, and who know our past and present modes of "fighting the good fight of faith." I do not reckon that the press of Melbourne, or the publicans of Victoria, would sum us up as "effeminate," or "selfish" types of character, and the records of Melbourne Gaol where we suffered for obeying Christ can tell another tale.

If I write warmly it is because I feel warmly the

insult and wrong which links me to Christ's enemies, and brands me as an effeminate coward—and all this in the name of philosophy, science, and Christianity.

I would be unworthy of my Lord in His great goodness to me did I not feel warmly, and repel warmly, the attack made upon the Gospel and Ministry of Divine Healing: for the progress of Christ's Kingdom is in no small degree dependent upon their triumph in the world.

But of the final issue there can be no doubt

"Oppositions of science, falsely so-called," have in all ages led Christian professors to swell the ranks of those who have "erred concerning the faith " But "the faith" cannot be shaken by false science—it is not only unchangeable but imperishable For that "faith once delivered to the saints" I will earnestly contend and will "guard that which is committed unto me "

Suffering millions from beds of pain shall not for ever appeal in vain to a Church which has, alas, forgotten so long that He "who went about doing good and healing all who were oppressed of the devil" is still the same Healer and Deliverer · for "Jesus Christ is the same yesterday, and today, and forever."

The doctrine of Divine Healing is not new, or it would not be true.

" 'Tis the old time religion,
And 'tis good enough for me "   .

_____

(Written July 10, 1886,—forecasts political situation—exhorts to faithfulness.)

Beloved Wife.

After my long letter of Wednesday you will not expect much today.

God is very good to me in many ways recently, and I feel sure He is leading, and it will be in a way to still better work for Him. If He would but graciously grant us increased means, we could do so much more, even with our present opportunities.

All I ask for is "enough;" and although the answer is sometimes delayed to the last moment— **it always comes.**

Amongst my recent letters, I have had one from Mr. O—, who went down to Auckland, New Zealand, lately, as you will remember.

He sent me a photo and some lithographic views of the recent eruption; and it seems to me that they are of a very serious nature and may be followed by volcanic outbreaks on this continent.

Earthquakes are among the latter day signs; and in every sense there are earth tremors about—who can tell the moment when the unquenchable fires of hell, underlying the Rotomahana of Modern Society here and in Europe, will burst forth into the conflagration?

Many in power are now making great display of their riches before the eyes of Europe. It is like displaying diamonds before the covetous hearts and greedy eyes of armed brigands. All men are worshiping in society the Australian Golden Fleece; and British society, from the Queen down, are doing it daily reverence. What if the Bear of Russia, and the Eagle of France, and possibly other powers, combine to try to steal these jewels and fleeces? They will sweep down upon Australia and India, if they can— and, then? War is almost as disastrous to the victors, as to the vanquished—historical facts prove it often to have been ruinous to a people to have been successful in war. France in this century, and Spain, in modern ages, comparatively, are illustrations; and in ancient times Rome and Greece, Egypt and Babylonia, are proofs that empires built of blood must perish. Gladstone is beaten—what next? A Tory Government holding power for seven years, as it may do, will probably plunge the Empire into war after war in every part of the world and make reforms and reformers throughout all its provinces to be, in its eyes, criminals and rebels. **Oh, what Seas of Blood the na**tions are nearing! God will preserve His Israel; but **they will suffer who sin.** I feel "Redemption draweth nigh." for the King of kings, whom **kings dishonor** and peoples disown, is coming. Therefore the terrible days are coming. Now let us continue the cry, "Behold the Bridegroom cometh!" We must tell men everywhere to be "ready"—**spirit, soul, and body**—for His coming, and we must be sure we are ourselves.

"The time is short;" and we must well employ it. God willing, we shall spend the last three months of this year in revisiting New South Wales, and in New Zealand, and Tasmania, in a Salvation, Healing and Holiness Mission; and I can see plainly God is so leading. We are being **thrust out**, as well as led out, and called out; and, perhaps, the permanent establishment (humanly speaking for nothing here is permanent) of the work in Fitzroy will depend upon our going out This is becoming very clear to me On Thursday night last, I had a similar experience to that which we had in October, 1884, before we went out on our first Faith Healing Mission to Ballarat—you need no description: for we can never forget "the lights." Had you any special experience on the same night— say about 1 o'clock on Friday morning last? My bedroom was full of glory, and there's more to follow Pray over all this matter, and look upward with increasing **faith**, go forward with brighter **hope**, and let us work with more self-denying, self-consuming **love**— God's **faith**, God's **hope**, God's **love**. We are working for God and for eternity—what higher calling can there be than this which we have in Christ? He has a work for us such as we have never dreamed of, if we are only faithful

Quite unusual has been the leisure hour which has enabled me to write the foregoing, which is but a little of what I would like dearly to talk to you about. I sometimes do so want you so much to be here. We have been so much together these last four years, and for the first five of our married life, that separation comes hard. I miss you most when some heavy piece of work is done, and I want a quiet hour with you. And perhaps you miss me, too; and our re-union will be the sweeter, if we do all God's will shows us whilst we are apart for a few weeks longer. "Life is to do the will of God," someone has said. All else is Sin and Death.

The work goes on in every department, and I keep "pegging away." We had some good temperance, salvation, and healing cases this week.

A million kisses for yourself and our darling; and with kind remembrance to all, I am,

Ever yours in love in the Lord,

John Alexander Dowie.

(Written July 17, 1886—tells of strange unveiling of his own nature —able to penetrate into thoughts of others.)

Beloved Wife:

I write these lines just in time to catch the mail by going on board the steamer. I have had a wondrous week in conection with the healing work, and a new gift of the Holy Spirit, and new light on the whole subject of the mystery of life in Christ, has quite suddenly been given to me. I cannot **write** about it; but I should like to talk heart to heart with you just now. Do come home again not later than Wednesday week—I cannot do without you any longer. It is all so strange; I can **see** as spirits— God's "ministering spirits" do. Four times in two days, I was able to penetrate into the **deepest, most secret thoughts** of four separate men; and that after a night of **strange unveiling of my own nature** by the Word and Spirit of God.

I have not had an average of more than four hours'

sleep out of every twenty-four; but I am not only well, but look it, and feel stronger in every way than during any former period of my life. It is a fresh baptism of "Power from on High;" and I am sure it is given me for witness and for service. I am so firm, cool, calm; but so changed in feeling. Wave after wave of Holy Power has come upon me, and it remains. All else seems trivial compared to this. Christ is unspeakably dearer, clearer, and nearer to me in all things. Abraham's God is mine; and I will, God helping me, **be faithful as he was.** Pray for me, for yourself, for all whom we love, and who love us. If you are like Sarah of old, we shall have a glorious future here and hereafter.

Abraham and Sarah were the Friends of God— are we?

Christ says we are. Do not let us fear, but love.

When you return I want to tell you all that has happened, since Friday week—I cannot write it.

Externally, work has gone on very busily during the days, and early parts of the nights. I have had a continued rush of visitors and ran away from them yesterday—yet I saw nineteen yesterday forenoon and evening.

I have been praying for your healing, and I am sure you have got it—is it not so? Come back strong.

I am,

Forever yours in love Divine,

John Alexander Dowie.

(Written to an "auld Covenanter.")

Many thanks for your kind message from an "auld Covenanter," and your kind gift, the Treasurer's receipt for which I inclose herewith. I, too, am of the Scotch Covenanter stock, and our family suffered with "patience" for Christ's Crown and Covenant in the days of Claverhouse and earlier. Some of my ancestors devised, in dark days, the crest and its motto which is at the head of this page, and from my childhood I have asked God to enable me to carry, like the dove, (emblem of the Holy Spirit) with unwearied constancy, the olive branch (emblem of Gospel Peace) of God to weary hearts over the sea of life. Amidst many dangers and trials this is our one great aim, and I am grateful to all whom God moves to help us in our work for Christ.

May the grand and holy fire of our fathers burn more brightly in our hearts and lives—the fire of zeal for God's glory, and of love for our Lord and King; and may you and all your dear ones join above that glorious company of all who have faithfully witnessed for Jesus throughout all the ages, as did our fathers who sealed their testimony with their blood in the hills and glens of dear old Scotia. . . . .

(Written to a friend.)

. . . . In default of news, I will give you another hymn which I wrote on Saturday evening last. My favorite tune "Praise" will go to it.

> Approach, my soul, with reverent love,
> Gather the manna from above,
>   Rained daily down for thee:
> Eternal food, so freely given,
> Gives sweetest antipast of heaven,
>   Wherever thou mayest be.
>
> Dost thou the weary desert tread,
> Thirsty, with scorching sun o'er head?
>   Behold Him at the well!
> Art tempest tossed on wintry sea?
> Stilled are its waves; O mystery:
>   He doeth all things well.

Dear Saviour, cast out all my fear,
Be Thou my only comfort here,
 My Anchor, firm and sure!
Daily renew my strength in Thine,
Let all Thy will be wholly mine,-
 Thus shall I be secure.

(On board S. S 'Rotorna" at sea from Taranek to Nelson, New Zealand, April 25, 1888—Leaves of Healing launched)

Dear Brother in Christ

Your very welcome letter reached me on 16th inst , on my return to Auckland with Mrs. Dowie, after a journey of about fifteen hundred miles down and up the east coast of these islands, during which we had very interesting, important, and successful meetings with the Associations which we formed, by the grace of God, last year.

We found much need for our visit : for the work had got into unholy hands, and the Associations were being used to serve personal interests by some few misguided persons But they are now all on a healthier footing, and the evil leaven has been removed, so far as men can see at present. Many new members have been added—thirty on Monday evening last in Auckland alone, and the Associations are unanimously with us.

A new magazine, **"Leaves of Healing,"** of which I enclose a prospectus, is about to be published for all the Australasian Associations and I want you and all the friends to subscribe and get as many subscribers as possible.

We hope the Lord will greatly use the magazine; and all our friends will keep in constant touch with us through its pages, as well as with each other. I hope to get the first monthly issue nearly ready by the time I leave Christ Church on May 14th for Auckland and proceed, after a few meetings, on our journey to America per "Mariposa," leaving there on Monday, May 21st, and due in San Francisco Lord's Day, June 10th. . . . .

A very severe storm began whilst I was writing the foregoing, and compelled me to desist; but we are now this morning safely in the harbour, and the sea all around is looking so calm and beautiful: the high mountains around the Bay, some of them capped with snow, are like giant sentinels over the bright blue waters which reflect their glory.

We much need the Lord to send us "the silver and the gold" required for what lies immediately before us; and we do not doubt for a moment but what it is coming in His own good way and time. Keep on praying for us, and watch against the Tempter assailing you from within the church. Does it not seem incredible that John, "the disciple whom Jesus loved," who was received by our Lord into the closest intimacy, should have been insulted and rejected by a Diotraphes in his old age, a fellow minister, a leading member, probably of a church which the apostle himself had founded? Then should I wonder if I also suffer from such a person? But they are not of God. "Beloved, imitate not that which is evil, but that which is good. He that doeth good is of God: and he that doeth evil hath not seen God."

With Christian love to you all, I am,

Ever yours in Jesus,

John Alexander Dowie.

———

(*Excerpt from a letter written to a friend in* 1888.)

. . . . I have no love of restless change, and that which I do is given to me of God, and is a part of my ministry in the Lord, as the facts of my life have abundantly proved. The one fact that He sustains me in the course which I pursue is of itself a proof: for

I have gone out entirely without financial resources, and have undertaken work which has cost me ten times any ordinary minister's salary every year But "he who excuses, accuses," so says the French proverb, and so I will not excuse my course of life and ministry, neither can I expect others to understand it, since they have no knowledge of the inner as well as the outer facts which vindicate that course. I have learned to leave personal vindications with the Lord, and I never defend myself against the countless attacks which have appeared against me in the press, having only written once to a newspaper in five years to correct misrepresentations. I have defended the truth committed to my charge, but at no time have I ever cared to defend myself as a personal matter. God is my Judge He never makes mistakes, and He corrects all the false, and mistaken, judgments of men. Oh, it is good to know that He alone sits on the Throne!

Many persons cannot understand that a man does not need to belong to a denomination to be a Christian, or to be a sworn member of a secret or semi-secret society to be a good citizen, and a social reformer. My faith in Christ is broader than the limits of a sect, and my love for humanity forbids my being narrowed down to a mere spoke in a social or political wheel of fortune, turned to and fro at the pleasure of clever men or women, who talk of the wideness of their charity, but limit it to the cut of their clothes in some cases, or to the grip of their hand, or to their uttering some shibboleth. There is very little real independence of thought, and still less of action, in the things of to-day, and both church and state and reform movements have come to copy the German Army Regulations too closely, and have got a good way off from the liberty wherewith Christ has made His people free.

Do not imagine that I am averse to organization,

for it is the great need of the church and of the world. I would go right back to the organization in I Corinthians 12, and have every particle of it, and all the gifts, once more in harmonious, ecclesiastical, orderly operation; and there is none other that will do. . . . .

(Written in 1888—tribute to his wife—longs for old apostolic times— deplores lack of authority in modern churches—would not return to old way of "settling"—full of confidence and hope.)

. . . . Jeanie is invaluable in seeing the sick with me, and is an excellent helper in every way. We are very good friends, and don't have any serious difficulties, for we are the Lord's servants as well as husband and wife. I have every cause to be grateful to God for my wife.

We shall rest at home bye and bye, and will be able to talk with you on the deep things of God, and the practical things concerning His kingdom on Earth, which is now becoming clearer and clearer to me, and yet there is much that we do not know. Oh, for the old apostolic times, when the Timothys and the Tituses could find their Pauls, and be led by Divinely appointed men. I love the thought of the old apostolic rule and would rejoice to see it established once again, for what is needed above all things is first LOVE, and then AUTHORITY of the most absolute kind in matters of church work. There is no real authority any where. Rome is apostate, and the churches are all split up, apart from each other, and divided within themselves. The attempt to settle things by conferences and synods and councils is failing, for no one has any real consciousness that these are any real power at all, or that the Holy Spirit is owning them. "Come from the Four Winds, Oh Breath, and breathe upon these slain that they may live."

. . . . If I desired to "settle," as it is called, I could do so in any one of a score of places, to say the least, and there are friends and correspondents in England who are pressing me to go there, and who offer me a headquarters' free in one of the best parts of that country, near to Halifax. We are in the Lord's hands entirely as to the future, as we have been in the past. We have had many temptations and not a few severe trials of faith, indeed we have them all the time, in one form or another, but I would not return to the old way of "settling" for all the gold of Ophir. We have the entire freedom and independence which would be impossible, if we were to be dependent on the caprices of small-minded deacons or impudent and ignorant, purse-proud members of churches, who look upon the minister as a salaried servant, not of the Lord Jesus Christ, but of their little **syndicate**, which it might be more appropriate to spell with an i rather than y The Lord never sent forth His servants in this way when He was here on earth, and He has never left any other way of sending them out but at His charges It would be a strange thing for an Ambassador to be sent forth by any Government with the declaration that he was to be dependent upon the people of the country to whom he was sent, for a living. Every Government provides for its Ambassador from its own resources, and so does God. Paul lived of the Gospel, but he never was dependent upon the people, and rather than be that he laboured with his own hands. The Lord provided, and all the Messengers went forth in simple Faith that He would so provide When they returned they were able to say that they "lacked nothing." If we are faithful, we shall be able to say the same, and, if not, then we have failed somewhere and in something: for "God is faithful "

340

"We do not covet earthly store,
Beyond a day's supply;
We only covet more and more,
The clear and single eye,
To see our duty face to face,
And trust the Lord for daily grace."

And so we go on with our hearts singing, not without temptations and attacks from the Enemy who would fain make us fear if he could; but able thus far to say that we have never yielded to these temptations, and that God has been with us all the way as JEHO-VAH-JIREH, according to promise.

I tell you these things, because they are the very essence of our life, and all the other things which happen are because we are enabled by the Holy Spirit's power to trust in the word of our Lord, and to do His will according to our light. For this also we praise God, and give Him all the glory, from whom is all the Power.

. . . It is worth all the toil and trial and ten thousand times more, to have the real and unmistakable experiences of the years now passing by, so full of confidence and so full of hope and love do they make my life, giving me the needed grace for trials and toils and victories yet to come. The sense of all this being a kind of preparatory school, is one that increases steadily in my heart as the years go by. They whiten my hair, and put new furrows in my face, but my heart grows younger, and my faith is stronger and simpler, my hope is brighter, and above all my love is purer, for all these are more and more clearly Divine, His Faith, His Hope, His Love, and how could my heart be anything else but younger? Life has fewer real perplexities, and the solution of human difficulties is so clearly to be found in Christ alone that I have no other thought than just to get to know what He said, and did, and willed, and that is the path, and that alone, for me and for all the world beside. Whosoever says otherwise is a fool or a scoundrel, and perhaps both. I never did have any faith in what Tennyson calls "honest doubt," for I have always felt that to doubt our Lord Jesus Christ for a moment was a mean and dishonest thing, and now I never give it any quarter. It always arises from Sin, and oftentimes from very filthy forms of Sin The Church needs to remember that NOW God "commandeth men everywhere to REPENT " God is with me as I preach Repentance as the foundation of the Gospel, and this is the fundamental in all our preaching Salvation through Faith are all impossibilities to an impenitent sinner. People do not like to be told this, and that only confirms its truth and the necessity for preaching it Tens of thousands of persons are entering into fellowship with the Church who have never entered into fellowship with God, for they have never repented of Sin, and God never forgives those who do not repent It is an impossibility

(From the first copy of Leaves of Healing, issued June 1, 1888—"a monthly Australian magazine for the promotion of healing and holiness through faith in Jesus"—tells of farewell meetings, after sixteen years of ministry in Australia, upon his departure for America.)

It seems fitting that this record of our present and future work should have, for a link with our past work for the Lord, some account of the closing scenes of our nearly sixteen years of ministry in Australia Therefore, I will refer to our Farewell Meetings in the Free Christian Tabernacle in Fitzroy, Melbourne, of which I had charge from its erection in 1884, and, I may add, the Church meeting therein had recognised me as its pastor from its formation by myself, in February, 1883 It was no little grief to part from the dear people whose love and loyalty to me had stood the severest tests which Satan could devise, and who had never failed in unswerving fidelity to Christ's laws, even to "bonds and imprisonments," seeking to save the perishing on every side. But their love to God stood the strain of my resignation in November, 1887; and after long meetings for prayer, one an all-night with Jesus, both amongst the office-bearers and the people, a resolution, amidst many tears was unanimously passed on the evening of November 4, 1887, agreeing to accept my resignation, with expressions of loving regard similar to those afterwards embodied in an address hereafter referred to, but requesting that I should not retire for at least three months. Accordingly, I yielded to their wish, and my resignation, although accepted, was arranged not to take effect until February 19, 1888, on which date I announced I would preach my farewell sermons. Meanwhile, many precious seasons of spiritual communion were vouchsafed to us; and opportunities of witnessing together for Christ. One of these seasons was the Fifth Annual Commemoration of our Ministry of Healing through Faith in Jesus, which was held in the Tabernacle on Lord's Day 4th (three public meetings), and on Monday, 5th December last (one meeting).

Full reports of these four meetings have been published (M. L. Hutchinson, 15, Collins Street W., Melbourne,) in the form of a Record, which contains over seventy testimonies from those healed, taken down at the moment by a shorthand writer on the staff of one of the Melbourne morning daily newspapers, whose name is given. This Record has been much used of God, and, as nearly the whole of the first edition of 3,500 copies have been disposed of, it is our intention to reprint it (D. V.) in America. We thank our Lord, and one of His servants who bore the entire cost of printing and publishing it, that our last Annual Commemoration in Australia was so graciously used; for many have been led to the Lord as Saviour, Healer, and Sanctifier through its pages, wherein witness after witness declares that He is healing "every manner of sickness and every manner of disease among the people."

Then on the eve of the Centennial Day of Australia, January 21st last, we had an Ordination of Elders at midnight, and a most solemn and impressive All-night of Prayer and Teaching in the ever-to-be-remembered Healing-room attached to the Tabernacle, when two beloved ones, Elders Joseph Grierson and John S Wallington, were ordained, having been most manifestly "separated" for this work for some time by the Holy Spirit who had used them to many of God's sick ones in my frequent absences during the last two years. It is important to notice that the Holy Spirit first calls, then separates, and then ordains Christ's servants to the various offices in His Church—See Acts i. 15-26, and Acts xiii. 1-4, concerning the call to the first and most important of all offices in the Church (1 Cor xii. 28), the office of "apostle."

No greater misery can ever happen to a man than to be rashly ordained of men to any office in the Church to which the Holy Spirit has not already called and separated him, and it is a source of endless confusion among God's people, and a stumbling-block to the world, who mock, not without justice, at the impotence of man-made elders whom foolish or designing men have ordained

On Lord's Day, February 19th last, just five years from the date of my forming the Church in the Fitzroy Town Hall, I preached my three last sermons in the Tabernacle, and closed my pastorate there with the blessed ordinance of the Lord's Supper, the most glorious of all the Church's memorial services, looking backward to the Cross, looking upward to the Throne, and looking forward to the Blessed Hope of His Coming. Oh, how sweet and rich in heavenly blessing is it to meet with the Lord at His Table. Why do so many of His beloved ones neglect it, or infrequently appear at it? Is it not because so many portions of His Church only spread it once a month, or at even longer intervals, instead of following the beautiful practice of the Church in its primitive glory and power, when "upon the first day of the week (not of the month or quarter) we were gathered together to break bread"—Acts xx. 7.

We made that the occasion upon which I formally laid down my office as pastor, commending them to the Chief Shepherd at His own Table, and "so departed." But on the following Tuesday our dear people and many Christian friends met tegether in the Tabernacle under the presidency of a highly honoured brother, Mr. Elijah Stranger, and the following was presented to me, accompanied with a cheque for 100 pounds.

"Address to the Rev. John Alex. Dowie, on the "occasion of his retiring from the Pastorate "of the Free Christian Church, Johnston "Street, Fitzroy, on the eve of his departure "to America and Europe, to engage in the "Divine Healing Mission, to which the Holy "Spirit has called him.

"Free Christian Tabernacle, Fitzroy,

"Melbourne, Victoria,
21st February, 1888.

"Rev. and dear Sir :—

"We, the office-bearers and members of the Free "Christian Church, Fitzroy, with a large number of "Christian sympathisers from different parts of the "Australian Colonies and New Zealand, beg to present "this testimonial as a very small token of the love "and appreciation borne toward you for your untiring "and devoted zeal in bringing very many in these "lands from darkness into God's marvellous light, and "for the promotion of Divine Healing. You have been "made the Divine agent in doing many mighty works. "The Lord has, in a most manifest manner, heard your

"prayer of faith, and raised up many, in some cases
"more than ten thousand miles distant. Truly, the
"Lord has made you a chosen vessel, in leading hun-
"dreds, by your teaching from His Holy Word, to the
"sanctification of spirit, soul, and body. We cannot
"even estimate the number blessed under your min-
"istry,—eternity alone will reveal them—but we know
"that hundreds, who have been both saved and healed,
"regret, as we do, your departure from these shores.
"The loss of your spiritual exhortations, your kindly
"counsels, and your faithful prayers, will be deeply
"felt throughout Australasia; but your Church and
"people have felt, from the date of your letter of the
"16th April, 1885, to the London International Con-
"ference on Divine Healing, held at the Agricultural
"Hall, London, June 1st to 5th, 1885, till now, that
"the Holy Spirit was leading you to visit America and
"Europe, to preach Christ as the Saviour and Sanctifier
"of the spirit, soul, and body, and we submit to the
"will of our Heavenly Father, and pray that you may
"be used and blessed to a far greater extent than you
"have been, and that, if it be His will, you shall return
"again to this land.

"We herewith subscribe our names, on behalf of
the above,

"JOHN SAMUEL WALLINGTON,
"JOSEPH GRIERSON,

Elders."

We shall never forget the kind words thus spoken
to us, and will treasure the beautiful illuminated address in its handsome covering, which so fittingly en-
folds them.

But loving words came from all sides, and when
many had spoken, a gentleman left his seat and advancing to the chairman, asked him to present us with
a very beautiful Revised Version Bible, as a token of
love and gratitude. He had been blessed in the Taber-

nacle, and healed of a deadly cancer in his face. It was nearly midnight ere we could leave the building, where large numbers of eager friends crowded around us, not for the last time, for one more season was to be given to us of still deeper and sweeter communion with the Lord and our dear people there.

The next few days were largely spent in all the many duties and toils inseparable from the private affairs of this life, in disposing of our few worldly goods, "in doing things honestly in the sight of all men," and in preparing Our Little Pilgrim Band of Five for our long journeys and voyages. I may be permitted here to say that our two little ones accompany us on our travels, my son aged 11 years, and my daughter aged 7, and I would earnestly ask the prayers of all our friends in Christ everywhere for these dear children, and that we may be enabled to educate and train them up "in the admonition and fear of the Lord," amidst the many special difficulties which will attend this important duty. We felt it was quite impossible to leave them behind us for so long and uncertain a period of missionary journeying, and, therefore, we felt led of the Spirit to take them with us, believing the beautiful words of Joseph (Genesis l. 21) find a sweet fulfillment in Jesus, and are His words to us—"Now, therefore, fear ye not: I will nourish you and your little ones."

Again I say, beloved, "Pray for us daily." It will be an inexpressible comfort to know that you are so engaged, not only in your gatherings together but in your homes, around the family altar: for your faithful prayers shall be answered by our faithful God.

Friday, March 2nd, we held in the Tabernacle, Fitzroy, our last meeting with our dear people and many Christian friends from other Churches. It was a Farewell Consecration and Communion Service, and a time of great searching power, and of holy fire. During three hours, from 8 to 11 p. m., we sought the Lord for wisdom and knowledge, spreading Thessalonians 1:5 before us; and expounding it to those whom we were now so soon to part from, many of whom are our own children in the faith Verses 22 to 24, formed our closing exhortation ere the Table of the Lord was brought forth. Then we gathered around, and sought to see His face, and hear His voice. And not in vain: for in eternity we shall praise Him for the parting blessing then received

"Till He come" was then sung, and as we went homeward in the stillness and the starlight of the midnight hour, we could hear the loved voices still singing the words ·—

> "Sweet memorials,—till the Lord
> Calls us round His heavenly board,
> Some from earth, from glory some,
> Severed only, 'Till he come!'"

How often we have read the words, "and **when they** (the Lord and His first apostles) **had sung a hymn,** they went out unto the Mount of Olives." How we have longed to hear the voice and see the face of Him who led that song, ere He went forth to suffer and to die. Down through the ages its echoes still are ringing, and "the ransomed of the Lord" still "come with singing unto Zion" As we looked upward in that beautiful night, we saw the "many mansions" of light shining in the boundless vault of the heavens above They seemed to us, like heavenly silent singers, forming, from the Southern Cross, a glorious pathway of stars through all the Milky Way, with jewelled steps, upwards and onwards to the centre of all things—the Throne of God. And then Daniel's words of prophecy came to us poor Pilgrims of the Night, who were about to go forth to all the earth with Words of Life and Light and Love to countless sufferers who are fainting and groaning in pain on their earthly journey to Zion above—"They that be wise shall shine as the brightness of the firmament; and they that turn many to righteousness as the stars for ever and ever." And we were comforted: for the way of wisdom was lying clearly before us, and we knew our Guide, the unerring Spirit of God, would lead us in the steps of Him who sang the hymn and went forth to open the way of Salvation and Temperance, of Healing and Holiness to all who will trust and follow Him. All was peace, and the night soon passed away.

At mid-day on Saturday, March 3rd, we went on board the A. U. S. N. Co.'s S. S. "Maranoa," lying at Queen's Wharf, on the River Yarra, in the heart of the city, where we had been so tried and so blessed. Some hundreds of our friends "accompanied us to the ship" where we had a precious time of prayer and praise; and so amidst hymns and tears and blessings from grateful hearts we sailed away down the river and the bay, away out into the Ocean hearing the words, floating on the waters, of our sweet singers as we left the shore:—

> 'Beyond the swelling floods
> We'll meet to part no more."

In two days we arrived safely in one of the loveliest of all the earthly heavens I have ever seen—the beautiful harbour of Sydney.

The voyage had been very stormy until the morning of our arrival, but when the sun rose upon the giant cliffs of George's Head, a gentle breeze was beating over the fair face of the deep blue waters, and scenes of entrancing beauty burst upon our gaze, as we sailed onward close to the shores of the charming Illawarra country. The five islands, the pastoral uplands, the fertile cultured plains, and the mountains towering over all, with the joyous sea for an ever-changing foreground, made a grand picture. Onward we sailed past villages and towns which found fitting place in the ever-changing panorama. Passing the southern suburbs of Sydney itself, we sailed close under the high rocky steeps which front the ocean, and hide the great city beyond them. Then onward to the Heads which open out that wondrous channel, a narrow gateway of divine grandeur, into a harbour of surpassing loveliness stretching away north, west, and south on every side for miles into bays and coves, where it seems as if all the navies of the world might ride at anchor in perfect peace. More than one thousand miles of water frontage lie, I am told, within these Heads. And then how wondrous the effects of sun and sea upon these scenes of beauty which unfold as we pass onwards to the city. The green slopes and smooth lawns of rich men's homes, embowered amidst trees and flowers, mingled with views of virgin forest still remaining on the shores, are passed swiftly by as we thread our way onward past the pretty islands which are scattered over the lake-like waters. But now the city flashes forth from every height, crowned to their summits with houses, the homes and business places of hundreds of thousands of busy men and women. Wharves crowded with ships of all nations appear. Spires and towers and domes of great public buildings meet the eye in every direction. A great commercial city is before us, where a hundred years ago the silence of nature reigned, save for the cries of a few savage aboriginal tribes—a wondrous transformation.

But our vessel is soon berthed at the Grafton wharf, and we hear salutations of kind friends greeting us, who have been watching for our coming.

CPSIA information can be obtained
at www.ICGtesting.com
Printed in the USA
LVHW082337240620
658926LV00016B/312